GOODBYE TO THE USSR

The Collapse of Soviet Power

STEVE CRAWSHAW

BLOOMSBURY

To the memory of
Nicholas Ashford

First published in Great Britain 1992
Bloomsbury Publishing Limited, 2 Soho Square, London W1V 5DE

Copyright © 1992 by Steve Crawshaw

The moral right of the author has been asserted

A CIP catalogue record for this book
is available from the British Library

ISBN 0 7475 1167 5

Photoset by Parker Typesetting Service, Leicester
Printed by Clay Ltd, St Ives plc

Picture sources
Victoria Ivleva/The *Independent*: page 7
R. Koch/Katz Pictures: page 6 *top*
Katz Pictures: pages 1 *bottom*, 3 *bottom*, 4 *top & bottom*, 5 *top & bottom*
Jeremy Nicholl/Katz Pictures: page 8 *top*
Popperfoto: pages 6 *bottom*, 8 *bottom*
Sygma: page 1 *top*
R. White/Sygma: pages 2, 3 *top*

CONTENTS

ACKNOWLEDGEMENTS

For help and hospitality during my constant invasions of the Soviet Union in recent years I am grateful to many colleagues: to Rupert Cornwell and his successor, Peter Pringle, in Moscow; to Michael Tarm and Susan Viets in the Baltic and Ukraine; and to Edward Lucas in the Baltic republics and eastern Europe. Special thanks are due to Helen Womack, who has been extraordinarily – and typically – generous in opening up her notebooks and sharing her observations and insights. I owe her a considerable debt. Thanks, too, to Conor and Zhanna O'Clery for their kindness during difficult times.

I am grateful to Jonathan Eyal for reading the manuscript and for valuable comments. I would like to thank Andreas Whittam Smith and Godfrey Hodgson, editor and foreign editor of *The Independent*, for encouraging me and making it possible for me to write this book. Thanks, too, to Bill Hamilton – whose phone call in spring 1991 prompted the idea of writing a book about the end of the Soviet Union and who provided much good advice.

Finally, and above all, thanks to Ewa for her tolerance, scepticism and encouragement, in equal abundance and at all times.

1 Before the Deluge

Seryozha's words, at a party in a cramped Leningrad flat one summer evening in 1976, seemed hauntingly Soviet, the very spirit of the Brezhnev era. He insisted, repeatedly, that the Soviet system was a model of liberty, envied throughout the world. Eventually, at the end of a long evening − vodka, beer, tea, wine, mixed freely, in the time-honoured style, in no particular order − I asked him: given that he believed the Soviet Union was so strong on freedom, was he surprised to hear that some Russian acquaintances made it clear that I should not advertise the fact that I knew them, because they might have problems with the authorities? Only the previous week, a friend had asked me to pretend to his mother, when I had visited his apartment, that I was not foreign at all. My accented Russian could be explained by saying that I came from the Baltic republics; her son said she would be frightened if she knew that a visitor from the *kapstran*, the capitalist countries, was a guest in the flat.

As I recounted my experience, Seryozha looked faintly embarrassed. Then he muttered, 'To be honest − in my case, too, perhaps it would be better if you did not talk too much about our knowing each other.' The great defender of the Soviet system was, it turned out, himself too frightened to let the authorities know that he was acquainted with a foreigner.

That blend of unquestioning certainty and residual fear was everywhere. Again and again, you could meet those who aggressively proclaimed their loyalty to a system that was − to the outsider's eye − rotten to the core. I was a student at Leningrad State University, living for a year in a hostel on Vasilievsky Island, a short tram ride away from the Winter Palace, where the cruiser *Aurora* had fired the first fateful shot of the Revolution. Like most Westerners, my circle of friends consisted almost entirely of sceptics who lived a bohemian life on the fringes, deliberately closing out the Soviet world. They laughed, drank and mocked the realities of their Soviet life. Some − not political dissidents in the active sense of the word, just quiet rejecters – took delight, in the half-privacy of their own apartments, in not giving a fig for the system, which was no longer as murderous as it had once been. 'Please, sergeant, don't interrupt us!', one theatrical friend used to complain into the telephone receiver whenever there was a problem on the line. But even she and her family also felt fear. On some occasions – following the dictates of paranoia, or of common sense (in the Soviet Union it did not always make much difference) – they would cover the telephone receiver with a pillow if a conversation in the apartment was intended to be private.

It was easy to imagine that all Soviet citizens were equally disaffected. To the Western visitor, it seemed logical. Western newspaper reports gave copious coverage to the tiny circle of dissidents and their activities. But the disbelievers – cheerful, gloomy or indifferent – were not representative in any real sense. The Seryozhas of the Soviet world were more typical: boasting about the virtues of their country and desperate not to face up to the contradictions which they themselves half-felt. Talk to your fellow-passengers in a bus, train or plane and you would, as likely as not, find yourself talking to a Seryozha.

Most Russians knew little of Alexander Solzhenitsyn, the Nobel-winning author (and ex-inmate) of *The Gulag Archipelago* who was bundled on to a plane for Germany in February 1974 and stripped of his citizenship, or of Andrei Sakharov, the nuclear physicist whose criticisms of the Soviet system later led to his being exiled to the city of Gorky. For many years, both men were far better known in the West than in their home countries. In the Soviet Union, only a tiny minority sought or had access to the illegal *samizdat* (literally, 'self-published') copies of *Gulag* and other banned works – well-thumbed, sometimes barely legible carbon copies of typescripts which passed from hand to hand among those who trusted each other not to betray. Solzhenitsyn, Sakharov and those who filled the camps stood isolated in their own land.

There was sullen indifference, even resentment, of those who chose to rock the boat. People simply did not become involved in the political world. Life was easier if you kept your head down. Those who did otherwise were unpatriotic, hooligans, a disgrace. Some listened – despite the difficulty with jamming of Russian-language broadcasts – to Western radio stations, to hear an alternative version of what was going on. But there was a deep, generalized fear of too much knowledge, even of what others were doing. I remember, on a crowded bus in Leningrad, the horrified hush that descended when one small boy – ten years old, perhaps — told his friend, in a piping voice: '*We* listened to Voice of America last night, you know.' In the Stalin era, the authorities would have arrested the boy, found his parents and carted them all off to a Siberian labour camp, where they would probably not have survived. By 1976 it was unlikely that anybody would bother to pursue the matter. Still, the bus passengers froze with horror as the child prattled on. Listening to foreign radio stations was not uncommon. But to talk openly of it was to break a holy taboo. This was a society which, in every sense, did not wish to know. Foreign travel, too, was impossible for ordinary mortals, so that the stories that came back about Life Out There were few and far between.

The authorities went to extraordinary lengths to ensure that the block on information was complete. Much later — in an era when everything could be said out loud and when political miracles were two a penny — Soviet newspapers reported that in the Brezhnev era there had been an official ruling which banned all scenes from Western supermarkets from being shown on Soviet television or cinema screens. It sounded incredible and yet it was probably true. It was part of the everyday insanity of life at that time.

The creation of *homo sovieticus* — Soviet man, for a Soviet era — was real enough. The main distinguishing feature of *homo sovieticus* was the ability not to think for yourself. Everything else flowed from that. Conformism was important in everything: in clothes, in the arts, in literature, in science and, of course, in politics. Though, in reality, politics hardly existed. You had the State and the Party, which ruled your life. Politics suggests argument — and there was none of that, except in private, late at night, around the kitchen table.

Already, there were two great differences between life in Brezhnev's Soviet Union and the Stalin era. On the one hand, the climate of fear was no longer as absolute as it had once been. Making anti-Soviet statements in private no longer got you killed; it was unlikely even to get you arrested, unless you tried to tell the whole street. In that sense, Soviet society had 'progressed'. On the other hand, Soviet society had lost the overwhelming self-confidence which was its most distinctive feature during the Stalin years.

In the heyday of Stalinism, in the 1930s, millions of Russians could see that their society's might was growing, year by year — and millions genuinely believed in the rightness of the cause. As the slogan had it: 'Thank you, Comrade Stalin, for our happy life.' Stalinism gave a confidence to an entire nation — and impressed even foreign visitors.

This was how Walter Duranty, Moscow correspondent of the *New York Times*, described the Soviet capital in 1935:

> New Moscow needs space to breathe, so that its citizens may feel themselves indeed free men and women, as unhampered by relics of the past as they are released from tsars, landlords, and gendarmes ... Nowadays, there is an air of purpose and energy, of intense united concentration towards a common goal, which is to be seen nowhere outside the USSR.

Duranty said that the Soviet capital had been 'transformed in the most amazing way', and suggested: 'Moscow may – who knows? – one day become capital of the Federated States of the World.' The Soviet Union had already entered the most brutal period of its history. But Duranty was by no means alone in his optimistic vision. Millions died – perhaps as many as ten million – during the man-made famine in the Ukraine following the forced collectivization of the 1930s. And yet Bernard Shaw and other Westerners visited the Soviet Union during the famine and returned insisting that all was well. Shaw said he had not seen a single undernourished person and mocked reports of hunger. Malcolm Muggeridge's searing reports for the *Manchester Guardian* were a shining exception that proved the depressing rule.

In the 1930s, those who retained an independent way of thinking and who kept an un-Stalinist vision of life rightly feared for their lives. In the words of the writer Isaac Babel: 'Today, a man only talks freely to his wife, in bed, with the blankets drawn over his head.' With views like that, it was perhaps not surprising that Babel himself was later executed. But millions were loyal to what they saw as the achievements of Stalinism – Duranty's 'concentration towards a common goal'. To every question, there was a right and a wrong answer. The Soviet Union supplied the right answer. And that was that. Even those who lost relatives in the Siberian camps convinced themselves that all was well. Sasha, a friend in Leningrad whose grandfather died in a labour camp, said that his family had always insisted, at the time, that the arrest was a simple mistake. Families deluded themselves in the same way across the country. As Sasha remarked: 'Millions of families believed that the arrest of others was justified – but *their* relative had been arrested "by mistake".' Such evasions of reality became a national disease.

The Soviet propaganda machine lied with a certainty that brooked no contradiction. The endless films of socialist progress – building another tractor factory here, bringing in another rich harvest there – showed young, smiling faces who marched onwards to an ever-better future. Those convictions moulded an entire population. When Stalin died in 1953, the streets of Moscow filled with those who wished to pay their respects to the dictator. As Russians later ruefully confirmed, the tears were real.

After Stalin's death, the reign of terror never quite returned. Nikita Khrushchev, who succeeded him, condemned the repressions of the Stalinist era in his 'secret speech' of February 1956, which was soon widely published in the West and officially saw the light of Soviet day over three decades later. Unlike Stalin, Khrushchev did not suggest that the Soviet Union was already stronger than the West, nor did he believe that it was necessary to kill large numbers of people in order to make his country purer and stronger. He talked, instead, of direct competition with the West. The Soviet Union was about to move into the lead. 'We will,' said Khrushchev, 'overtake America.' The phrase led to the creation of a pastiche slogan that was popular long after the table-thumping Khrushchev was dead and gone. 'The West is teetering on the edge of the precipice – and we, comrades, are about to overtake them.'

According to the official version, Communism was always just around the corner. Stalin told the Soviet Union in 1936 that socialism – first stepping stone on the road to Communism – had been achieved. In 1961, Khrushchev announced that the next stage, full Communism, would be achieved by 1980. Then, as the deadline for achieving Utopia drew nearer, Brezhnev acknowledged that there had been some slippage in the timetable. He therefore announced an on-hold version of Communism called 'developed socialism', which remained the basis of party ideology, even in the *perestroika* era.

Under Khrushchev, at the beginning of the 1960s, came the first thaw – the description was taken from a novel by Ilya Ehrenburg and reflected the sense of many Russians that the ice was cracking, at last. Some of the camps still existed. But Khrushchev allowed details of the worst horrors of the Stalin era to be published. It was during this period that Solzhenitsyn's classic tale from the Soviet camps, *One Day in the Life of Ivan Denisovich*, was published. For a while, it even had the blessing of the authorities: *Pravda* supported the book's nomination for the Lenin Prize. Out on the streets, too, there was a hunger for this kind of writing. The literary magazine *Novy Mir*, which first printed *Ivan Denisovich*, sold its entire, enlarged edition within a few hours; altogether more than a million copies were published – and quickly sold out. Brief though this thaw would be, some early seeds of doubt were sown. As one friend from Leningrad who had read Solzhenitsyn at that time commented later: 'It was impossible to read *Ivan Denisovich* and still remain a Stalinist.'

But, if people began to breathe for a while, it did not last. In October 1964, Khrushchev was ousted in a palace coup by Leonid Brezhnev, his loyal aide. When Brezhnev came to power he presided over a cut-down version of the fat-cat society. The propaganda still talked, for good measure, of moving towards the Communist millennium. But nobody was expected to believe it. Instead, you were encouraged to participate in a society of hypocrites. You merely needed to keep your head down, say nothing and do nothing. If you said nothing and did nothing with sufficient conviction, then you had a chance of joining the rarefied spheres of the *nomenklatura*, the layer of privileged officials who ran the country – Communism's ruling class.

The *nomenklatura* establishment was dominated by the Communist Party, but it was not an absolute requirement that you should be a party member in order to partake of the privileges. Nor, conversely, did party membership bring you automatic access to privilege: Communists on the bottom rung had extra duties, but gained little; the party's closed shops were not accessible to the rank and file. The most important requirement was to be of a conventional frame of mind. Family background also helped. If you came of good Bolshevik stock, or if your parents were already part of the *nomenklatura*, then it was certain that you would inherit their privileges. For a child of the *nomenklatura* to lose his privileges – better shops, foreign travel, an apartment of your own – was as unlikely as for the son of an earl or baronet to be dispossessed of 5000 acres on the Scottish moors. The occasional rebel fell foul of the system. But the exceptions only proved the unwavering rule.

Some argued that it was a matter of character – that the Russians were constitutionally incapable of rebelling and were historically doomed to live without democracy. Certainly, pre-Revolutionary Russia was already regarded by many foreigners as a hopelessly dictatorial mess. In the nineteenth century, the most famous traveller in Russia, the Marquis de Custine, was horrified by the tyranny that he found, as were other visitors to the country. The 1914 edition of *Baedeker's Russia* passed a judgement which was echoed, in modified words, by many visitors in the Soviet era:

The Russians cling obstinately to their traditions, and are full of self-sacrificing devotion to Tsar, Church and feudal superior. They are easily disciplined, and so make excellent soldiers, but have little power of independent thinking or of initiation. The normal Great Russian is thus the mainstay of political and economic inertia and reaction ... Here we have the explanation of the want of organization, the disorder, and the waste of time which strike the Western visitor to Russia.

Thus, *homo tsaricus*, even before the birth of *homo sovieticus*, was regarded by many as a lost cause for democracy. In the Khrushchev and the Brezhnev era, there seemed little reason to modify that view. Resistance was sporadic, and harshly repressed. In post-war eastern Europe there were frequent attempts at rebellion: the East Berlin workers' uprising of 1953; the Hungarian rebellion of 1956; Czechoslovakia's liberalization in the Prague Spring of 1968. Most notably, Poland achieved a remarkable hat trick – an early testimony to the reality of people power – when popular protests in 1956, 1970 and, most dramatically, in 1980 forced three successive changes of Communist Party leader and a number of Communist Party retreats.

Russians, on the other hand, could, at the time of Brezhnev's death in 1982, claim few successes against the regime. In June 1962, there were riots in the southern city of Novocherkassk. At least twenty people died in the suppression of the unrest by Soviet troops. A number of people were sentenced to death for carrying placards with slogans like 'We demand meat, butter, and a pay rise'. The incident was officially hushed up and the protests did not spread. There were occasional explicitly political protests, too. But these were sad, isolated affairs.

When the dissident Vladimir Bukovsky and two others were convicted for staging a brief protest in Pushkin Square, Moscow, in 1967, the prosecutor argued that they had committed a gross breach of the peace. 'Gross, because of its impudence – impudence as shown by the fact that they criticized existing laws and the activities of the security services, thereby undermining their authority.' It was an interesting definition. But the number who turned up at such demonstrations was always tiny. Those who did risk their liberty could expect little support from their fellow-citizens.

A protest in 1968 against the Soviet-led invasion of Czechoslovakia was attended by just eight people on Red Square, with slogans like 'Freedom for Dubcek', 'Hands off Czechoslovakia' and – a slogan which would take on considerable importance two decades later – 'For your and our freedom'. The demonstrators were convicted of carrying slogans which contained 'deliberately false fabrications discrediting the Soviet state and social system', and were sentenced to between three and five years in jail or exile.

In the Brezhnev era, there was a twofold social contract. On the one hand, there was the economic contract summed up in the popular saying, 'They pretend to pay us – and we pretend to work.' Nobody took work seriously, it would have been absurd to do so; equally, your salary could buy you nothing. And on the other hand there was the political contract: keep your nose clean and you will have no trouble. Vaclav Havel aptly described the totalitarian absurdity in his classic essay written in 1978, 'The Power of the Powerless'. He muses on the shop manager who puts up a poster in the window that declares 'Workers of the world, unite!':

> What is he trying to communicate to the world? Is he genuinely enthusiastic about the idea of unity among the workers of the world? . . . I think it can safely be assumed that the overwhelming majority of shopkeepers never think about the slogans they put in their windows, nor do they use them to express their real opinions. That poster was delivered to our greengrocer from the enterprise headquarters along with the onions and carrots. He put them all into the window simply because it has been done that way for years, because everyone does it, and because that is the way it has to be. If he were to refuse, there could be trouble. He could be reproached for not having the proper 'decoration' in his window; someone might even accuse him of disloyalty. He does it because these things must be done if one is to get along in life. It is one of the thousands of details that guarantee him a relatively tranquil life 'in harmony with society', as they say . . .

This is what Havel called living within a lie. If, he suggested, people learnt to live in truth ('one day, something in our greengrocer snaps'), then the totalitarian system itself might start to crumble. Back in the 1970s, however, most people believed there was little chance of that happening in Czechoslovakia, let alone the Soviet Union. The meaningless posters were here to stay.

In contrast to the Stalin era, fear did not need to be a direct part of daily life, unless you were brave enough to challenge the authorities. In that case, you could expect petty harassment, or you might be sent to prison, psychiatric hospital or a Siberian labour camp. In the Brezhnev era, you were unlikely to be taken away at night and shot. But few people, by this time, had the bright-eyed young Stalinist's belief that all would be better in a brighter future. Tomorrow did not belong to them. People simply lived with what they had – there was enough to survive, and there was always plenty of cheap vodka – and questioned little. All that was expected was compliance, and complacency.

Complacency there was, in staggering measure. Leonid Brezhnev kept awarding himself more and more medals. 'We congratulate Comrade Brezhnev on his Order of Lenin,' one Red Square slogan read, after yet another decoration was pinned on to the old man's chest. In that sense, the later official buzzword was entirely accurate: this was indeed the *vremya zastoya*, the era of stagnation.

But, stagnation or not, it did not yet seem that the system was ready to implode. A leading dissident, Andrei Amalrik, asked in a book published in 1970, *Will the Soviet Union survive till 1984?*. But few saw the decline as so imminent. Solzhenitsyn, in *Gulag Archipelago*, his epic account of the Siberian camps, suggested that it might be impossible for his words to be legally published in Russia for generations to come. Even his half-optimistic comments suggested that change lay far, far, ahead. 'Some day in the future, this Archipelago, its air, and the bones of its inhabitants, frozen in a lens of ice, will be discovered by our descendants like some improbable salamander.'

And yet Solzhenitsyn seemed to speak not just for the past, but also to predict the future, when he wrote: 'History is for ever springing surprises even on the most perspicacious of us. We could not foresee what it would be like: how for no visible compelling reason the earth would shudder and give, how the gates of the abyss would fly out before they slammed to, to stay shut for a long time to come.' Those words were written in 1967, just a few years after the brief Khrushchev thaw. It would be almost twenty years before the gates opened again – at first just a little and then wrenched off their hinges by a hurricane, never to be replaced.

2 Mikhail the Saviour

Late at night on 10 March 1985, the old world ended. A small group of old men gathered in the Kremlin to decide on the successor as Soviet leader to Konstantin Chernenko, who had died in a closed hospital for the Kremlin elite, in western Moscow, earlier the same evening. Chernenko was the third to go in less than three years. First Leonid Brezhnev died in November 1982; Yuri Andropov, the KGB boss who introduced some reforms and a crackdown on corruption, was next, in February 1984; and now Chernenko, apparatchik and former Brezhnev aide. New blood was clearly needed. As Nikolai Ryzhkov, who later became prime minister, remarked: 'We knew that if we chose an old man again, we'd have a repeat of what we'd had three years in a row – shaking hands with foreign leaders at funerals.'

Formally, the appointment was not confirmed until after a meeting of the central committee, which took place next day. The official announcement of Chernenko's death came almost twenty-four hours after the event; then, barely four hours later, the mournful music gave way to the announcement that Mikhail Sergeyevich Gorbachev was the new general secretary of the Communist Party of the Soviet Union. In *Pravda* the following day, the dead Chernenko did not even merit a front-page portrait: Gorbachev pushed him on to page two.

Internationally, too, Gorbachev was of greater interest than the man he replaced. The state funeral was less a farewell to Chernenko than a hello to Gorbachev, of whom the British prime minister, Margaret Thatcher, had said – when she met him in Britain a few months earlier – that he was 'a man we can do business with'. It was clear that Gorbachev spelled change. But none – including, as he later acknowledged, Gorbachev himself – dreamed of quite how radical that change would prove to be.

Gorbachev, who had a law and an agricultural degree, was the first Soviet leader since Lenin to have higher education. But he had risen in the traditional way – through loyalty and patronage. He was appointed to the Politburo by Leonid Brezhnev, to whom he had been introduced in 1978 by Yuri Andropov as a likely lad from the south. Andropov had introduced his protégé at the old railway station in the Russian spa town of Mineralnie Vody ('Mineral Waters'), when Brezhnev was returning from a visit to Azerbaijan and when Gorbachev was the party boss in the southern town of Stavropol. It was a meeting that brought together Brezhnev and his three successors as Communist Party leader: Brezhnev the current boss; Andropov the KGB man; Chernenko the loyal aide; and Gorbachev the enthusiastic local party secretary.

Brezhnev — still at that time in command of his old-guard senses — fetched Gorbachev to Moscow a few months later, as a central commit-tee secretary in charge of agriculture. Gorbachev's tenure of the agricul-ture post was disastrous: indeed, the harvest figures were so much worse than in previous years that they had to be suppressed. Still, as was traditional, this did not impede his career. Gorbachev became a full member of the Politburo in 1980 and continued to rise, steadily.

None the less, he was fully aware of the absurdities of Brezhnev's legacy. In this he was not alone. By the time of Brezhnev's death, the leadership was beginning to realize that things must change. Gorba-chev's ascetic mentor, Andropov, was appointed in order to introduce reform and during his thirteen-month occupation of the general secre-tary's chair, he succeeded in doing so. Things began to move for the first time in decades.

After Andropov's death, the old apparat took fright at the prospect of yet more change. The dying Andropov hoped to see the young(ish) fifty-three-year-old Gorbachev as his heir apparent. But the old guard were happier with Konstantin Chernenko, seventy-three. After a Polit-buro meeting, Dmitry Ustinov (defence minister, seventy-six) put his hand on the shoulder of Nikolai Tikhonov (prime minister, seventy-nine) and — using the familiar names of both the main contenders for the Kremlin throne — declared confidently: 'Kostya will be more manageable than Misha.'

Still, when Chernenko, too, died after barely a year in office, even the Kremlin's rulers knew that (to use Gorbachev's own phrase) 'we can't go on living like this'. Gorbachev was propelled into the driving seat; Andrei Gromyko, the old-timer foreign minister, told the central com-mittee that Gorbachev had performed 'brilliantly, without any exagger-ation'. Gorbachev's brief was to get things moving — which he did. Many Russians could not believe the energy with which he approached his task. The new Soviet leader quickly became immensely popular.

When he went on street walkabouts, people reacted with genuine enthusiasm to the sight of a leader who so obviously enjoyed his direct contact with the Russian people, the *narod*.

Instead of hiding inside his curtained limousine, as all his predecessors had done, Gorbachev bounced straight into public view. He revelled in his meet-the-people sessions. At one such meeting, in Leningrad in May 1985 – just two months after his appointment – the crowds clustered eagerly round him on Nevsky Prospect, while he, the all-powerful Soviet leader, asked them for advice on what he should do. 'Get closer to the people,' said one woman. 'How can I get closer than this?' he replied, amid laughter all round. The citizens of the Soviet Union had become accustomed to the idea that they would always be ruled by senile time-servers, or worse – men who did not care a jot about what the people thought. Now, they saw this man, so full of energy, prepared to step out on to their grimy pavements – and with a sense of humour, to cap it all. He seemed sent from heaven.

Gorbachev made it clear from the start that he thought Soviet society had become bogged down. It needed energy to get Communism moving once more. An old Russian word *perestroika* – 'restructuring' or retuning – received a new lease of life as the buzzword of the new era. The old word *glasnost* – openness or 'proclaiming things loudly' – was also dusted off as *perestroika*'s propaganda twin. The new Soviet leader had a simple, impossible agenda: to drag his fellow-citizens away from the fantasy world in which millions of them had comfortably lived for so many years. He wanted the Soviet show back on the road, and he would do anything to kick it back into life.

Certainly, energy would be needed, as became plain during four weeks spent in the unexceptional Soviet town of Vitebsk, a few weeks after Gorbachev came to power. 'We have no serious problems. We are making steady economic progress,' said the chairman of the town council when he was filmed for a television documentary about life in Vitebsk. In a much publicized speech, Gorbachev told Soviet managers. 'Manna does not come from heaven.' But in Vitebsk, such talk was, as the saying had it, *kak z gusya voda* – water off a goose. Quote Gorbachev's words about the need for radical change and officials looked perplexed – or retorted, warily: 'I am not aware that he said those words.' No changes were needed, they said. So, Gorbachev was wrong? No, no, came the Pavlovian response. Everybody knew that a Soviet Communist Party leader could never be wrong. What, then, did they think needed changing in Vitebsk? No answer; this left them stumped.

It was in the Vitebsk sky that Marc Chagall had painted his fiddlers and flying cows seventy years earlier. In his native city, however, as throughout the Soviet Union, Chagall was a non-person — despite his stint as Commissar for Art here after the Revolution. Imagination was no longer in vogue. Now, Vitebsk — a quiet, Intourist-free place, in the western republic of Belorussia — was conventional in every respect. The unquestioning loyalty of the officials, and of the crowds, in Vitebsk and a thousand other towns like it was, in one sense, an advantage for the system. No chance of rebellion here. But, as the remarks by the chairman of the town council so clearly showed, this acceptance of reality was also a problem for the new Soviet leadership. In the Vitebsks of the Soviet world, the establishment was not yet ready for change.

Vanya, a baker, told how his working life was dominated by the plan: the central plan required his bakery to produce more black bread than was needed; conversely, there was not enough white bread to satisfy demand. 'They'd give us a plan to bake 100 tons of black bread. We'd bake 100 tons of bread — but the town wouldn't need 100 tons. So the bread would be left over. It would go mouldy, be spoilt.' It was just one of many absurdities of the senseless Soviet economy. Vanya seemed pleased about the arrival in power of the energetic Gorbachev, though he was careful not to criticize his predecessors. At this stage, that would still have been quite taboo.

Vanya was an exception in that he was prepared even to acknowledge the existing problems. The plump and sweaty manager at the carpet factory where Vanya's wife Faina worked insisted that there were no serious difficulties. When pressed, he told us: 'Our main problem today is ...' he paused for a moment — '... the lack of workers, here in Vitebsk.' The reason for the alleged lack of workers: 'The province and town of Vitebsk were totally destroyed and suffered greatly during the Great Patriotic War.' Four decades after the conflict had finished, officials still took refuge in the comforting old explanations. Not a word about the visible inefficiencies, the waste, the chaos, the drunkenness, the lack of initiative, and the fact that most of his workers were already underemployed. Even with the words of the Communist Party leader to prompt him, the factory manager could not get his mind round the idea that the party line had now changed. If there was a problem, it could only be connected with the Nazis and the Second World War.

Slogans boasted of the decisions of the 'April plenum' — referring to the plenary session of the Communist Party central committee, just a month after Gorbachev came to power, which was allegedly intended to shake everything up. But everybody knew that plenums came and went. All you needed to do was to praise the party, and pass the vodka, and you could allow the world to pass you by. Thus it had always been, and nobody saw any reason why it should change.

Still, one change at least was quickly felt. Soon, it was more difficult to pass the vodka. One of Gorbachev's earliest, and most energetic, campaigns was against alcohol, a taboo topic throughout the Brezhnev years. With a typically Gorbachevian energy, it was a question of all or nothing. *Pravda* started talking about the 'ugly phenomenon' of drink and said that the new campaign would 'remove this evil from our society'. Whole vineyards were destroyed, as vodka, wine and brandy suffered the equal brunt of the new campaign. Gorbachev came to be known, with a hint of popular resentment, as Mineral Secretary instead of General Secretary. But the eradication of alcohol was, in any case, not going to shake the foundations of the Communist state. It was just another campaign.

In the political arena, it soon became clear that the new man wanted to sweep the place out with a new broom. Gorbachev went much further, much faster, than Andropov had done. In his first months in office, he got rid of a number of Brezhnevites and appointed new men – including the Georgian Communist Party leader, Eduard Shevardnadze, as foreign minister. Shevardnadze replaced Gromyko, who was so famous for using the Soviet veto at the Security Council of the United Nations that he came to be known in the West as Mr Nyet.

Then, in December 1985, Gorbachev got rid of one of the most prominent members of the old guard, Viktor Grishin, who had himself been touted as a possible rival for the party leadership. Grishin was replaced as party leader in the city of Moscow by a little-known but energetic man from the Siberian city of Sverdlovsk – a fifty-four-year-old professional member of the apparat called Boris Yeltsin. Yeltsin had been recommended for promotion by a fellow-Siberian, the crusty but almost equally energetic Yegor Ligachev, who had himself been promoted by Gorbachev. It was Ligachev who made the phone call to Yeltsin in Sverdlovsk in April 1985, to persuade Yeltsin that his presence was essential in Moscow.

There can be little question of the positive role that Gorbachev played at this time. Even Yeltsin later acknowledged: 'What he has achieved will, of course, go down in the history of mankind . . . He could have draped himself with orders and medals, the people would have hymned him in verse and song, which is always enjoyable. Yet Gorbachev chose to go quite another way.'

At the Communist Party congress in February 1986, Gorbachev continued his unprecedented assaults on those who were resisting change. But he retained a classically Soviet optimism too. One of his main slogans at this time was *uskorenie* – acceleration – in other words, a retuning of the Soviet economy, to make it work better than ever. He announced that national income was planned to double. With a very Soviet exactitude – never mind the reality, admire the decimal points – Gorbachev told his comrades, during a five-hour speech in the Palace of Congresses in the Kremlin, that productivity was to increase 2.3–2.5 times, while energy consumption per rouble would drop by 28.6 per cent before the year 2000. In the five-year plan to 1990, Gorbachev announced that the intention was to double the growth rate of farm production and to ensure a substantial increase in the consumption of meat, milk, vegetables and fruit. He was stern about the implications. 'Can we do this? We can and we must.' And so it went on. Gorbachev concluded his report to the congress, which was repeatedly punctuated by the obligatory prolonged applause, with the upbeat declaration: 'That is the only way we will be able to carry out the behests of the great Lenin – to move forward energetically and with a singleness of will. History has given us no other destiny. But what a wonderful destiny it is, comrades!'

This was a clean-up operation against Brezhnev and on behalf of Lenin. 'The life-giving impetus of our great Revolution,' Gorbachev said, 'was too powerful for the party and people to reconcile themselves to phenomena that were threatening to squander its gains.' He curtly dismissed any talk of a hidden agenda. 'To put an end to all the rumours and speculations that abound in the West about this, I would like to point out once again that we are conducting all our reforms in accordance with the socialist choice. We are looking within socialism, rather than outside it, for the answers to all the questions that arise.' ('Socialism', it should be noted, was used in the Soviet Union as a synonym for the one-party Communist system; any connection with policies espoused by socialist politicians in Western 'bourgeois democracies' was purely coincidental.) Gorbachev insisted:

We must be on the offensive in exposing ideological subversion and in bringing home truthful information about the actual achievements of socialism, about the socialist way of life. We have built a world free of oppression and exploitation and a society of social unity and confidence. We, patriots of our homeland, will go on safeguarding it with all our strength, increasing its wealth, and fortifying its economic and moral might.

Glasnost should not, he insisted, be toned down. 'There can only be one answer to this, a Leninist answer: Communists want the truth ... Those who have grown used to doing slipshod work, to practising deception, indeed feel really awkward in the glare of publicity ... Therefore, we must make *glasnost* an unfailingly operative system.' That, in February 1986, was the Gorbachev creed.

Just how unfailingly operative that *glasnost* would prove to be was demonstrated with lethal clarity in the wake of the explosion that took place two months later, at 1.24 am on Saturday, 26 April 1986. Sixty miles north of Kiev, at a power plant called Wormwood – in Russian, Chernobyl – came the worst nuclear disaster that the world had seen. Government leaders in Moscow knew about the emergency within hours. But they remained silent for three days. Only when Swedish scientists noted abnormally high radiation levels was Moscow forced to come up with a public explanation. Finally, on Monday evening, Tass news agency issued a single, brief communiqué. 'An accident has occurred at Chernobyl nuclear power station. One of the atomic reactors has been damaged. Measures are being taken to eliminate the consequences of the accident. Aid is being given to the victims. A government commission has been set up.' For Soviet newspapers, there was an extra sentence: 'It is forbidden to publish anything but this Tass bulletin.' It was, in other words, *glasnost* as usual. The following day, an additional short statement was issued, declaring that the radiation had been 'stabilized'. Soviet television carried the news about Chernobyl as an also-ran towards the end of the programme – after items about women's fashion and new electricity lines to Bulgaria.

Secrecy and neglect bedevilled the entire operation. Evacuation of the immediate area did not begin until more than thirty-six hours after the explosion. The May Day celebrations, just five days after the disaster, went ahead in Kiev as though nothing had happened. There was dancing, music and a marchpast. Tens of thousands were officially encouraged to be there – despite the known, possibly lethal consequences, in the months and years to come. The contrast between the cheerful atmosphere and the underlying reality was, as one of those present later remarked, 'bizarre, pure Kafka'.

The Chernobyl disaster contained many lessons. It was the result of an over-ambitious test that went badly out of control. As things started to go wrong, those who conducted the experiment — which served a good Soviet purpose, to increase output — chose to override all the warning mechanisms that had been built into the system. They ignored danger signs and switched off safety devices while disaster could still be avoided. Each time, they preferred to plough ahead with the experiment, rather than giving up entirely and making the reactor safe. Finally, they accepted that the experiment was beyond rescue and must be abandoned. There was a frantic attempt to shut down the reactor and to save the plant. By now, however, it was too late for the experiment to be safely aborted. The overheating of the system was so great that catastrophe had become inevitable. Only two people died in the moments of the explosion itself, but the Chernobyl disaster poisoned an entire region, for years and decades to come. It was easy to see, in the horror story of that night, a grim, apocalyptic parable for the fate of the Soviet Union itself.

Gorbachev finally appeared on television three weeks after the accident and half-defended the Soviet cover-up: 'We had to make a quick and competent analysis. As soon as we received trustworthy information, we issued it to the Soviet people and sent it abroad through diplomatic channels.' This was untrue; the Soviet authorities continued to conceal whatever they thought they could get away with. Nothing was revealed until the Soviet hand was forced; and even basic information, like the time of the explosion, was only revealed ten days after the disaster. It would, however, be several years before things changed so much that Soviet newspapers dared to challenge a presidential lie.

Chernobyl was a human, ecological and political catastrophe. But it also marked a positive turning-point in terms of the pressure for change. Chernobyl made it clear that *glasnost* had to be something more than just a pretty word. Those who spoke out were promoted. Vitaly Korotich, for example, an editor in the Ukraine, was summoned to Moscow, where Gorbachev offered him the job of editing *Ogonyok*, an illustrated weekly magazine which, until then, had embodied all the worst aspects of the Soviet Thank-you-dear-party-for-our-happy-life mentality — full of smiling Pioneers (crisp white shirts, red scarves and Lenin badges) and triumphs at the collective farm.

Korotich later described the kind of sycophancy that was endemic when he arrived at his post. On his desk, under the perspex cover, he found a list of the birthdays of all the members of the Politburo, together with details of what sort of birthday portrait to print. Korotich asked the central committee: was it an official party decision that such portraits should be printed, or was it up to the editor? 'There was a long silence. Then they told me there'd been no official decision. But — nobody had ever protested.'

This kind of lackeyism was an inbuilt part of Soviet society. But, under Korotich, that style now went out of the window. *Ogonyok* and other liberal papers began to chip away at some of the old-means-best mentality. The policy of greater openness was relative, at best. The list of taboos was still long. None the less, the changes were real.

Changes continued in other areas, too. At the time of Chernobyl, the Soviet Union's camps and prisons contained hundreds of political prisoners. In early 1986, Gorbachev was still denying their existence. He told *L'Humanité*: 'About political prisoners — we don't have any. Likewise, our citizens are not prosecuted for their beliefs. We don't try people for their opinions.' Of Andrei Sakharov, who had been exiled with his wife, Elena Bonner, to the city of Gorky since 1980, Gorbachev declared: 'It is common knowledge that he committed actions punishable by law.' None the less, Sakharov's exile, and the existence of the political prisoners, continued to be internationally embarrassing, at a time when Gorbachev wanted to improve relations with the West. After the KGB made propaganda use of a secretly filmed medical examination, the frail Sakharov declared that he and Bonner would from now on refuse all medical treatment. Then, in December 1986, one of the Soviet Union's best-known political prisoners, Anatoly Marchenko, died after a four-month hunger strike. Before his death, he had repeatedly been put in freezing punishment cells. His death caused a renewed outburst of international condemnation. The danger of Sakharov dying, in similar circumstances, was real — and would be, in public relations terms, disastrous. Suddenly, the policy changed.

Sakharov had written to Gorbachev in February 1986, calling for the release of all prisoners of conscience. Gorbachev received the letter, but did not reply. Suddenly, however, it was all different. Just a week after Marchenko died, a telephone was unexpectedly installed one night by KGB engineers in Sakharov's house (until then, in order to ensure his isolation from the outside world, he had not been allowed a phone; the house in Gorky was guarded by the KGB and the city was out of bounds to foreigners). Sakharov was told to stay indoors and to expect a call. At 3 pm the following day — Sakharov had got bored of waiting and was about to go out to buy bread — the telephone rang. 'Mikhail Sergeyevich is calling,' said a Kremlin switchboard operator. 'I am listening,' said Sakharov. The unbelievable was about to happen: Gorbachev told

Sakharov that he and Bonner could both return to Moscow. Sakharov said that others should also be freed. Gorbachev replied: 'I don't agree.' But Sakharov's release was in itself a momentous event that paved the way for the much greater changes to come.

Sakharov and Bonner packed their bags and caught the train to Moscow. On arrival at the Yaroslavsky Station, on 23 December 1986, they were besieged by a mob of well-wishers and reporters. Microphones were thrust towards them and hundreds of cameras flashed. It took forty minutes for Sakharov and Bonner to make their way through the crowd, back to a Moscow which was on the point of being transformed. After seven years of exile, Sakharov – the man who had, to use Vaclav Havel's phrase, always lived in truth – was back at the centre of things. Until now, he had been ignored or rebuffed by his compatriots; soon, however, Sakharov would be the most popular and respected politician in the Soviet Union. By the time of his death, in 1989, he was, at last, a prophet with honour in his own land. That change of heart was good news for Russia, even more than for Sakharov himself. Within a few months, too, 140 political prisoners – who, only a year earlier, Gorbachev insisted did not exist – were released, with a 'pardon' for their alleged crimes.

Meanwhile, Gorbachev was getting into his stride in his battle with the hardliners. At a central committee meeting in January 1987, he delivered sharp attacks on the Brezhnev era and suggested what amounted to a revolutionary development, by Communist standards: that party secretaries should be elected in secret ballots. Still, however, 'restructuring' continued to be regarded as the panacea for all the Soviet woes. It was both obligatory and uplifting. As one typical billboard in Gorky Street, in central Moscow, declared: '*Perestroika!* Democracy! Optimism!' It was like saying: 'Towards the successful fulfilment of the 12th Five-Year-Plan!' or 'Soviet Union – Bulwark of Peace!' Like the greengrocer's exhortations for the workers of the world to unite, the *perestroika* slogan did not mean anything – nor was it expected to. It was simply a way of decorating the streets.

In the international arena, there were many successes, although things did not always go as Gorbachev hoped. In Iceland in October 1986, the US President, Ronald Reagan – who had coined the phrase 'evil empire' for the Soviet Union – met Gorbachev for what seemed set, at one point, to be a historic summit. Meeting at the clapboard Hofdi House in Reykjavik, they came close to achieving agreement on a clutch of arms issues, but eventually the talks foundered on Reagan's attachment to the

Strategic Defence Initiative, or Star Wars. By the time that the two superpower leaders parted, there was such bitterness they seemed unable even to look each other in the face. But the failure of Reykjavik was soon forgotten in a string of diplomatic triumphs that followed. In February, Gorbachev announced the Soviet Union's readiness to strike a deal on medium-range nuclear weapons in Europe – which would be the most important arms reduction deal that had yet been seen. Time and again he showed himself to be a nimble performer; his mental alertness contrasted sharply with his opposite number in Washington, who was often muddled about even the most basic aspects of the arms control.

For the moment, Gorbachev was still in control of the reform process which he had launched. He spent most of the time trying to kick the process forward, not holding it back. And, despite all the odds, he kept succeeding. Occasionally, fate would play into Gorbachev's hands – such as when a nineteen-year-old- West German, Mathias Rust, flew unintercepted more than 500 miles through Soviet air defences, circled a few times over the Kremlin and landed his single-engined Cessna plane beside St Basil's Cathedral on Red Square. It was an extraordinary humiliation: how could a mixed-up teenager pull off such a stunt, against all the might of a superpower, without being noticed – let alone stopped? Rust's adventure was almost certainly made easier because it took place on 28 May, Border Guards' Day, when those who should have been checking their radar screens were celebrating with illicit vodka. Gorbachev took the opportunity to carry out a complete shake-up of the Soviet defence bureaucracy, sacking both the defence minister and the air defence chief.

Even now, the official 'openness' was far from all-embracing. This was more than a year after Chernobyl, the watershed for *glasnost*. But the evasiveness was familiar. Thirty-six hours after Rust's dramatic landing, a forty-five-word story in *Pravda* announced only that the citizen of the Federal Republic of Germany M. Rust had violated Soviet airspace and landed 'in Moscow' – no embarrassing mention of Red Square. That was the first that the Soviet reader was allowed to hear of the matter. The announcement nestled under an exciting item about Soviet athletes accepting an invitation to the fifteenth Winter Olympics in Calgary. The sacking of Sergei Sokolov, the defence minister, did not even make the headline of the communiqué where his ousting was revealed.

A small comparison indicates how far the Soviet Union was out of step with the more liberal parts of Communist East Europe at this time.

MIKHAIL THE SAVIOUR

In 1986, one of Poland's most popular writers, Tadeusz Konwicki, had published a set of stories and essays called *New World and its Surroundings*, in which the authorities are directly challenged. Konwicki dares the authorities ('I know that Mr Censor is twisting in his chair at this point . . .') to strike a blue pencil through his words, which question the Communists' right to rule. At another point, Konwicki declares: 'I know that Mr Censor is tormenting himself now: he wonders if he should remove the whole chapter − or just cross out what might offend or anger somebody − or even incline them to make a telephone call.' The Polish censor, keen to demonstrate to a resentful nation that 'liberalism' ruled, left the book without cuts.

Anybody reading words of similar defiance in the Soviet Union at this time − or at almost any time up to 1990 − would have been (a) dreaming, (b) reading an illegal publication or (c) both. In due course, the spirit of rebellion would infect Russia and the rest of the Soviet Union, too. But that lay in the future, several dramatic years down the road. In 1987, Gorbachev was still under little domestic pressure from below. Instead, he continued his attempts to steer Communism off the rocks. During the summer of 1987, while on his summer holidays in the Crimea, he produced a book called simply *Perestroika*, devoted to the Gorbachev view of life.

In *Perestroika*, he talked − and this was the blunt kind of talk that turned Margaret Thatcher into an early, dedicated admirer − of the 'absurd situation' in the Soviet economy, where the world's biggest producer of steel, raw materials, fuel and energy suffered shortages, because of waste and inefficiency. Gorbachev highlighted the paradoxes of the Soviet system more honestly than any of his predecessors had ever done. 'Our rockets can find Halley's comet and fly to Venus with amazing accuracy. But side by side with these scientific and technological triumphs is an obvious lack of efficiency in using scientific achievements for economic needs. Many Soviet household appliances are of poor quality.'

Certainly, few would quarrel with the last sentence. The shoddiness of Soviet products was legendary, sometimes lethal. Exploding television sets, for example, caused 18,000 fires in the five years to 1987; 1000 people died. 'How can it happen,' *Ogonyok* magazine asked mournfully, 'that one of the greatest achievements of mankind be turned into a bloodthirsty enemy of the people?'

Alongside the bluntly critical talk, *Perestroika* contained endless laudatory references to Lenin and his achievements. Lenin, said

Gorbachev, was an ideological source of *perestroika*; an inexhaustible source of dialectical creative thought, theoretical wealth and political sagacity; an undying example of lofty moral strength, all-round spiritual culture and selfless devotion to the cause of the people and of socialism – and much more of the same. It was laid on more thickly than the rule book demanded, even at this time. The love of Lenin continued to be the cornerstone of Gorbachev's declared philosophy to the very end.

Meanwhile, the changes continued. The anti-alcohol campaign was followed by a campaign against 'bureaucratism', which was a useful catch-all phrase. That, in turn, was accompanied by an upsurge in the campaign against corruption and privilege. You could not open a Soviet paper without reading some horror story about a local official who had strayed from the Leninist straight and narrow. The anti-corruption campaign was not, in itself, new. It had originally been launched by Andropov. But this went much further. By 1987, even Brezhnev's son-in-law, Yuri Churbanov, was under investigation (and later jailed), in connection with a corruption scandal in the Central Asian republic of Uzbekistan. The scandal was, in effect, a Soviet version of Gogol's *Dead Souls*, where the idea had been to make vast profits by selling thousands of serfs who existed only on paper. In the updated version of Gogol's plot, billions of roubles were paid out for cotton (the 'white gold' of Central Asia) which did not, in reality, exist. The fraud was only discovered when satellite photographs of the region allegedly under cultivation showed that there was nothing there.

Other sensitive topics began to be tackled, too. After more than two decades of silence, Stalinism was back on the agenda. The Georgian film-maker, Tengis Abuladze, made a film in 1984 – while the hardline Chernenko was still in power – which tackled extraordinary taboos. The filming was possible because of the patronage of the then Georgian Communist Party leader, Eduard Shevardnadze. But filming was one thing; public release was another. *Repentance* remained 'on the shelf'. Abuladze's film was, despite its dream-like style, a clear and powerful allegory of the Stalinist era. When it was finally released in 1987, it caused a furore. The film gnawed away at the lies of Soviet history as never before. Indeed, a main theme was not just the crimes that had been committed by the Stalin figure, but the failure of later generations to admit that those crimes had taken place. Effectively, the film banned the option of comfortable amnesia, which so many millions of Soviet citizens had chosen. In that respect, it was a turning-point.

Still, however, there was much caution even about tackling such subjects. Gorbachev himself began publicly to address the issues of Stalinism. In November 1987, he attacked the Soviet Union's Stalinist legacy, as Khrushchev had done during his secret speech three decades earlier. But Gorbachev's speech provided a partial condemnation, at best. He talked of the repression of 'thousands' of people, rather than the millions who had died. It was a gently revisionist version of history – partly because of the pressure of hardliners, who were already horrified at the extent of change. Gorbachev also delivered a sideswipe at unnamed 'over-zealous' comrades – a reference which would soon be spelt out clearly for the world to see. For, in the meantime, Boris Yeltsin, the self-described 'awkward person' from Siberia, had grown increasingly frustrated with what he saw as the slow pace of change. Yeltsin later summed up Politburo meetings thus:

> After the general secretary's remarks, comments were solicited around the table from left to right, to give all the members (they usually spoke for from two to five minutes, sometimes less), the chance to have their say, 'Yes, yes, very good ... it will influence ... improve ... broaden ... deepen *perestroika* ... democratization ... acceleration ... *glasnost* ... alternatives ... pluralism.' The members were beginning to get used to the new buzzwords and enjoyed repeating them. At first the emptiness of our sessions was not so noticeable, but the longer I took part in them the clearer it became that what we were doing was often pointless ... I cannot recall anyone at those meetings attempting even once to voice a serious disagreement.

During his two years as party boss in Moscow, Yeltsin gained huge popularity for his head-on attacks on corruption and the privileged lifestyle of the elite. He made a point of arriving, unannounced, in food shops and exposing yet another of the scams with which all Moscow was rife. Little of the meat which arrived in the shops was sold, legally, over the counter. Instead, it was sold at the back door – metaphorically and literally – for those who had the right connections, or paid the appropriate sweeteners, or both. Yeltsin's tactics were a populist move – an easy way to gain support. But they struck, too, at the heart of the way that the Soviet distribution system worked. Not surprisingly, he did not endear himself to the hardliners, who resented his very real disturbance of the status quo.

Throughout 1987, Yeltsin became increasingly restless. He was convinced that Gorbachev did not support him in his battles with the hardliners – most notably, with Ligachev, the head of ideology, who had talent-spotted Yeltsin, but who was now the most important brake on change. Yeltsin wrote to Gorbachev during the summer holidays, threatening to resign. But Gorbachev postponed discussion of the matter. Yeltsin, easily riled, was having none of it. At the end of a Communist Party plenum in October 1987, the tension finally exploded. Yeltsin asked for the floor, in order to raise 'a number of issues that have been causing me some concern'.

As ever, he did not bother to mince his words. He pointed out that the early 'tremendous surge of enthusiasm' for *perestroika* had already begun to ebb away. This happened because time was spent drafting documents, which did not reach the people. The party's authority had drastically fallen because of its failure to act. All of this was heresy enough. But it did not stop there. Yeltsin complained directly that nothing had changed 'in the style of work of the secretariat of the central committee – or of Comrade Ligachev'. And, implicitly attacking the holy of holies, the Communist Party leader himself, he complained that the power of the party was put into a single pair of hands, and that one man was totally immune from all criticism. He complained of 'absolutely unacceptable' adulation of the general secretary. Then, to round off his system-shattering speech, he offered his resignation from the Politburo.

Gorbachev was enraged. He asked Yeltsin: 'Are you so politically illiterate that we have to give you classes?' He defended Ligachev and turned on Yeltsin, saying: 'Is it not enough for you that the whole of Moscow revolves around your person that you now want the central committee to spend time on you as well? Have you reached such heights of self-admiration and is your opinion of yourself so great that you have put your own ambitions above the interests of the party and of the cause?' The details of the plenum were not published at the time, but soon began to leak out nevertheless. At an official news conference on 31 October – ten days after the plenum – it was admitted that Yeltsin had offered to resign, though a message from Tass 'categorically' forbade Soviet news organizations to print the sensational news.

Once the seventieth anniversary celebrations of the Bolshevik Revolution, on 7 November, were out of the way, the party knives could be publicly sharpened. Now was the time for settling of scores. On 9 November, Yeltsin went into hospital, after what he described as a stroke. Two days later, Gorbachev telephoned him in hospital and ordered him to attend a special meeting of the Moscow city party committee which had been called. Yeltsin protested that the doctors had forbidden him to move, but Gorbachev insisted. Yeltsin described the atmosphere as being that of a 'a pack of hounds, a pack ready to tear me in pieces'. A long line of people went up to the rostrum and 'flung themselves on me at the bidding of the chief huntsman: tally-ho!' It was a pro forma business. To have stood up for a dissenter would in those days still have been almost unthinkable. Yeltsin was sacked as Moscow party leader, for the 'gross shortcomings in the leadership of the Moscow city party organization'. None the less, his radical credentials were strengthened, a hundredfold. For the moment, it seemed that this was the end of Yeltsin's career. Indeed, Gorbachev told him as much. But Yeltsin's defiance of Gorbachev on this occasion would stand him in good stead in the years to come.

It was impossible, after Yeltsin's sacking, for anything positive to be written about him in the Soviet press. But, for the first time, there were hints of the possibilities to come. For the moment, it was just a matter of letters to the newspapers and a few small protests, but it was a sign that things were no longer what they had once been. Factory workers in Moscow committed an unheard of breach of Communist etiquette by refusing to endorse Yeltsin's sacking. A group which wanted to hold a demonstration 'in support of glasnost and perestroika' was refused permission to do so — because the group was known to be pro-Yeltsin. Change, in other words, but only on the authorities' terms. The contradictions were just beginning to show through. In late 1987, all this was little more than the first few shoots of early spring, poking up through the half-frozen ground. With a severe frost, it seemed that such new growth could easily die. None the less, the shoots were there.

Many Russians were still sceptical that the basics would ever change. The old system seemed firmly in place, as the sacking of Yeltsin showed. But the hardliners were already beginning to worry. For them, things were already changing, too fast. Soon they would feel impelled to act.

3 Spanners in the Works

The half-hidden drama — perhaps the greatest upheaval in the three years since Gorbachev came to power — began on the day the Soviet leader left for a visit to Yugoslavia, on 13 March 1988. Under the overall heading *Polemics* and under the headline 'I cannot give up my principles', the daily *Sovietskaya Rossiya* published a letter from Nina Andreyeva, an unknown chemistry lecturer in Leningrad. Her 'letter', which covered an entire page of the paper, praised *perestroika* (that was obligatory, for everybody), but also complained about ideological confusion, the blackening of Soviet history and the 'obsession' with attacking Stalin. Andreyeva criticized the champions of 'left-wing liberal socialism' saying: 'They try to make us believe that the country's past was nothing but mistakes and crimes.' Now, she said, 'the subject of repressions has been blown up out of all proportion ... and over-shadows any objective interpretation of the past'.

In one sense, there was little strange about Andreyeva's complaints. Such views were widely shared on Rusia's streets, where there was a widespread nostalgia for the moral certainties of the past. But, in a country where diversity of opinion and political debate were still prohibited, the letter was a bombshell. Nobody had seen anything like it before. People guessed (rightly) that this was the beginning of a would-be palace coup.

It was, to use a favourite Soviet propaganda phrase, 'not by chance' that the Andreyeva letter was published at this moment. While the boss was away, the hardliners could play. *Sovietskaya Rossiya* was edited by Valentin Chikin, a friend of Ligachev, and Andreyeva's unsolicited letter provided the perfect ammunition for a broadside attack on reform. Ligachev (though he later tried to dissociate himself) approved the article before publication and Chikin slipped it into the paper at the last moment, replacing a page that had already been prepared.

Once the letter was published, Ligachev worked fast. He called a meeting of senior newspaper editors and praised the article as 'marvellous, very instructive material'. Tass, the Soviet news agency, was ordered to distribute the article at once, so that it could be reprinted in regional newspapers across the country. Communist Party meetings were called in connection with the Andreyeva letter, at which a return to the old ways was supported. Within a few days, all the changes of the past three years began to be put into reverse. For Russians watching the process unfold – the letter, the publicity, the old-style party meetings – the prospects seemed grim. Tatyana Zaslavskaya, a leading Gorbachev supporter, later reminisced: 'We all remembered the sudden end of Khrushchev's thaw. This thaw had lasted longer – now we felt that it, too, was ending. We had returned to the system that freezes everything.'

But, not for the first or the last time, Gorbachev turned defeat into victory. On his return from Yugoslavia five days after the publication of the Andreyeva letter, he deployed all his formidable tactical skills and used the article as a weapon *against* the conservatives. He forced Polit-buro members to declare their loyalties and introduced an anti-Andreyeva campaign before Ligachev's pro-Andreyeva bandwagon had truly begun to roll. Soon, *Pravda* and other newspapers delivered sharp attacks on the Andreyeva letter. *Pravda* described it as 'an anti-*perestroika* manifesto', in an article that was obediently reprinted and commented on, approvingly, throughout the Soviet press. There were no dissenting voices. In the traditional humiliating style, *Sovietskaya Ross-iya* even delivered a withering attack on itself – as if the paper's editors were participating in one of the Stalinist show trials of the 1930s, where the defendants were required to hurl accusations at themselves before being taken out and shot. *Sovietskaya Rossiya* said that it fully agreed with 'the critical assessments, propositions, and conclusions' contained in the *Pravda* editorial. It regretted publishing the letter, which 'leads us all away from the revolutionary renewal of society on the basis of democracy and *glasnost*'. *Perestroika* was once more safe and under control.

On the one hand, publication of the Andreyeva letter was alarming, in that it showed that the hardliners were still strong – in case anybody harboured any doubts on that score. On the other hand, the unanimous, concerted attacks on it also served as a reminder that the alternative to Andreyeva was not open discussion. That was still banned. *Perestroika* was the Correct View, which could be published. Critics of *perestroika* – whether liberal or (as in this case) hardline – held the Incorrect View, which could not. The Andreyeva letter was a traditional, closed-doors drama. At the time, the 'facts' were confined to paranoia, rumour and tea-leaves. Power struggles at the top were still as taboo as they had been when Brezhnev seized power from Khrushchev in 1964. The articles which, on Gorbachev's orders, rubbished the Andreyeva theme did not refer, even obliquely, to the blazing rows in the Kremlin that had taken place. (Describing one Kremlin confrontation, a witness said later that if he had been in Ligachev's place, 'my heart would have exploded'.)

Gorbachev was still, at this time, under little pressure from below. Never again, however, after the failed mini-coup of spring 1988 would the hardliners hold so many cards. The people, out on the streets, were not yet allowed to have their say, either for or against. And, more importantly, they were not pressing to do so. Within a year, that would change.

Meanwhile, the defeat of Ligachev was accompanied by yet more changes in the international arena. In December 1987, Gorbachev and Reagan had signed the most radical nuclear arms treaty that there had ever been. All talk of evil empires, and the high dudgeon of Reykjavik the previous year, was forgotten. Symbolism was rife. Reagan gave Gorbachev a pair of cufflinks depicting Isaiah beating swords into ploughshares. The Soviet gift to the Americans was a painting of St Sebastian pierced by arrows. According to the terms of the INF treaty, both sides agreed to destroy thousands of their medium-range nuclear weapons. In the words of Gennady Gerasimov, the Soviet spokesman and chief phrase-maker, the two sides had crossed a Rubicon.

Now, in May 1988 — just as the press campaign against Andreyeva was in full swing — Moscow began to disentangle itself from the political and military misadventure that it had embarked on eight years earlier. Like the pictures of the US helicopter lifting off from the roof of the American embassy in Saigon in 1975, the scenes of the Soviet tanks pulling out of Afghanistan represented international humiliation at the end of a meaningless war. When the first column of armoured vehicles rumbled across the Friendship Bridge over the river Oxus and into the small Soviet border town of Termez, they were greeted by cheering crowds, blaring car horns and military fanfares. The slogans proclaimed: 'Welcome to the soldier-internationalists who have courageously fulfilled their duties.' But the reality, impossible to conceal, was different. The war had brought only international isolation and military defeat; 13,000 Soviet soldiers died, for their 'internationalist duties'. It was a wound which would be difficult to heal.

At home, Gorbachev appeared to have a firm grip. In June 1988, a special party conference was held at which everything seemed to go his way. The hardliners received a thorough going-over, though they, too, gave a robust performance. Ligachev reminded his comrades that politics was 'not as easy as eating cabbage soup'. Yeltsin, still out in the cold, begged for his political rehabilitation, saying that he deeply resented what had happened to him. But his bid failed. Ligachev turned on him and, in what became the single most famous phrase from the conference, told him: '*Ty, Boris, nie prav!* You, Boris, are wrong!' The phrase would be thrown back in Ligachev's face, time and time again, in the months to come, as the crowds chanted: 'You, Yegor, are wrong! *Ty, Yegor, nie prav!*' The party's rejection of Yeltsin only deepened the popular alienation from the party itself.

Nevertheless, the party conference approved a set of changes which would prove to be crucial. It was agreed to hold partly contested elections, in spring 1989, to the new Congress of People's Deputies, a 2250-member parliament which would meet a few times a year. From the members of the Congress, a smaller permanent parliament, the Supreme Soviet, would be drawn. The elections would be Communist-controlled and seemed almost foolproof. A few multi-candidate elections had already been tried – and the system scarcely trembled. As Ivan Polozkov, the hardline Russian Communist Party leader, later remarked: 'When I tried multi-candidate elections, my party workers complained: "Don't play with us. We know it's only a formaility. However many choices we have, we know whom to pick. Why are you wasting our time?"' None the less, the hidden dangers of contested elections for the status quo were many.

Already at this time, there were the first public atempts to push things beyond what Gorbachev and his party comrades were then prepared to accept. For, from now on, it was no longer only the Andreyeva-style hardliners who attacked the authorized version of *perestroika*. On 7 May 1988, a radical new group, the Democratic Union, was formed – in explicit opposition to the ruling Communist Party and calling for a multi-party system. Dozens of the participants in the founding meeting were arrested, as was Sergei Grigoryants, editor of the banned magazine *Glasnost*, who put his apartment at the Democratic Union's disposal.

The new group was small and, theoretically, harmless. But its importance lay in the fact that it went beyond what was already allowed. In terms of its effect on Soviet politics, it was a no-lose strategy. If the Democratic Union was left unmolested, then that was a victory in itself, since it meant that the limits of the permissible had changed; it would thus pave the way for the formation of other opposition groups. If, on the other hand, the Democratic Union suffered at the hands of the authorities, then — following the law of popular perversity which had long existed in eastern Europe and was now beginning to take hold in the Soviet Union — support for radical ideas, and hostility to the Communist authorities, would be certain to increase. In the event, the authorities alternated between suppressing and attempting to ignore. The illegal protests of the Democratic Union in central Moscow grew through the summer of 1988. They were violently dispersed, again and again, but that only focused attention on the opposition, as never before, giving the Democratic Union a significance out of all proportion to its small size. A new riot squad was formed to deal with the protests, and with unrest in the republics, called Special-Purpose Militia Units: *Otryady militsii osobovo naznachenia* or Omon, for short. In eastern Europe, the authorities had needed special police squads — Zomo in Poland, for example — to keep the people in check; but in Russia, never. The formation of Omon — which would play a notorious leading role in the years to come — was thus another small tribute to the changes that were beginning to take place.

Meanwhile, other aspects of ordinary life were beginning to change. Small co-operatives — in effect, private businesses — began to open up, especially in the big cities, where restaurants or workshops charged a real price in return for a real service. The black market for craftsmen had always existed — moonlighting was an essential way of life, with payment in vodka plus cash. But the co-operative system formalized it; in many different fields, from plumbers to fashion design, co-operatives began to spring up.

Other changes, too, emphasized the more human face of the new regime. The Church began to be accepted and many churches werre rebuilt. For decades, the freedom to practise religion, solemnly proclaimed by the constitution, had been a lie. In reality, everything was done to suppress religion. Churches were destroyed; others were used as storerooms for potatoes or grain. Lenin wrote in 1922: 'Famine is the only time when we can beat the enemy over the head. . . . Victory over the reactionary clergy is assured. . . . We must crush their resistance with such cruelty that they will not forget it for decades.'

By the Brezhnev era, Lenin's brutal vision had receded. But there was no acceptance of religion. The Orthodox Church tried hard — notoriously hard, some argued — to maintain good relations with the Soviet authorities. It had little to show for it. For anybody of working age, regular churchgoing was a sure way of destroying your career; the churches only contained a clutch of *babushki* — old women in headscarves, with nothing to lose. Still, there was a curiosity about religion and the impressive Orthodox ceremonies, even in pre-Gorbachev days. At Easter especially, the few churches that were allowed to remain open were packed. The crowds were undeterred by the militiamen surrounding the churches, who tried to stop young people going in — allegedly, they were seeking to prevent hooliganism (I did not again see so many Soviet militiamen, looking so suspicious, until the mass anti-Kremlin protests of the Gorbachev era). At Easter, Soviet television used to show films from the West — an almost unheard-of rarity at the time — in order to persuade people to stay away from the incense-filled churches.

Gradually, the official hostility faded and the restrictions were lifted. Under Gorbachev, that process was accelerated tenfold. In 1988, the Orthodox Church publicly celebrated a thousand years of Russian Christianity, in a way that would have seemed impossible only a few years earlier. In the next two years, thousands of churches were reclaimed and reopened. It was a remarkable change.

None the less, these official concessions did not strike at the heart of the system. Indeed, it was remarkable, considering the Soviet and international hullabaloo, how little had yet changed in the Soviet power structures, the Soviet way of life or the Soviet economy (the co-operative businesses were few and expensive, and scarcely impinged on most Russians' lives). There was one main exception to the no-change rule. Between 1985 and 1988, the press was transformed beyond recognition. As later events would show, it was a crucial change. The Communists still ruled, unchallenged. But the seeds of later rebellion were planted at this time.

For years, everybody had become accustomed to reading newspapers back to front: you ignored what was on the front page of *Pravda* or *Izvestia*, with a picture of a prize-winning milkmaid or honoured steel-worker, and looked for the one-paragraph items that might be tucked away and could, if you were lucky — and if your antennae were sensitive enough — include hidden nuggets of information. Those were the glory days of Western Kremlinologists, where the dissection of news items, line by line, was almost all that anybody had to go on to understand the comings and goings in the corridors of power.

By 1988, there was still more than a whiff of the old style. *Pravda*'s front page continued to represent the Communist theatre of the absurd. But other papers began to touch on the ills of Soviet society and prided themselves on seeing how far they could go. *Ogonyok* magazine, under

Vitaly Korotich, became a standard-bearer of *glasnost*. So, too, did the once-propagandist *Moscow News*.

Even the liberal press could not yet challenge the status quo. Saying things that the Communist Party leader did *not* want to hear only came much later. In 1987 and 1988, the absolute sceptics were still forced to operate illegally – like Grigoryants and the impudently titled *Glasnost*; he and his journalists were constantly harassed and arrested. None the less, the achievements of the liberal wing of the official press were real, as the frequent attacks on them by the hardliners made clear. The hardline attacks, however, only increased the popularity of the liberal media. *Ogonyok* and *Moscow News* became such hot properties that each copy was read many times over. If somebody was sitting reading *Ogonyok* on the Metro, several other people were always reading it at the same time. Battered back numbers, several weeks old, were sold on the street at well above their original face value.

Many of the most important taboos vanished. By now, it was open season for attacks on Brezhnev – the phrase 'era of stagnation' entered the official vocabulary. Historical figures were reassessed: a clutch of leading Bolsheviks, murdered by Stalin and non-persons for decades, were rehabilitated, with dozens of newspaper articles about their fate, and the show trials of the 1930s were publicly condemned. Lenin was still firmly in place in the gallery of official Soviet heroes, but other former leading lights found themselves on the historical rubbish heap. Indeed, they themselves became taboo. Librarians were told to remove political material from the Brezhnev and Chernenko era and – in the unlikely event of anybody asking for it – to say that the material was 'borrowed'.

Most tellingly of all, the school history exams for 1988 were cancelled. So many conventional wisdoms had been overturned in the previous months that the existing Soviet history books became useless. The decision to cancel the history exams was one of the most revealing public admissions that the whole way of looking at Soviet life had begun to change. In the old days, things were simpler: when Stalin's secret police chief, Lavrenty Beria, was disgraced and then executed in 1953, it was necessary to wipe him out of people's minds. Subscribers to the *Soviet Encyclopedia* received a special additional article on the Bering Strait and were told to stick this over the Beria article. From a mixture of fear and obedience, many people complied. Now, the rewriting of history was no longer so Orwellian. Instead, it represented an attempt to come face to face with some of the lies of the past decades.

The crimes of Stalin were part of the staple diet of the liberal press. *Moscow News* talked of the 'genocide' of the forced collectivization of the 1930s, in which millions died. There were reports, too, on the excavations in the forest of Kurapaty, in Belorussia, where tens of thousands had been shot and buried in shallow graves in 1937. The authorities attempted to prevent demonstrations being held at the site. Already, however, the idea of popular protest – especially on such an apparently unexceptionable subject – was beginning to take root. *Ogonyok* noted that this conviction on the part of the authorities that 'they know what is best' was typical. 'Have you seen one of our ideologists speaking to a crowd these days? There is no sadder spectacle to be seen.'

Social taboos were broken, too. Three years after it began, the anti-alcohol campaign was admitted to have gone badly wrong. The campaign had not reduced the amount of alcohol being drunk – it had merely driven it underground. The loss to the state coffers was so dramatic that it caused a reported drop of more than 2 per cent of the country's gross national product. But the vodka trade itself continued unabated. At several points in the city, taxi drivers waited all day and all night – ready to sell you vodka, at a price, out of a crate in the back of the car. It was illegal, but unhampered; the appropriate authorities received their cut.

The reduced vodka production led to other ways of making up the shortfall. Almost half a million people were charged, in a single year, in connection with the production of *samogon* (literally, 'self-brew'), the Russian moonshine. As a result of the explosion in *samogon* production, sugar was soon in short supply and had to be rationed in many areas. But sugar was only the safest of a number of ingredients used in lethal concoctions – from shoe polish to eau de Cologne. One man from a remote area of northern Russia complained to an interviewer from Moscow that the capital was better off than the provinces, because 'you have cheap eau de Cologne – we only have the expensive brands out here'. More than 11,000 died during the anti-alcohol campaign – 'almost as many as we lost in Afghanistan', *Ogonyok* remarked. It was a stark reminder that the best intentions could go lethally wrong.

At the same time as the polemics in the press and the greater honesty on social issues, barriers in literature and the arts were being pushed back, too. Many banned works were published, including Boris Pasternak's *Doctor Zhivago*, which gained its author a Nobel Prize and unleashed a torrent of abuse against the 'hidden enemy filled with malice' for his work which 'spat in the face of the people'. Vasily Grossman's *Life and Fate*, which Brezhnev's chief ideologist said would never be published in 200 years, had seen the light of Soviet day. The 'anti-Soviet' memoirs of Nadezhda Mandelstam, widow of the poet Osip Mandelstam, were published. There were hints that Solzhenitsyn might soon be published in his own country, for the first time since his expulsion in 1974.

In the cinema, too, things began to move. *Repentance* had provided a launchpad for *glasnost*, in its examination of the Stalinist past, in 1987. Now, it was a matter of tackling the present day. Some films took *perestroika* as their starting point, battled with all sorts of allowable punchbags (corrupt bureaucrats and similar) and concluded that, in this new, wondrous age, everything was now perfect. At a time when so little in the system itself had truly changed, it was a depressingly pliant view. But other films went further.

Little Vera – the title could also translate as 'A Small Belief' – was, in the conventional sense, a depressing film. It told the story of a hopeless teenager and her hopeless life in the Soviet provinces. The only chink of light in her life is a passionate liaison, which leads nowhere. Not much reason for taking heart, you might think. And yet, to watch a film like that – in the newly opened, crowded *videosalon* on Arbat Street in central Moscow in 1988 – was to feel your spirits lift. At last, th era of yes-men seemed to be drawing to a close. The film portrayed real, grimy Soviet life. And, at the same time, it did not pretend that there were simple solutions. The good fairy of *perestroika* would not wave a wand and turn Vera's life from grim to magical. When Gorbachev saw the film, he was reportedly shocked at the sex – in itself a reminder of the deep conservatism of Soviet society, since the single, simple love-scene was by no means provocative. More important, however, was the film's no-punches-pulled candour, which seemed to hold the key to the birth of a free spirit, as yet scarcely dreamed of. It was no surprise to find that the writer of the screenplay had almost got herself thrown out of film school when *Little Vera* was conceived.

Even the most surprising places sometimes gave a glimpse of the changes that were on the way. The Exhibition of Economic Achievements of the USSR had always been one of the most hideous monuments in Moscow: expanses of Stalinist propaganda, with immense and immensely ugly pavilions detailing Soviet brilliance in every sphere from cattle-breeding to space travel. It represented Stalinism incarnate. As *Ogonyok* wrote:

It isn't simply a model, it's a symbol of our great country, covering an area of 750 acres. A symbol 'exalting' us to the shining heights, where cramped communal flats and squalid five-storey prefabs are transformed into splendid sculpted palaces; where instead of queues for dirty-pink sausage which you wouldn't give to the cat, we see a rich abundance of veal and sturgeon; and where antediluvian educational machines are replaced by gleaming electronic miracles of scientific and technological progress – of strictly limited availability, of course. How sweet it used to be to wander around this fantasy world, blissfully murmuring to oneself: 'We *can* do it if we try . . .' We never used to doubt the ennobling power of this lie, never paused to think that all lies degrade us, liers and lied-to alike.

The description was deadly accurate. And yet, here at the Exhibition of Economic Achievements, during a damp weekend in autumn 1988, one could see the contradictory changes that were on the way. One event that weekend was described as a 'discussion-fashion show', which took place in a hall under a scarlet-and-white banner declaring, 'We will fulfil the decisions of the 27th party congress'. Several fashion co-operatives were showing off their best. Many of the audience did not like what they saw and there were boos from the floor. Those who were involved in presenting the show got a rough reception: a man stood up and accused one of the fashion designers of wearing 'foreign clothes' herself. She was, he implied, a sell-out and a hypocrite. As it happened, the woman was wearing clothes that she had made herself, from Soviet materials. None the less, the distrust in the crowd of anything that was different was palpable.

Younger members of the audience were disappointed at the hostile reactions. A woman in her twenties, almost in tears, commented that if on the Metro a girl wore a simple, fashionable skirt, she immediately got critical comments from her fellow-passengers. 'People will laugh and point at you for being different. It's an aggressive psychology here.' Soviet society was itself, she implied, sick at heart. Another member of the audience complained of the Soviet Union's long isolation. 'We're not ready for the avant-garde. How could we be?' A third man said: 'The Gulag archipelago has destroyed our ability to think innovatively.' But, if the conservatism was real enough, it was also notable that people were not frightened to discuss the reality. In print, the taboo of *The Gulag Archipelago*, with its devastating analysis of Soviet state repression, had not yet been broken. But the fear was already receding.

In the same exhibition grounds – whose most conspicuous feature was the massive Stalinist statue of the Worker and Collective Farm Girl, wheatsheaf raised high above their heads, which towered over the entrance – a different kind of discussion meeting was organized the following day. If the fashion meeting served as a reminder of the deep conservatism of much of Soviet society, this second meeting made it clear that it was no longer possible to accept the old argument that Soviet society was incapable of change. All the old certainties were turned upside down.

Here, for the first time, I saw Russians speak openly, and unharassed, in a public place. It was an extraordinary experience. Many of the subjects raised at that meeting could not possibly have been touched upon in the press: there was criticism of the KGB, and of the Communist Party, too. That, in itself, was important. Crucially, though, most of the crowd packed into the exhibition hall – standing room only, and not much of that – were not the dissident intellectuals who had always been waiting for the opportunity to speak out. This was almost as mixed a crowd as the crush that filled the Metro to bursting point day after day. True, they had come along to an *Ogonyok*-sponsored meeting, which put them in the 'liberal' category. But some were there almost by chance, out-of-towners who were visiting the exhibition during a brief trip to the capital. Everybody seemed to have a different agenda. But there was one thing they had in common: they all wanted change.

Those frozen moments on a Leningrad bus back in 1976, when the little boy horrified his fellow-passengers by chattering about Voice of America, were part of another era, which could not easily return. People demanded answers. They assumed that KGB men were standing somewhere in the room, taking notes. There were jokes to that effect. But it no longer mattered. They knew that they were there together – and how could the KGB arrest the whole hall? In 1984, in a memoir concerning the then-imprisoned Russian poet, Irina Ratushinskaya, a friend of hers from student days had described a brief stage sketch that somehow slipped past an obtuse Soviet censor:

It lasted no longer than half a minute. At first the stage was dark. Then a flashlight beam landed on the scared face of a mime, who said: 'What can I do alone, anyway?' Another beam, another mime: 'What can I do alone, anyway?' There were about twenty of them on that stage. Their faces appeared out of the darkness one by one, and each of them said: 'What can I do alone, anyway?' They marched away backstage, chanting all together, their voices almost cheerful: 'What can I do alone, anyway? What can I do alone, anyway? What can I do alone, anyway?'

It was a telling image of not-yet people power. 'What can I do alone?' was a sentiment that could be heard, again and again – sometimes in those exact words – throughout the Soviet bloc during the 1980s. All that was needed was a little more illumination on the stage and each of those individuals would realize how much could be achieved. The discussion meeting, in one corner of the Exhibition of Economic Achievements of the USSR, served as a reminder that these dissonant, questioning voices would not necessarily remain alone and in the darkness for ever. There was an excitement in the room that day as a hall full of Russians began to realize that no taboo need be for ever.

The Soviet Union, by now, was full of such improvised meetings. An important forum for the airing of alternative views was provided by the *nieformaly*, the 'informal organizations', which, in the words of one Soviet paper, were springing up 'like mushrooms after rain'. By 1988, there were tens of thousands across the country. The earliest groups all dealt with subjects which appeared to be innocuous – the environment, cultural history or simply *perestroika*, a codeword for anything and everything. But these grassroots movements were another important sign of what was on the way.

One of the best known of the *nieformaly* was Memorial, whose honorary chairman was Sakharov and which was devoted to ensuring that the Stalinist legacy should be fully acknowledged and publicly repented. That continued to be a sensitive subject. The authorities did everything they could to hamper Memorial when it held a founding conference in Moscow in January 1989; publication of the organization's draft statute was delayed, and a bank account for money for a monument to honour those who died in Stalin's purges was frozen.

Even those *nieformaly* with the most innocent titles could be a Trojan horse for more subversive ideas. At a meeting of the Movement for Democratic Perestroika (what could be more ideologically sound than that?) in a university institute in the south of Moscow, it was already possible to sense the cat-and-mouse game that was being played. Theoretically, this was no more than an innocuous discussion group. Those at the meeting were keen not to confront the authorities head on: they rejected the Democratic Union's policy of illegal demonstrations, for example. Many of the group's supporters were themselves Communist

Party members and they did not want to be seen as – in the words of one of those at the meeting – 'a frankly dissident group'. But this discretion did not protect them from official displeasure. The meeting had to be moved, at the last moment, because of a ban on using the official hall. As one man put it: 'The institute gets a headache from our meetings.'

Despite their apparent innocence, these groups consciously paved the way for more radical change in the future. Igor, a mathematician involved with the informal organizations, talked about the huge problems that they faced. He acknowledged that the hardliners still wielded considerable power. And yet, he argued, change already had an unstoppable momentum. The regime had lost its ability to instil real fear. As one (half-daring) badge declared: 'Say – what you think!'

Many believed that the process could still be reversed. After all, they argued, the Soviet Union had been here once before, twenty-five years earlier, during the Khrushchev thaw. Then, one fine day, the curtain came down – and it was as if the past had never been. The hardliners had already tried it a few months earlier, with the Andreyeva letter. And they could try it again, with tanks. Igor argued cautiously that there was still a case for optimism, however much those in the Kremlin might want to hold on to a version of the status quo. 'I don't see any sign of the party giving up its hierarchical rights. But it's difficult to imagine now that things would go backwards completely.' Already, he argued, there was beginning to be a place in society for Rosa Luxemburg's *Andersdenkende*, those who think differently. 'Solzhenitsyn was alone – and yet he still played an important role for his generation. He was an influence. Now, there are many, many more such people. Today, it would be much more difficult to get rid of them.'

One of the periodic crises in the Kremlin at this time – crises that were becoming increasingly frequent – illustrated the way in which the Soviet Union was suspended precariously between the old and the new style. Days of mounting rumours culminated in a special session of the central committee that was called urgently, for 30 September 1988. The Supreme Soviet, the Soviet parliament, was convened for a special session the following day. Shevardnadze cut short a visit to the United Nations in New York; Dmitry Yazov, the defence minister, returned from India; Sergei Akhromeyev, the chief of staff, came back from Sweden. The Soviet press said nothing, even though news of the central committee meeting had been made public to foreign journalists and was filling the front pages with speculation worldwide. The liberals were worried: was Gorbachev's head on the block?

In fact, as on so many occasions to come, Gorbachev sliced through the hardliners. Ligachev was demoted from ideology to agriculture — where he would be a suitable scapegoat for everything that was certain to go wrong. Other hardliners were scattered. Gromyko, who had served as foreign minister for almost three decades, before being kicked upstairs to the then powerless post of president in 1985, was now eased out entirely.

On the one hand, Gromyko's departure marked an important symbolic break with the past. But the way that he went was the same as in the old days. The central committee plenum, with its dramatic sackings, was all over, with almost no discussion, within an hour. The special session of the Supreme Soviet — for which some of the 1500 delegates had flown from the remotest parts of the country, through more time zones than between London and Tokyo, at one day's notice — was equally unreal. The delegates were not the limousine-driving classes: they knew that they had only walk-on parts to play. They had a few privileges — they were, for example, allowed to bump ordinary citizens off overbooked aeroplanes — but they were not members of the true elite. Again and again, a ritual was played out: 'In favour? — Against? None. — Abstentions? None.' Unanimous vote after unanimous vote — including the vote for the 'election' of Gorbachev as chairman of the Supreme Soviet, or president.

Watching from the balcony, one could see that many of the delegates — arranged regionally and some wearing their local national dress — had scarcely survived the long journey; they slept throughout the proceedings. Instead of listening to the dull speeches, delegates compared the booty found on a tour of the shops during the brief, expenses-paid visit to the Soviet capital. An illustrated children's book which several delegates from the Soviet Far East had bought caused especial interest as it was handed around during Gorbachev's speech. There were schoolroom japes, too: one delegate found himself being tickled on the back of the neck as everybody waited to be allowed home again.

At that time, three years into the Gorbachev era, it would still have been unthinkable for a delegate to get to his feet and argue with the views of a speaker at the rostrum. Debates, disagreement, dissent — these were still alien concepts. Demonstrators on the streets were still being locked up; the alternative press was banned. But the countdown had already begun.

It was still easy to find devoted supporters of Gorbachev. For many

Russians, as they began to emerge from a lifetime of fear and lies, he was what one Russian described as a *tsar-batyushka* — lord-and-master and fairy godmother rolled into one. For some, it was little short of hero worship. Like the cinema ticket-seller I talked to, who worried about those who were 'putting on the brakes'. Of Gorbachev, the Communist Party leader, she had only this to say: 'May God preserve him. May God preserve him.' — whereupon she crossed herself fervently, twice.

But not all Russians were inclined to be so solicitous. Gorbachev had promised that *perestroika* would begin to deliver the goods within a couple of years. He talked of a steady improvement in the people's standard of living and of raising people's well-being to a qualitatively new level. The reality was different. As the surface grime was cleaned off the Soviet machine, it became more obvious than ever that the machine itself was seriously flawed. The command economy began to collapse, but there was nothing to replace it. People's living standards dropped, sharply — as did their morale.

In 1987, there were the first indications of the rebelliousness to come. There were a number of reports of small strikes (euphemistically described as 'stoppages') in many corners of the Union. They were mostly small and isolated: a few hundred workers on strike at a bus factory here, protests over food supplies in a truck factory there. Nevertheless, the strikes hinted at the problems that lay around the corner if the economy was not seen to improve.

The turning-point in Gorbachev's domestic popularity was probably his visit to the Siberian city of Krasnoyarsk in September 1988. He popped up there after his summer holiday break, for a televised walkabout. So far, so normal: there had been plenty of those before, where Gorbachev had been mobbed by the adoring crowds. In some ways, the walkabout was the same as those that had come before. There was the elegant Raisa, smiling delphically and signing autographs in the background, while the KGB men in their well-cut suits observed the crowds with the calmly suspicious gaze which marks out secret servicemen the world over. But, in other respects, these encounters were different.

There were moments of enthusiasm. But, again and again, there were angry complaints, too, and complaints about the empty shelves. 'There's no sausage, there's nothing, not even hot water,' said one man. Another man interrupted Gorbachev in full flight about the miracles yet to come, saying: 'It won't happen. And I'm not the only one to think so.' 'Will this be on television?' asked a third, sceptically. In the event, much of it was shown — if only in an attempt to prove that *glasnost* was real. But the halo had been punctured. Within months, Russians would have a public forum where all their pent-up grievances could be aired. The formation of a new parliament, where the Communists could no longer call all the shots, was only months away. In one corner of the country, meanwhile, the Soviet system itself was already under attack — and would shortly be defeated.

4 Unlocking the Side Door

By the end of 1988, the Russian federation — heartland of Soviet power, an immense republic that stretched from Leningrad to Vladivostok — was barely starting to grapple with the implications of the changes that were under way; the revolution from below had not yet begun. But, in the Baltic republics, a breathtaking revolution was almost over.

Disaffection in the western republics of Estonia, Latvia and Lithuania had always been greater than elsewhere in the Soviet Union. According to one compulsory schoolroom song: 'My address is not a house, nor a street — my address is the USSR.' For those in the Baltic republics, that was a poor joke. If the Balts could have sent out collective change of address cards, they would happily have done so. Throughout the Brezhnev years, there was no expectation that change could come in the foreseeable future. But the resentment at living according to Moscow's rules was at least as great in the Baltic republics as in those countries of central and eastern Europe which had become part of the Soviet bloc after the Second World War.

Homo sovieticus, with his obedient way of thinking, had never quite taken over in the Baltic republics. All three Baltic states were annexed by Stalin in 1940, under the secret terms of the Molotov-Ribbentrop pact between Nazi Germany and the Soviet Union, signed the previous year. In the West, the protocols were published after 1945, on the basis of copies that survived in the Nazi archives. In Moscow, their existence was denied for fifty years, even though every Balt knew that they were real. The language of the secret protocols was blunt, talking of a 'territorial and political rearrangement in the areas belonging to the Baltic states' and describing, line by cynical line, where the new border between Germany and the Soviet Union should go after the two countries divided up the spoils.

The Baltic states, like long-divided Poland, only regained their independence in 1918, after years of being part of the tsarist empire. But their sense of nationhood was strong. As one Estonian remarked, in

1988, of the inter-war period of independence: 'Those twenty years have spoiled us, for ever.' The sense of separateness had been strong even during the tsarist era. Now, the Baltic republics felt that Soviet rule had brought them nothing but political and economic hard times. The Balts looked enviously across the Baltic Sea to Scandinavia. Estonia felt especially close ties with Finland – the two languages are related and Estonians were able to receive and understand Finnish television broadcasts. The melancholy 'What if . . .' game was almost a national disease. Stalin had launched a war in 1939 against Finland – which had also once been part of the tsarist empire – but had eventually withdrawn. As the efficient Balts gazed at the affluence and stability of Finland, they wondered what life would be like if they, too, had ended up on the other side of the curtain.

The official version was that there had been a revolutionary action of the working people against the bourgeois regime. In the Estonian capital, for example, this is how the guidebook told it:

On the morning of 21 June 1940, the factory whistles in Tallinn gave the signal for the beginning of revolutionary action of the working people. The fascist bourgeois dictatorship was overthrown. On 6 August 1940, the Supreme Soviet of the USSR complied with the request of the State Chamber of Deputies and accepted Estonia into the Union of Soviet Socialist Republics as an equal Union Republic. Tallinn became the capital of the Estonian Soviet Socialist Republic. The red flag of freedom – the state flag of the republic – fluttered over the ancient tower of Pikk Hermann, Tall Hermann.

Nothing there to hint at the reality – the secret clauses to the deal that Vyacheslav Molotov, Stalin's foreign minister, and Joachim von Ribbentrop, his German counterpart, had toasted in vodka and champagne, together with Stalin, in the Kremlin on the night of 23 August 1939. The Soviet Union's annexation of the three Baltic states in 1940 – officially denounced by the West but soon accepted de facto – proceeded smoothly. According to the official history books, at least. The truth was that hundreds of thousands of Balts were deported to Siberia, where many of them died, in an extraordinary attempt to crush any possible national resistance to the Soviet takeover and to engineer a permanent population shift. As a Lithuanian MP later pointed out – to Moscow's fury, for there was no greater shibboleth – the Balts had, proportionally, lost more people in Stalin's camps after the annexation of the Baltic states than Russia lost to the Nazis in the Second World War. A strong partisan resistance movement, involving tens of thousands, continued for several years after the war.

Eventually the resistance ended; only the anger remained. Nevertheless, the contrast with the rest of the Soviet Union was always clear. In the Brezhnev era, the Baltic republics were sometimes described as the *sovietskaya zagranitsa*, the 'Soviet abroad': better clothes, better cafes, better shops, than in Russia proper. Tallinn and the other Baltic capitals were used by Soviet film-makers as a stand-in for Western locations – understandably so. Tallinn, like the Latvian capital, Riga, was a Hanseatic port and the medieval, European legacy was strong. The winding streets of the Old Town and the steep red-tiled roofs of the merchants' houses created an atmosphere closer to the Baltic ports of Lubeck and Gdansk than to anything in Russia, to the east. When I first visited the city in 1976, with friends from Leningrad, there was no mistaking the fact that Tallinn, with its cafes and self-confident charm, was part of a different world. Even Estonia's taste in popular music was closer to that of the non-Soviet world outside. Tallinn's bars (fewer drunks, and a greater variety of drinks, than anywhere in Moscow or Leningrad) were playing records that were fresh in the Western charts. After living in Leningrad, that came as a shock: I had become accustomed to the idea that Western pop music, when played in Soviet public places, meant easy-listening hits from the previous decade. (If music was not saccharin, then it was frowned on by the Brezhnevite authorities and even banned. 'Alternative' music was almost in the same dangerous category as illegal, *samizdat* literature.) To my surprise, too, people were not routinely rude in restaurants. Truly, this must be *zagranitsa*.

Yet it was only half-true. In the end, the system was more powerful than national identity. An old East European joke told of the Russian who took a train to Paris and the Frenchman who took a train to Moscow. Both got out in Warsaw, convinced that they must already have arrived. The Frenchman saw the almost-empty shops and the grey look of the city, and thought this had to be Moscow; the Russian saw the greater variety of goods and more fashionable decoration than he had ever known, and was convinced he had arrived in Paris. The Baltic republics were a similar kind of halfway house: they, too, seemed shockingly poor and primitive to the outsider arriving from Helsinki or Stockholm, and shockingly rich and sophisticated to the visitor from Leningrad or Moscow.

With their different historical baggage, it was hardly surprising that the Baltic republics were the first to explode, once half an opportunity presented itself. The prologue to the dramatic events in the Baltic republics came in August 1987, when – despite threats from the authorities – demonstrations were held against the Molotov-Ribbentrop pact. There were some arrests and there were tirades in the Soviet press against the 'paltry group of aggressive extremists' who had gathered for 'anti-Soviet hate rallies'. Then came huge ecological protests in autumn 1987, over seemingly non-political issues like open-pit mining in Estonia and a nuclear power station in Lithuania. But all of this was a mere warm-up for what was about to come.

It was in spring 1988 that the juggernaut of change seriously began to roll. By now, when *perestroika* was officially being heralded as containing the solution to all the world's problems, the Balts were beginning to realize that the new party line – reform, democratization, streamlining the economy – could have a hidden pay-off. All they needed to do was proclaim loyalty to *perestroika*. The rest would look after itself.

On 13 April 1988, Estonian Television held a live discussion in the weekly series called *Let's Think Again*, which had become immensely popular because of its tendency to break new ground. It was the familiar television format – moderator, panel of learned guests – which usually goes on interminably and gets nowhere. This night's programme was, however, historic by any measure. It was only a month after the publication of the Andreyeva letter and the radicals in Russia were not yet beginning to stir. Here, though, in quiet, sensible Estonia, the Communist world was about to end. Participants in the debate, following up an idea first tentatively floated at a meeting of Estonian writers and artists a fortnight earlier, argued that a mass-movement pressure group should be created for reform. It could, for example, be called a Popular Front. An appeal was issued to viewers, on air: what do you think? The programme's participants became enthusiastic about their proposed new project and the programme itself was extended beyond its usual running length. And then, after the programme was over, the participants stayed behind in the empty television studio. Together, until the early hours, they wrote a draft version of the manifesto for the as yet non-existent organization.

If one single event marked the moment at which the collapse of Soviet power became inevitable, then it was probably that television programme – which set Estonia alight, but of which the huge majority of the Soviet Union's 300 million citizens remained unaware. The response to the television appeal, and to the Popular Front's manifesto, was instant and overwhelming. This was no longer about the lofty kind of change, a 'restructuring', imposed by politicians inhabiting what they believed to be the corridors of eternal power – in the Kremlin and in the Communist Party central committee headquarters on Old Square in Moscow. Rather, this movement drew its strength only from the popular will. Without popular support, the idea would have been stillborn, but, backed by mass demonstrations, there was nothing that a Popular Front could not do. In the weeks and months to come, the pace of change in Estonia – and, soon afterwards, in Latvia and Lithuania – would sweep everything else before it.

The official name of the new Estonian organization was the Popular Front for the Support of Perestroika. It sounded well-behaved and manageable. But the reality was that a death knell was being sounded for the Union of Soviet Socialist Republics and for Communist rule. The movement was popular as nothing in the Soviet republic had ever been before. In June 1988, the Popular Front organized a huge rally in the song festival grounds on the edge of Tallinn. By now, the Front had 50,000 signed-up supporters and its rallies brought crowds of up to a quarter of a million – one in six of the population. Most dangerously for Moscow, the local Communist Party – already wary of marginalizing itself by being too harsh – gave up repressing the radicals and gave the Popular Front an official platform.

Some of the changes were, on the face of it, to do with greater economic autonomy. As one Estonian politician pointed out, 'In our own republic, we are not entitled to fix the price of a cinema ticket, a cake recipe, or the cost of a jar of Tallinn sprats.' Put like that, it sounded like a good piece of *perestroika* talk, which encouraged decentralization of decision-making for greater efficiency. In fact, Moscow soon began to understand that there was an alarming sub-text: most Balts did not wish to be part of the Soviet Communist economy at all. They were ready to deal with the Communist economy, as a partner, but they dreamed of being quite separate, just as they had once been.

The Soviet authorities could not decide how to react. Sometimes, they helplessly went along with the fiction that this was just what the *perestroika* doctor had ordered. Sometimes, the propaganda pendulum swung the other way. In an article about the Estonian Popular Front in August 1988, *Pravda*, for example, talked of a venomous hatred for all things socialist, hiding behind a screen of *glasnost*, *perestroika* and democracy. But the Estonians were unabashed. When the Popular Front held a huge rally in September – a song festival that celebrated the changes that had already taken place – the new reformist Communist Party leader, Vaino Valjas, was among those who attended. The Estonians began, without exaggeration, to talk of the events of 1988 as their 'singing revolution'. The Popular Front became part of the establishment (and indeed, many of its leaders had emerged from the establishment); some Popular Front leaders were co-opted into the new Communist Party leadership. One-party rule was being destroyed, from within. The implications for the Kremlin were disastrous.

The euphoria of these months would never be repeated: the much greater victories that were to come would seem an anti-climax by comparison with the extraordinary nature of the events of 1988. But, like the birth of Solidarity in Poland in 1980, the Balts' early victories (followed, as in Poland, by many apparent defeats) provided a regional cornerstone for all the other changes in the next years.

Every few weeks in 1988, the Balts slaughtered another sacred cow. On 16 November, the Estonian parliament (still Communist-dominated – its elected successor would feel able to be even more radical) rejected amendments to the Soviet constitution which sought to increase Moscow's control. Estonia declared its own sovereignty – for the moment, still within the Soviet Union – and gave itself a veto over Soviet laws. It was a quite unthinkable challenge to Moscow. Theoretically, Article 72 of the Soviet constitution gave republics the right 'freely to secede from the USSR'. But that was only for decorative purposes. It was never intended to be taken seriously. Moscow was worried at the implications of what had taken place. By now, Gorbachev's patience had snapped. 'We are one family, we have a common home. Some people omit that now, and try to idealize the bourgeois period in the development of the Baltic republics. But we know how backward Lithuania was, or when the greatest number of people left Estonia because life there was impossible.' Gorbachev dispatched Viktor Chebrikov, a former head of the KGB, to give the Estonians a dressing-down and get them back into line. Chebrikov's mission, unsurprisingly, had no effect.

In the other Baltic republics, the changes were equally dramatic. Latvia and Lithuania also formed Popular Fronts, whose aims were similar to that of Estonia. Lithuania's equivalent was called *Lietuvos Persitvarkymo Sajudis* – literally, Lithuanian Movement for Perestroika. It was not long before no Lithuanian bothered with the Perestroika. They did not want restructuring of the existing system. They wanted a different system altogether. Soon, it was just the Movement – Sajudis. Each of the three republics was different in its approach, but each played an important part in the drama that was just beginning to unfold. In October 1988, Rupert Cornwell, then the *Independent*'s Moscow correspondent, described the atmosphere of wonderment at the huge rally that took place to mark the founding congress of Sajudis, in the Lithuanian capital, Vilnius.

> The crowd gathered from every direction, slow streams of people carrying candles, torches and the long-banned red, green and yellow flags of 'bourgeois' Lithuania. As they approached the square, the streams became rivers of their own, of old and young, children on their fathers' shoulders, walking to the soft rhythmic chanting of patriotic songs which everyone knew by heart. Finally, there were 200,000 of them, crushed together under a night sky like black crystal. The mood was of rapture, barely suspended disbelief, as they listened to songs and poetry long prohibited ... Sajudis was formed only three months ago, as a ginger group for reforms. This showed that it was already far more: an independent movement, whose leaders' speeches were less platforms for change than torrents of pent-up nationhood, and of an anger at Stalin's crimes against Lithuania, only sharpened by forty years of historical ties.

The old towns of Tallinn, Vilnius and Riga were as tranquil as ever. But every political taboo was smashed. There was a remarkable confidence that it was too late for the clock to be fully turned back. Sitting in the office of the Estonian Popular Front in Tallinn in March 1989, where posters condemning the Molotov-Ribbentrop pact hung on the wall, one of the Front's leaders, Marju Lauristin, talked of a possible 'dying colossus' scenario, where the Balts would be wounded by an angry flick of the tail during the imperial monster's final agonies. Lauristin, a sociology professor at Tartu University, argued that the break-up of an empire did not need to be violent. 'After all, you British have lived through the break-up of an empire.' But Lauristin − who later gave up her Communist Party card and became the leader of Estonia's Social Democrats − insisted, too, that if Moscow did try to introduce a crackdown, it would solve nothing, and would ultimately only lead to the same outcome. 'It will be a catastrophe, tanks on the streets. But things have gone too far. The Soviet economy is in such deep crisis − it could not survive the backlash.'

Baltic independence was not yet on the official agenda in early 1989. But you did not have to scratch hard to find what lay underneath the talk of autonomy. One Estonian shrugged half-apologetically when I suggested that the Baltic secession he was talking of must surely lead to the collapse of the Soviet Union itself: once things had started to unravel, it was clear that the Balts would not be the only ones who wanted out. The response was simple. 'The Roman Empire was supposed to last for ever. The Third Reich was supposed to last for ever. And now this Soviet experiment is coming to an end.' Arriving from Moscow in early 1989, that kind of heresy made you gasp. But this was not some fringe crazy who was speaking: Andres Raid was a political commentator with Estonian Television. I asked if he was really so sure that the imperial game was finished. He paused and then came out with a reply which was, if anything, still more heretical, in its explicit rejection of Soviet rule. 'To be on the safe side: I am not certain. But I hope.'

Theoretically, anti-Soviet talk was still a state crime at that time. But, in the Baltic republics, Soviet laws were fast becoming an irrelevance. Already, the reference in the official Tallinn guidebook to the 'red flag of freedom' flying over Pikk Hermann was out of date. In February 1989, Estonia's blue, black and white flag was officially raised, where the hammer and sickle had flown for the past four decades. Nothing was sacred any more.

Each of the three Baltic republics was now racing ahead with radical change. Gorbachev encouraged a limited decentralization of power; what began to happen was de-Sovietization. In Vilnius, a banner hung over the main street, still known − though not for much longer − as Lenin Avenue. The slogan declared, 'Lithuania without sovereignty is Lithuania without a future.' Remarkably, this was not even a Sajudis banner, but one belonging to the Lithuanian Communist Party. Sovereignty was a useful word for everybody at this stage of the Baltic revolution. It could make the most cautious politicians sound radical, which was useful for the Communists, in order to please the people; and it made the radical politicians sound moderate, which was useful for the implicitly pro-independence movements, who did not yet want to be out in the open. Nobody, after all, could seriously quarrel with the idea of sovereignty, which merely meant that the Balts should have more rights. It was, however, dangerous terrain for Moscow. A Lithuanian saying declared: 'Gorbachev was only joking. The problems started when the Lithuanians took him seriously.'

Even in Latvia, the quietest of the three republics, the transformation of the republic was happening at a greater speed than anybody there could ever have guessed. A glance at two rival statues in Riga gave a hint of what was happening. At the end of Lenin Avenue stood a huge statue of the founder of the Soviet Union himself, with his cap crumpled in his left hand and his right arm raised to the sky. At Lenin's feet were an unhappy five tulips and seven carnations, laid out individually by an official delegation. A few hundred yards behind his back, further along Lenin Avenue, on the bridge leading across to the Old Town, was the Freedom Monument, erected in 1935 in commemoration of Latvia's independence in 1918. At the base of the Freedom Monument were thousands of flowers — from simple bunches of snowdrops and violets to elaborate bouquets — together with the national flags of Latvia, Lithuania and Estonia. Until recently, anybody who tried to pay tribute at the Freedom Monument was bundled off by the police. Now, however, it became a crucial focus, as the nation began to find its confidence once more.

Latvia was more cautious than the other Baltic republics — not least because of its ethnic mix. Latvians accounted for barely half of the inhabitants, following an intensive policy of Russification in all three Baltic republics after the Second World War (before the war, Russians had formed 12 per cent of the population in Latvia). Ethnic Russians in Latvia and the other Baltic republics formed pro-Soviet pressure groups and, certainly, the needs of the local Russians needed to be addressed in all three republics. The Russification policy, which was intended to pacify and neutralize the Balts, had radically changed the population mix in each of the republics. In Estonia, about 40 per cent of the population were non-Estonian, mostly Russians (before the war, 86 per cent of the inhabitants of the republic were Estonian and only 8 per cent Russian). Even Lithuania, ethnically 'purest', had a 20 per cent non-Lithuanian minority — partly Russians and partly Poles who lived in territories that had once formed part of Poland.

Movements were formed in all three republics which claimed to be internationalist in spirit: Inter-Movement in Estonia, Inter-Front in Latvia and Unity in Lithuania. In reality, the internationalists were often more chauvinist than the breakaway nationalists. Few Russians who settled in the Baltic republics felt it was appropriate to learn the local language; they took it for granted that the locals would learn Russian. But, despite this ill-defined sense of power, Russians also resented the fact that Balts lived better, on average, than they did. Many Russians were convinced that it was *they* who had sacrificed themselves for the benefit of the Balts.

It had long been one of the paradoxes of the Soviet bloc that Russia itself was worse off in material terms than many of the central European countries where the Kremlin called the shots. Central Europeans deeply resented Moscow for destroying their economies and their lives. But many Russians, in turn, resented the fact that Poles, Czechs and Hungarians lived better than they did. Thus it was, too, within the Soviet Union. The Baltic republics were many times more affluent than Russia, which they blamed for all their misfortunes. Even in the Caucasian republics of Armenia and Georgia, life was less hungry and less oppressive than in the Russian Federation. It was a uniquely unbalanced relationship. Most empires are rich and take from the poor. The Soviet empire, on the other hand, was poor — and (apart from its huge army and ambitious space programme) remained poor, even while it controlled the destinies of other, more prosperous nations.

Despite the resentments, the pro-Kremlin groups in the Baltic republics never gained mass support on the same scale as the Popular Fronts, even among the ethnic Russian population. None the less, there was hostility towards the idea of independence, especially at this early stage. There were strikes and protests throughout 1989 as the position of Soviet power was eroded. At demonstrations on the anniversary of the Soviet annexation, banners in Tallinn complained of the 'Estonian falsification of history'. At a ship repair yard, Russian strikers argued that new language laws — which made Estonian, not Russian, the republic's main language — meant that they, the Russians, were now second-class citizens in the republic. One woman at the yard was angry that managers were obliged to know both Estonian and Russian in order to communicate with the workforce. 'Now, they want us to learn Estonian. We just can't do that. They've cut us out from start to finish. Now, a factory manager has to be able to speak Estonian. It's *very* offensive.'

She and her comrades made it clear, too, that they were unhappy at the undermining of ideology in the Baltic republics. 'The Soviet Communist Party is working for socialism. But the Estonian Communist Party is working for a return to bourgeois rule. They want to restore the republic as it was, before 1940 . . . Maybe Estonia was an independent country. But I think they've lost *nothing*.' Yevgeny Kogan, with a bushy beard and the build of a Sumo wrestler, was one of the Russian minority's most vocal representatives in the Estonian parliament. He insisted that Estonia must drop any fanciful ideas about independence. 'I'm not responsible for what Stalin did fifty years ago. Now, Estonia is part of the Soviet Union. We have to begin with the realities.'

For the moment, many Russians unquestioningly accepted that view.

The old beliefs had not yet been shattered. On an overnight train from Tallinn to Riga, I shared a compartment with a young Russian conscript in an encounter that provided a reminder of how fear and ignorance were still an essential part of Soviet life in spring 1989. The conductor brought us tea, from the samovar to be found at the end of every Soviet train carriage, and we chatted for a while as the train rumbled into the darkness. Then, from some throwaway comment that I made about Britain, the soldier suddenly realized that he had been drinking tea with a citizen of a real-McCoy capitalist country, a representative of the *kapstran*; until then he had apparently assumed from my foreigner's accent that I was a Balt. He looked shocked and nervous, as though mentally checking what he might have said wrong during our innocuous conversation. I reassured him, with difficulty; the worry in his eyes gradually faded. That fear was in itself indicative: it would have been impossible to encounter such fear among the Balts, at this time, and would soon be a rarer commodity in Russia, too.

As important as the fear, however, was the ignorance. The soldier talked, wistfully, about the resentment that he and his comrades encountered among the Balts. I agreed that it was sad, but added, as casually as possible, that this resentment was understandable, because of the secret protocols to the Molotov-Ribbentrop pact that everybody knew about – did they not? – and whose very existence was still officially denied by Moscow. My travelling companion again looked unsettled. Like millions of his compatriots at that time, he clearly felt that the Baltic republics were a natural part of the Soviet Union. He had never had any reason to question that view. After a moment, uncomfortably, he returned to the subject. 'Those secret protocols you mentioned – what exactly are they supposed to have said?' I explained the outline of the sordid deal, so well known to every Balt, young and old. As he listened to the details of the Stalin-Hitler carve-up, his young, loyal face seemed devastated. 'Well, I see,' he said, finally.

There was no artifice about his reaction: until this moment, it was clear, he had not known the truth. Not surprisingly, Moscow had been keener to stay silent than to deny the undeniable. The secret protocols therefore marked a black hole in the Soviet version of history. Admittedly, he, like millions of other Russians, had not asked the right questions – nor had he talked to Balts. None the less, he could hardly be blamed for his innocence. Only now was the ignorance being chipped away at, even in Russia. And, as that happened, the loyalty to the old regime would begin to crumble, fast.

In Moscow, the worries continued to grow through 1989. In February, *Pravda* complained that, under the cover of democracy and *glasnost*, of national self assertion, 'overt criticism of our system is voiced' and that there had even been 'attempts to create political structures in opposition to the party organs'. This was, of course, a heinous crime. Democraticization and *perestroika*, yes. Overt criticism of the system, or opposition to the party, absolutely not – only a month before the allegedly 'democratic' elections of March 1989. A few months later, *Pravda* pointed out, with reference to the demands of the Baltic republics and resolutions passed by the Popular Fronts: 'in total, although nobody talks about this directly, they [the resolutions] make sense only if their authors have in mind the complete secession of the three republics from the Soviet Union.' 'Perhaps you're right,' the Balts appeared to retort. 'And if so – what do you propose to do?'

To that, Moscow had no answer. The Soviet authorities could accept the inevitable; they could bluster; or they could use tanks. At different times during the next two years, they would do all three. But the final result was always the same: an acceleration towards the final collapse of Soviet power.

Meanwhile, the most important change in the Baltic republics was yet to come. The elections of March 1989, in which the Popular Fronts swept the board, were to the all-Soviet parliament in Moscow. They enabled the Baltic radicals to show their muscle and to be heard across the Soviet Union. But, in the Moscow parliament, the Balts were only a small part of the Soviet whole – three out of fifteen republics, whose voices could easily be drowned. Baltic politicians emphasized that the important turning-point would be the republican elections, originally due to take place in autumn 1989 and then postponed to spring 1990; those would be entirely controlled by the Balts themselves. By the time that things went so far, much would have changed elsewhere in the Soviet Union, too.

5 Birth of Politics

The Balts, in spring 1989, were already talking about a multi-party system (meaning an end to Communist power), a market economy (ditto) and political independence (ditto). Eastern Europe, too, was cracking open. In almost all of Soviet Russia, however, hardly anything had begun to move. The city of Kalinin, halfway between Leningrad and Moscow, supplier of train carriages to the nation, was just one of many cities all across the federation where pessimism ran deep. '*Perestroika k nam nie doshla*,' said one disheartened young man. '*Perestroika* hasn't reached us here.' Others shared that gloomy view. In the Baltic republics, they had already cracked open the Soviet *shampanskoe* in celebration of victories gained and in anticipation of what was yet to come. But in Kalinin, and throughout the Russian federation, there seemed little to look forward to.

Many were sceptical about what real change the elections could bring. It was, after all, clear that the Communist Party still called all the shots. Kalinin, like so many other towns, still seemed locked into the old Soviet certainties. There was a contest between candidates. That much was new. But this was a contest designed for *homo sovieticus*. Openly to have supported an anti-Communist platform would have been unthinkable – as *Pravda*'s horrified reaction to the Baltic republics had made clear. One candidate in Kalinin was a member of the Communist Party regional committee; his opponent was an organizer of political work in the army. Naturally, both were keen to attack 'bureaucrats'; but their vaguely worded programmes – democratization, improved living standards – were more or less interchangeable.

Here in Kalinin was ordinary Soviet life, almost unchanged since Brezhnev's day, except, perhaps that things were rather worse. In the main department store, a queue snaked down the stairs and around the block for a consignment of desirable Hungarian sweaters. Downstairs, there was another queue, for razorblades. Outside was another long line, for some unappetizing sausage being sold from the back of a van. In short, a very ordinary scene. The official slogans on the walls talked upliftingly of *perestroika* and progress – the party, as ever, was the *rulevoi*, the guiding helmsman of the Soviet Union's great history. The reality in the Kalinins of this world was no change, except for more rhetoric and less to buy.

Everything that had happened since April 1985, when Gorbachev's first plenary session of the Communist Party central committee launched the wave of reform ('The decisions of the April plenum – into life!', as the ubiquitous slogan declared), was little more than a warm-up for the revolutionary changes that were about to begin. As the suspicious reception for Gorbachev in Siberia had emphasized six months earlier, *perestroika* was badly in need of a dose of legitimization in order to be able to move forward. The elections of March 1989 were intended to provide such legitimacy. But serious attempts were also made to keep out those who seemed too outspoken. Meetings for the selection of candidates were rigged in an attempt to exclude liberals, like Korotich, the editor of *Ogonyok*. Whole regions of Russia did not have a single non-party candidate.

Until well beyond the eleventh hour Andrei Sakharov and many other radicals seemed to have been excluded, definitively, from the electoral process. In January, Sakharov failed to win nomination by the Soviet Academy of Sciences for one of the thirty seats allotted to it in the new parliament. Eventually the leadership of the Academy changed its mind – but only after embarrassingly large demonstrations in Sakharov's support and after a rebellion by the Academy's own members against the presidium's decision.

Already, however, Russia was beginning to stir, in a way that few Russians had believed possible. One Sunday afternoon in early 1989, it was possible to witness what had by then become an occasional ritual. Supporters of the Democratic Union held a rally in Pushkin Square, at which demonstrators unfurled the non-Communist blue, white and red Russian flag, to scattered cheers. Each time a flag was raised, a snatch squad would dart into the crowd to arrest a troublemaker. Then, after a few minutes, another flag or banner would be raised. One man was even arrested for waving a plain red flag, standard prop of countless official demonstrations.

The slogans harked back not to Lenin (as Gorbachev still constantly did), nor to the tsar – but to the first, February Revolution, which had ended tsarist rule and which ushered in eight months of chaotic not-yet-democracy, before the Bolsheviks put an end to any thought of multi-party rule for the next seventy years. There were attacks on the Communist Party of the Soviet Union itself. 'CPSU – enemy of the people,' said one placard in the square. Perhaps more significant than the slogans – written, after all, by a tiny handful of people – was the reaction of the passers-by. Even among those who were on their way home, or heading off to stand in yet another queue, it was difficult to find anybody who thought the police were right to be making arrests. There were angry mutterings of 'Fascists' as the police moved in and dragged demonstrators away to the waiting vans. 'And that's what they call "democracy",' said one old lady, scornfully.

Such a willingness to condemn the authorities, and to side with the different-thinkers, was in itself an extraordinary shift. A decade earlier – as the small, courageous band of dissidents had discovered to its cost – the support on the Gorky Street trolleybus for non-regime views had been negligible. Even in the early Gorbachev years, you would have found many who complained of the *huligani*. Now, in 1989, there were many who still felt that way, but, for many more, it was only a sense of hopelessness and the long tradition of passivity that kept them from joining the demonstration. There was little active support for the demonstrators – but there was even less support for the status quo. This was not yet a revolution – not by a long way. But, for the authorities, it was already a most dangerous change.

The elections themselves provided hidden possibilities for undreamed of change. The electoral campaign, certainly, was full of contradictions. The Communist Party – which had voted in favour of the change in June 1988 – seemed to hold all the cards and was determined not to give them up. The newspapers were full of electoral exhortations and empty of facts. The candidates were mostly identikit apparatchiks, in Moscow almost as much as in Kalinin. At an electoral meeting in *The Independent*'s local constituency, the Tagansko-Proletarsky district, in a hall decorated with frescoes of collective farm girls bringing in the harvest, the audience pressed Alexander Samsonov, director of Moscow watch factory No. 1, on how he would distinguish his programme from that of his only rival – Valery Nosov, director of state ball-bearing factory No. 1. Messrs Samsonov and Nosov, both Communist Party members for twenty years and both 'for *perestroika*', seemed at a loss for a reply.

Yet this was the time when the Soviet people first had a chance to break loose – if only in the most limited way. The result would be remarkable. *Glasnost* still had a long way to go. In the press, there was almost complete silence about the one candidate who everybody had heard of, everybody was interested in and every Muscovite had the opportunity to vote for. Boris Nikolayevich Yeltsin, who had fallen out with Gorbachev because of his reformist zeal, was still – as far as the *vlasti* (the powers that be) were concerned – a non-person. There were almost no references to him, and to his campaign, in the most important electoral battle of all, for the 'territorial' constituency of Moscow. (Everybody had two votes: one for a local constituency candidate and one for a candidate in the larger, 'territorial' constituency.) After a fierce series of behind-the-scenes battles, there was a single live television debate between Yeltsin and his rival, Yevgeny Brakov, the director of the Zil factory which – among other things – produced limousines for the use of the party leadership. Apart from that, there was silence. As Yeltsin later pointed out, the official tactics were disastrously misconceived:

I used to wonder what I would do if I were put in charge of a campaign to scupper Yeltsin as an election candidate for a people's deputy. Certainly I know very well what stupid errors I would not make. To start with, I would remove the shroud of secrecy and mystery from the name of Yeltsin ... I would immediately allow – no, I would force – every newspaper and magazine to interview him at least twice. .... And of course, I would make sure that he was often seen on television, on every suitable, and unsuitable programme. .... Before long, the electorate would be absolutely fed up with hearing his thoughts and ideas. Then, I might have a hope of sabotaging the election chances of the undesirable Yeltsin.

But this, he remarked, was the reality:

The official press has kept silent about me, and the only interviews with me to be heard are those broadcast by Western radio stations. Every new move against me only makes the Moscow voters more and more indignant. .... The upshot is that my enemies have been doing everything possible to ensure that Yeltsin is elected deputy for the Moscow city no. 1 constituency.

Yeltsin was right. The official attempts to spike his guns backfired, spectacularly. On the streets it was almost impossible to hear a word against Yeltsin. Every new sign that the party leadership and the apparat disliked him only redoubled his popular support. Badges declared simply: 'Boris – you tell them!' Never before in the Soviet Union had ordinary people been prepared so openly to defy what the party leadership wanted them to do. The election – in which Boris Yeltsin was, after all, a legitimate candidate – gave the people a kind of political immunity, allowing them to defy the authorities without fear of retribution. It was an important moment of self-liberation.

At an election rally in Kuntsevo in western Moscow, the growing desperation of the *vlasti* could clearly be seen. Other candidates' meetings – like the session with Samsonov and Nosov just a few days earlier – were pre-arranged, publicly advertised (although, understandably, few people turned up) and went ahead tediously and without hindrance. But nothing in Yeltsin's campaign could be like that. Muscovites who came to the Kuntsevo meeting had found out about it only by chance: they saw some of the handful of stickers which were plastered up on some Metro stations at the last minute; or they knew somebody who had spread the word. It was almost as if this was some illegal opposition meeting which could only be publicized by word of mouth. As if to emphasize how far Yeltsin and his supporters were at odds with the status quo, two busloads of policemen came and parked at the site several hours before the rally began.

But there was one important difference from any old-style opposition meeting. In previous years, ordinary Russians had been indifferent or hostile to the troublemakers. Now, they were passionate. The crowd was excitable, longing for Boris the Hero to show up. When some of his leaflets were distributed, people threw themselves upon them as greedily as if this was a free handout of oranges, scarce vodka or *Ogonyok* magazine. Yeltsin's meeting at the Kuntsevo cinema had, it turned out, been hijacked by the district party committee. The 'public' meeting was by invitation only. Half-shamefaced, half-defiant invitees confessed that they had been issued tickets by their local party offices. Foreign journalists – privileged, as ever – were allowed in. But ordinary electors, who had traipsed across Moscow to see their hero, were not permitted to attend.

Yeltsin, when he arrived, was furious. In the end, he held two meetings: he addressed the faithful in the cold outside, before going into the cinema hall for his encounter with the chosen, pro-party audience. Using only a single megaphone as he stood in front of the crowd outside the hall, his words were barely audible to most of his audience. But that did not matter. They knew that they supported him, whatever he said. For them, Yeltsin represented their chance to hit back at the system which they had never before dared to loathe. That, in itself, was a prize beyond all dreams.

Support for Yeltsin in Moscow was not quite unanimous. One could still hear mutterings about his alleged demagogic tendencies. There were charges too, of hypocrisy: some claimed that he still made use of some party privileges, even while he publicly attacked them. A frequent question at electoral meetings was about his family's living conditions, which hospital they used, which schools their children went to. Yeltsin insisted that he had given up all the *spets* (short for *spetsialny* or special) privileges that formed part of the fabric of Communist life − including the *spets*-schools, the *spets*-shops and the *spets*-hospitals.

The results of the election, on 26 March, spoke for themselves. Yeltsin was elected to the parliament by an 89 per cent majority. It was a stunning gesture of defiance to the powers that be − including, implicitly, Gorbachev himself, who had assured Yeltsin that he would never return to power. Gorbachev himself received 98 per cent of the vote − but not from the people. He was approved by the Communist Party central committee, the only electorate he subjected himself to, which had a large number of pre-allotted seats.

Soviet officials put a brave face on the Yeltsin triumph, calling it a 'vote for *perestroika*'. But the reality was more serious: it was a vote against what the Soviet leadership, including Gorbachev, so clearly wanted. Nothing would ever be the same again. Gorbachev still placed his faith in playing factions off against each other and indulging in the art of compromise, in order to retain the support of the decaying but vengeful party apparatus − without whom, he believed, progress was impossible. Yeltsin chose, instead, the support of ordinary Russians. Already, he was beginning to rely on the support of the crowd as resentment of the Communist establishment grew. The *Boy's Own* character in him, brought up on old Stalinist films full of larger-than-life heroes, warmed to the possibilities of direct confrontation with the powers-that-be.

Gorbachev continued to invest in the Communist Party − a dubious proposition, as it became clear to all that the party was morally and politically bankrupt. Yeltsin, on the other hand, with his reliance on the power of the street, found himself a gilt-edged investment, which during the next two years would compensate for his earlier humiliation many times over.

During the heavily rigged selection process, radicals only got through by sleight of hand, and sometimes not at all. When, however, it came to the election itself — in other words, when people were allowed to choose for themselves — it was the conservatives who fell by the wayside. In the republic of Ukraine, described by its inhabitants as 'a Brezhnevite nature reserve', the unpopular Communist Party leader, Vladimir Shcherbitsky, ensured that he was elected unopposed. But even that trick did not always suffice. In Leningrad, the regional party leader, Yuri Solovyov, was defeated *despite* standing unopposed. So many people angrily crossed his name out — 'One candidate on the ballot? Do you really call that an election?' said one indignant voter — that he failed to gain the necessary 50 per cent of the vote. The party leader for the city of Leningrad, Anatoly Gerasimov, gained a humiliating 15 per cent of the vote. In many areas, there was no real choice. None the less, in almost every case where electors had a clear choice between radical and conservative, they voted for the more radical candidate. It was an important lesson for what was yet to come.

The new parliament, the Congress of People's Deputies, was dominated by conservatives. It could not be otherwise, given the way that the selection process had taken place. But even the light peppering of radicals in the parliament would soon make a dramatic difference to the way that the country was run. The obstacles to change were still many. Even Yeltsin, who had the most impressive electoral majority in the country, failed initially to be elected to the Supreme Soviet, the smaller of the two parliamentary chambers, which was to sit throughout the year. Many of his fellow-deputies, elected on a Communist ticket, were unhappy that the spurned radical had returned to haunt them. Yeltsin only gained a seat after yet another sleight of hand when a university lecturer from the Siberian city of Omsk gave up his seat in the Supreme Soviet, on Yeltsin's behalf.

Now, the real explosion could begin. It did not take long. When the Congress of People's Deputies opened, on 25 May 1989, the Soviet Union fell through a deep hole into another era. One taboo after another was destroyed. A deputy from Latvia kicked off by demanding that the events in Georgia — where Soviet troops had killed twenty peaceful protesters six weeks earlier — should be publicly accounted for. That was not the end of the surprises. The growing tensions in Armenia, the official treatment of Solzhenitsyn, the powers of the KGB — all of these subjects could now be publicly raised. Even Gorbachev himself became fair game.

Radicals were not always well received. One Afghan veteran angrily accused Sakharov of slanderous insults in connection with Afghanistan and declared. 'More than 80 per cent of us are Communist – but no one has mentioned Communism. Let me say three words I haven't heard this week: state, motherland and Communism.' Led by Gorbachev, the hall gave him a thunderous ovation. In a speech that was repeatedly and angrily interrupted by Gorbachev himself, Sakharov called for the party's leading role to be abandoned and for the KGB's powers to be reduced. Gorbachev ordered his microphone to be switched off and asked him angrily: 'Do you respect the Congress?' Sakharov replied: 'I respect the Congress, but I also respect the people who are listening to me at the moment. I respect mankind.'

That broader constituency – the millions who were listening to proceedings on television and radio – proved to be crucial. If the parliament had not been televised, nationwide, the end of Communism would never have come so soon. All over the country, during those early weeks especially, people were glued to their sets for hours and days at a time, as they watched the taboos of a lifetime being destroyed. For a nation which until now had access only to a filtered, Kremlin-spun version of reality, it was an extraordinary, exhilarating (and, for some, alarming) process. Suddenly the Soviet nation was able to hear the voices of the radicals – Sakharov, Yeltsin, the Balts – direct, instead of in the distorted rendering of the television news and the official press. During the weeks to come, the televised proceedings of parliament were little short of a national obsession. At home, all other viewing took second place. And at workplaces, too, people gathered round as though watching a crucial football match. Even the economy began to suffer: a 20 per cent fall in industrial output during the first session of the Congress of People's Deputies was officially attributed to the nation's political square eyes.

Nor was there an alternative for anybody who wanted to sense the changes that were under way. Invariably, the most controversial highlights of the day were edited out of the version of events presented in the official press or on *Vremya*, the television evening news. If you didn't see it as it happened, then you didn't see it. This gave a unique sense of urgency to Soviet politics. The Congress demonstrated clearly to the rest of the Soviet Union that the different-thinkers did not need to be an isolated minority. Overall, the parliament gave the impression of being what one leading radical described as the 'aggressively obedient majority'. Nonetheless, there were enough no-sayers to hearten would-be renegades throughout the Soviet Union. After all, how could anybody – even out in the conservative provinces – be blamed for criticizing the

Soviet leadership or the KGB if the same criticisms had already been voiced in the Soviet parliament? Local hardliners did not like that line of argument. But it was a powerful alibi.

This was a country in which several generations had been taught that there was only one answer to every problem: the Communist answer. The party, was, in the words of the official slogan – to be seen on street-hoardings and factory walls across the country – the 'brains, honour and conscience of our epoch'. The party always knew best. With the advent of *perestroika*, that had not changed. Suddenly, though, those certainties were destroyed. Even in the many Vitebsks and Kalinins of the Soviet world, the changes would leave their mark. The party bosses would fight as hard as they could. Soon, however, even they would be in full retreat.

On television, remarkable taboos began to be tackled – often to the fury of the *vlasti*. On the current affairs programme *Vzglyad* (literally 'Viewpoint'), which soon gained a healthy reputation for impertinence, Mark Zakharov, a theatre director, even voiced the suggestion – during a live discussion in April 1989, on the anniversary of Lenin's birth – that the founder of the Soviet state might be removed from his mausoleum to a cemetery, almost as if he were an ordinary human being. This outrageous suggestion caused uproar. Heads had to roll. Alexander Aksyonov, the head of television and radio, apologized publicly to a Communist central committee plenum a few days later, on behalf of Soviet television. He said that it had been a gross error and a shocking statement. He explained that the programme had been live. 'Nobody expected anything like that. We have given this incident the strictest assessment and it was discussed and denounced at a meeting of television workers, arranged at short notice.' But even this breast-beating was not enough. Within weeks, Aksyonov was sacked.

And still the sacrileges multiplied. Soon, the new irreverence of Soviet politics would be formalized. With the beginning of parliamentary debate came the corollary: the beginning of a parliamentary opposition. The new Inter-Regional Group of People's Deputies did not, initially, describe itself as an opposition. That would have been impossible: opposition groups, after all, were still illegal. None the less, there was no mistaking the aims. At the founding meeting, at Dom Kino, the House of Cinema, in Moscow in July 1989, 250 radical members of the new Soviet parliament gathered to press for faster change. Yeltsin and Sakharov were among those elected to the collective leadership of the new group, whose creation – according to Yeltsin – proved that democratic consciousness had 'come of age'. There was criticism of Gorbachev for moving too slowly; there was criticism, too, of the 'deformed hybrid' of *perestroika*.

Meanwhile, battles continued to be won in the Baltic republics, where the final break was getting closer all the time. On 27 July, after months of refusal by Moscow, the republics finally gained the right to economic independence. Soviet television news said that the decision by the Soviet parliament was unprecedented. That much was true. But Soviet television also had its own interpretation, declaring that this would 'help the political and economic strength of the whole union'. In reality, as everybody knew, it would do nothing of the kind. Estonia's economic plans, first dreamed up at the end of 1988, officially went by the name of IME. Theoretically, IME stood for *Ise-Majandav Eesti* – 'economically independent Estonia'. But Estonians gleefully pointed out that *ime* was also the Estonian word for miracle. The label was appropriate. Once the Balts gained economic independence – which gave them the right (until Moscow tried to take it away again) to establish a market-based economy in their own republics – then everything else was certain to follow. For the Kremlin, still keen to set the rules, it was an enormous retreat. Worse, for Moscow, was that the Balts' economic independence was not a goal in itself. It was merely a stepping stone towards the political endgame, as Marju Lauristin – now one of the Balts' most powerful players – made clear in an article written shortly after the Moscow climbdown:

> We do not have wings. We have to climb the cliff carefully, securing our holds as we go. . . . Our economy has been totally destroyed, not because it was worse than any other Soviet republic – it is better, in many ways – but because its structure was diseased. The state of our economy is an obstacle in the development of independence. That is why the Baltic plans for economic independence were put forward before all the plans for political independence. There were many obstacles – but we have almost reached the finishing line.

Even now, Moscow still seemed caught between the impossibility of admitting old lies and the impossibility of sustaining them. In August 1989, for example, for a television film on the fiftieth anniversary of the Molotov–Ribbentrop pact, we talked to a Communist Party central committee adviser in Moscow who implied that the secret protocols to the pact did not exist. Yet the denials were senseless. In the main bookshop on the old town square in Tallinn, poster-sized facsimile copies of the Russian text – reproduced directly from the German archives – were freely on sale.

Even in Tallinn's staid municipal theatre, you could get a taste, not of 'Let's reduce the quotient of official lies', as in Moscow, but 'Let's try to tell the whole truth'. The theatre was showing a play called *Bedrooms*, written in Finland. The action took place in two sets of sleeping quarters – chez Mr and Mrs Brezhnev (Soviet leader and spouse) and chez Mr and Mrs Dubcek (Czechoslovak leader and spouse) – in 1968. Though blessed with some blackly funny lines, *Bedrooms* was, above all, a savage indictment of the immorality of the Soviet invasion of Czechoslovakia. Only three months before the revolution in Prague, the subject was still taboo in the Soviet capital.

After the performance, we went backstage in search of the actor playing Brezhnev. We asked the lumbering figure of Lembit Eelmae – who, stripped of his make-up, medals and spare eyebrows, turned into a human being in no way resembling Brezhnev – how relevant he believed the play was today. Eelmae did not hesitate. 'This play is about Czechoslovakia. But all the time, I'm thinking of Estonia.' By now, the world was gasping at the perceived international generosity of Gorbachev, as Solidarity prepared to take power in Poland. Here in Estonia, though, the Brezhnev doctrine – tanks, to prevent democracy – was already perceived as an obvious threat.

Edgar Savisaar, then deputy prime minister, who later became prime minister, agreed that tanks might be used. But he insisted that for Gorbachev or a successor to resort to such tactics would be useless. 'I don't want to make predictions. But in 1981, something similar happened in Poland. Not many years have passed since then. Yet Jaruzelski has been forced to negotiate with Lech Walesa. Nowadays, tanks can solve nothing.'

Others, too, showed the same mix of short-term pessimism and long-term optimism. Jaan Kaplinski, a leading poet, raised the spectre of Tiananmen Square, the massacre that had taken place just two months earlier and which hung heavy over East Europe through the heady days of change in summer and autumn 1989. 'They say you can't put toothpaste back into the tube. But it's not true. You can. It was possible in Prague, in 1968, it was possible in Peking.' Then he paused. 'But in the end, the general trend towards freedom and democracy is always there. We will win eventually, sooner or later. Modern society needs democracy and freedom, as fire needs oxygen.'

Certainly, the momentum seemed unstoppable. Finally, after months of persistent demands by Baltic politicians – backed up by petitions, signed by 1,500,000 in Lithuania alone – the Soviet authorities retreated once more. They allowed the liberal weekly *Argumenty i Fakty* to publish the protocols, just ahead of the fiftieth anniversary of the pact, in August 1989. It was, however, a Chernobyl-style decision – too late to defuse the indignation that was already set to explode. Even now, as the secret protocols were published, *Pravda* insisted that the Molotov-Ribbentrop pact had been 'not against, but in protection of Lithuania, Latvia and Estonia'. The pact had, said *Pravda*, set limits to the fascist expansion in East Europe. This was true, if only in a grotesque way. Stalin had set limits by saying to Hitler in effect: 'That much can be yours – as long as you leave the rest to me.' It was, perhaps, hardly surprising that the Soviet authorities were not keen to come to terms with the implications of the lie that formed the basis of the post-war Soviet state.

Valentin Falin, head of the Communist Party's international department, insisted, even as the genuineness of the protocols was admitted, that is was wrong to present the Nazi-Soviet pact as the collusion of two aggressors to divide Europe into spheres of influence. Because? Such an interpretation, said Falin, would cast a shadow on 'the legality of the territorial structure' in the region. Yes. Quite so.

Falin's logic was reminiscent of Lord Denning, the English judge who declared in 1980 that it was unthinkable to contemplate the possibility that the Birmingham Six, imprisoned for life for an IRA bombing, were innocent. Lord Denning pointed out that an appeal, if allowed, would indicate that police had deliberately lied, using violence and threats in order to achieve their conviction. Denning commented: 'This is such an appalling vista that every sensible person in the land would say, "It cannot be right that these actions should go any further".' Like Falin, Lord Denning explicitly acknowledged the devastating implications for the status quo of a change of line – and was therefore determined not to allow the facts to be re-examined. Better a convenient lie than an inconvenient truth.

When the innocence of the Birmingham Six was finally established, ten years later, and when police officers were charged with perjury, some in the legal establishment attempted to argue that the release of the Six, after years in jail, was proof of the essential soundness of the system: justice was, after all, seen to be done. Similarly, in Moscow, there were suggestions that the acknowledgement that the secret protocols were real was a tribute to *glasnost* and thus to the credentials of the Soviet system. In reality, the opposite was true. A late admission – given only after many refusals and after sustained pressure from below – was to be welcomed, on the 'better late than never' principle. But it provided evidence that the system was not naturally inclined to be open about its mistakes. It only surrendered when it had no choice. In those circumstances, the real credit went to those who felled the giant, not to those who finally admitted the lie.

Moscow's admission attempted to draw the sting of a protest that the Baltic republics organized for the fiftieth anniversary of the pact, on 23 August. But the Balts were unimpressed. The protest was the largest ever: a human chain of more than a million people stretched 300 miles from Tallinn through Riga to Vilnius. On the streets of Moscow, there were early rumblings, too. A few hundred people staged a demonstration in solidarity with the Balts. At the demonstration, as Tass reported, police 'correctly' detained seventy-five people.

The Soviet media went into top gear. *Vremya*, the television evening news, called the pro-independence movements in the Baltic naive, dangerous and hypocritical. *Pravda* accused pro-independence campaigners in Lithuania of moral and physical terror and warned that the consequences of secession would be unpredictable. Then, just four days after the anniversary, a central committee statement, taking up an entire page in the official press, delivered the most threatening blast yet. The tone of the statement was reminiscent of Soviet warnings before the invasion of Czechoslovakia in August 1968 and before martial law in Poland in 1981. 'The current situation in the Baltic republics is the cause of increasing concern,' it said. 'Developments there affect the vital interests of the entire Soviet people, our entire socialist Motherland.' The central committee statement complained that extremists and separatists had set up organizations resembling political formations of the bourgeois period and announced:

Things have gone far. The fate of the Baltic republics is in serious danger. People should know into what abyss they are being pushed by the nationalist leaders. The consequences could be disastrous for these peoples, if the nationalists manage to achieve their goals. The very viability of the Baltic nations could be called in question. We should say this openly, and with a feeling of responsibility before the Baltic and all Soviet peoples.

Nobody had seen or heard the like of it for years. Baltic leaders described the central committee statement as the most dangerous document since the days of Stalin. The difference was that Stalin knew that he was strong enough to stay in charge; so did Brezhnev when he ordered the invasion of Czechoslovakia in August 1968. By now, though, the Communist Party leadership could have had no such confidence. Apart from anything else, the Balts were no longer isolated. Elsewhere in the Soviet bloc, dramas were already taking place which would strengthen the Baltic cause.

6 Fraternal Allies Wave Goodbye

5 June 1989. Outside the Surprise Cafe, on Constitution Square in central Warsaw, a small crowd gathered round a bulletin board with a list of parliamentary candidates. Every few minutes another sticker with a distinctive little red logo was affixed to the board – and there were yet more cheers and laughter. People shook their heads in happy disbelief. Each of the stickers represented a victory by the Polish opposition, Solidarity, against the Communists who had ruled unchallenged for forty years. By the end of the day, the board was completely full. In the freely elected parliamentary chamber, ninety-nine out of a hundred seats went to Solidarity. The Communists, who had clung to power so tenaciously for more than forty years, had been forced to partake in their own electoral slaughter.

In the Soviet Union at this time (the Baltic republics apart), things were only just beginning to move. The Communists were still firmly in control. During the same month as the Polish elections, Gorbachev angrily attempted to silence Sakharov, with his calls in the Soviet parliament for a reduction in Communist Party power. Here in Poland, though, the old regime was in its death agonies. The Communists had rigged the elections so that they still held on to power in the main parliamentary chamber – but that, too, would not be for long. Outside the Surprise Cafe – which Solidarity had taken over as its campaign office – the silver-haired Andrzej Lapicki, one of Poland's best known actors, was mobbed by enthusiastic supporters. He was in no doubt of the significance of the elections that had taken place. With a can-you-believe-this smile as he signed a stream of autographs, Lapicki declared: 'This is the end of the system in its present form. And it is bound to give ideas to people in Czechoslovakia and East Germany, too ... The Baltic states will be independent in a few years' time. Now, everything is possible.'

He was right. In the months to come, the one-party unelected regimes collapsed, one after another, as each nation in turn found that it, too, could summon up the courage and the willpower to throw off a government that nobody wanted. This process – seen from afar, even through the distorting mirror of Soviet television news – would soon have incalculable effects in the Soviet Union, too.

The events in eastern Europe in 1989 were not entirely a bolt from the blue. From 1988 onwards, it had already been clear that cataclysmic change was on the way, whether Moscow wanted it or not. As the headline to a two-page report on eastern Europe in January 1989 pointed out, this was a region where goalposts were on the move. The ingredients were already all in place. Never before had eastern Europe faced so many uncertainties and so much pressure for change at one time. The catalogue of events spoke for itself:

In the last fortnight, dozens of protesters were arrested in East Germany, following increasingly outspoken opposition there. Czechoslovak riot police attacked large crowds in Prague, where the streets have in recent months been filling up with protesters for the first time in twenty years. Poland said it was prepared to legalize Solidarity, and Hungary passed a law which could turn it into a multi-party state by the middle of next year. With such developments, it is hardly surprising that, in predicting the future of the region, all bets are off.

It was clear that the dominoes must fall and that a political avalanche was on the way:

If Hungary gets anything approaching a multi-party system next year, can Poland be far behind? How can the Czechoslovaks remain quiescent if they see what is happening to the north and to the south? And where does that leave the Baltic states – Estonia, Latvia and Lithuania – which are hungry for change but hardly dare to voice their ultimate demand?

I, for one, never dreamed that the whole show would be wrapped up by the end of that same calendar year. None the less, for East Europeans, the overall trend was clear, as was the irreversibility of the changes taking place. Nowhere more than in eastern Europe at that time did Marx's doctrine of historical inevitability seem so apposite. Moscow was unhappy at the changes that were on the way. The attitude towards the growing pro-democracy movement in Czechoslovakia can be gauged from a Tass dispatch about a protest in January. It read, in full:

GOODBYE TO THE USSR

PRAGUE, 16 Jan 1989 — Mass unrest in the city's Wenceslas Square continued today as criminal elements, incited by anti-socialist groups, attempted to repeat Sunday's failed provocative demonstration. Riot police are using water cannon and tear gas to ease tensions. The centre of the city is cordoned off by militia and army controls. Item ends.

Water cannon and tear gas 'to ease tensions' — that was creative Kremlin-speak at its best. This, then, was the official Soviet view of events on the day that Vaclav Havel was arrested (and later jailed for eight months) for his part in a peaceful protest. *Pravda*'s comments had an equally interesting angle. The Soviet Communist Party daily declared that the demonstrations in Wenceslas Square sought to undermine the 'incipient process of democratization' allegedly taking place in Czechoslovakia.

The dramas of eastern Europe in 1989 had really begun in the shipyards of Gdansk nine years earlier, when the buried strength of people's power had showed itself for the first time — with important lessons for the Soviet Union in the years to come. It was in Gdansk that a nation first achieved astonishing victories against the resistance of a Communist apparat that appeared to hold all the cards. In Poland in August 1980, it was an extraordinary and moving experience to watch an unarmed people humiliate their unwanted leaders — and force the government to concede the impossible. For it *was* impossible; even the Polish opposition leader, Adam Michnik, believed that the calls for the legalization of an independent trade union were so unrealistic that he wanted to persuade the strikers to modify their demands. Luckily, as he himself said later, he was arrested before he could offer the strikers his helpful advice. For, after two weeks of mounting strikes, the Communists caved in. Gdansk — where the strikers, given the historical precedents, could reasonably have expected that guns or tanks would be used against them — showed, a decade before Communism's last bow, that the impossible could become almost simple, if enough people grasped for it at the same time.

Everybody in Poland understood how serious were the implications of that Great Retreat. Never before had the rulers been forced to give so much away to the ruled. The victory of Solidarity, eastern Europe's first independent trade union, was all the more remarkable in that it took place while Brezhnev — who had shown that he was prepared to use tanks in order to suppress change — was still alive. Even at that time,

Poles believed that the ailing Soviet Union could no longer afford to be as tough as it had once been. They also hoped that Moscow's exhausting new war in Afghanistan might discourage the Kremlin from taking on two battles simultaneously. Equally, however, it was clear that there was no room, in the longer term, for both Solidarity and the Communist regime. Officially, Solidarity described itself as an independent trade union. But that was a polite fiction, like the Popular Fronts 'for *perestroika*' in the Baltic republics. Solidarity, like the Popular Fronts, was above all a mass popular movement − which therefore implied the possibility of an alternative, non-Communist society in the future. For tactical reasons, it was unwise to say that out loud. But everybody knew it to be true.

Eventually, the Communists themselves were fated to go. In the short term, however, they still had enough strength to claw back the power that they were beginning to lose. After sixteen months of growing tensions between the rulers and the ruled − threats, promises and lies − martial law was declared in December 1981. The tanks attempted to put the lid back on a system that was already out of control. But this was not the end. The first legalization of Solidarity, and the destruction of hundreds of old one-party taboos during 1980 and 1981, created what one liberal Polish Communist Party paper in 1981 called − at a time when Gorbachev was still an eager new Politburo member, recently promoted by Brezhnev − a 'backbone that cannot be broken'. That analysis, suggesting the inevitability of permanent change, proved to be correct, and had important implications for hardline attempts to push things into reverse in the Soviet Union, too.

Gradually, the mass protests and strikes in Poland subsided, as people became weary after years of beatings and arrests. By the mid-1980s, it was easy to accept the official Polish version that Solidarity was a movement which had 'had its end'. But the resentment remained − and, especially as the regime weakened, it continued to explode. Again and again, Poles refused to accept economic austerity measures from their unloved regime. Finally, after another outbreak of pro-Solidarity mass strikes in August 1988, and as the economy continued to collapse, the Polish authorities agreed to start talking to the opposition once more. Round-table talks between government and opposition began, which led directly to the legalization of Solidarity − and to the Communists' subsequent electoral defeat.

Meanwhile, even as the logjam broke in Poland, small, surprising Hungary also paved the way for revolutionary change. There, too, the writing had already been on the wall. Hungarian radio's New Year cabaret for 1988 hinted at the dramas to come. A soundalike for Janos Kadar, then Communist Party leader, was asked who his successor might be. 'After me,' he declared sonorously, 'comes Comrade Deluge.' The Hungarian satirists – a hundred times more irreverent than any Soviet equivalent could yet dare to be – were right. Kadar was junked in May 1988. And his successor, Karoly Grosz, would find within the next few months that things were beyond his control, too.

In Hungary, one Communist politician played undertaker for the one-party system from late 1988 onwards: Imre Pozsgay. Communism in Hungary is a dirty word, so it is unlikely that there will be a monument to the man who, after playing politics too energetically, failed even to be elected to parliament in the free elections of 1990, unlike some of his party comrades. None the less, it could be argued that Pozsgay deserves a memorial for what he achieved. The bejowelled old Communist – a more thoughtful, less demagogic version of Boris Yeltsin – deliberately set about dynamiting the old structures. By early 1989, he was talking cheerfully of multi-party elections as a noble contest, at the same time that Gorbachev was condemning those who talked of a multi-party system as 'demagogues and irresponsible elements'. Then, on 29 January 1989, Pozsgay announced that the Hungarian counter-revolution of 1956 – as it had been officially described for thirty years – had in fact been a popular uprising. He chose his moment for delivering the bombshell: Grosz, the then party leader, was out of the country and the party was thrown into complete disarray.

Everybody understood the implications. Once it had been admitted that 1956 was a popular uprising, then – as night followed day – it was certain that everything else must unravel, too. The political system of 1989 rested on the legacy of the Soviet tanks from 1956; if it was officially admitted that those tanks had suppressed a popular uprising, then the system had thrown away its figleaf of fake legitimacy and could no longer survive. And so it proved. In June 1989, Imre Nagy – the former prime minister, who had been hanged after the 1956 uprising and whose body had lain for thirty years in an unmarked grave – was reburied with full honours. The game was over. As the changes began, Moscow growled. Tass complained that Hungarians should look objectively at all the circumstances, including the participation of reactionary emigrant circles in encouraging the 1956 counter-revolution. But the Hungarians no longer cared what the wounded bear (whose retreat from Afghanistan was already well under way) tried to say.

FRATERNAL ALLIES WAVE GOODBYE

All of this had startling implications for the country that East Europeans delicately used to refer to as 'our neighbours to the East', as though even to mention the name of the Soviet Union might bring bad luck. In Hungary in spring 1989, I talked to an official foreign policy adviser, who spoke with Hungarian calmness about throwing off the system that the country had lived with for forty years. Speaking of the changes in Hungary and elsewhere, Laszlo Lang insisted that there could be no way back. Things had gone too far. If the Soviet Union now tried to stop the pace of change, it would only destroy itself. It was the same argument that the Balts had used, and it seemed accurate enough. But what if the East Europeans changes were allowed to go the whole way – surely, in those circumstances, the ructions would eventually lead back into the Soviet Union and the system could not survive? Lang – who was obliged, according to the then prevailing rules, to allow at least a semblance of remaining dignity for the Soviet Union – fenced for a while. Then, momentarily, he dipped off-the-record, giving him the protection of anonymity. His reply was blunt and simple. 'No. Of course it can't survive.'

Gorbachev had two choices. On the one hand, he could say no. He could intervene, with tanks, to halt the changes taking place, which would mean intervening simultaneously in Hungary and in Poland, as a bare minimum – and in the Baltic republics, too. That would solve none of the region's economic problems, nor any of its political problems, but it would create the illusion of short-term stability. It would, however, be much more difficult for Gorbachev than in Brezhnev's time. Even Brezhnev, shying away from yet more political and military complications, avoided direct intervention in Poland in 1980 and 1981, and eventually persuaded General Jaruzelski, the Polish leader, to do the job for him instead. By 1989, Jaruzelski, bowing to popular *force majeure*, had come full circle and could hardly be expected to declare martial law a second time. Moreover, whereas Poland had been isolated in a sea of hardliners in 1980, it was now the old regimes, in eastern Europe and in the Soviet Union itself, which were under pressure as never before. Even the Baltic republics of the Soviet Union were almost off the leash. In addition, Gorbachev could no longer trust the Russian people to be as gung-ho for a clampdown on behalf of Communist rule as had once been the case. Would the factory workers – angry at the Communist Party and angry at the economic hardship – really turn out obediently to complain about anti-socialist activities in the fraternal countries, as they had done in the old days? And, as well as all this, any military intervention, apart from its futility, would unleash the anger of the West and plunge Gorbachev back into an economic and political Cold War that he could (to put it mildly) do without, as he tried to negotiate himself out of the arms race and encourage large-scale economic assistance and investment for the USSR. All in all, it was not a happy prospect.

On the other hand, Gorbachev could say yes. He could accept the changes one by one, as they happened, and look on the bright side. At home, he was still firmly rejecting the radical changes which eastern Europe was going through. He stood firm against a dilution of Communist Party power (though circumstances would soon change that, too). And he stood firm against the Balts returning to 'bourgeois rule'. But the rebellious parts of eastern Europe he could treat as ballast which, if thrown overboard, might conceivably save the Soviet ship – for a short while at least. The hardliners would complain, just as Polish hardliners complained when Jaruzelski proposed the re-legalization of Solidarity in January 1989. But Gorbachev could justly retort, as Jaruzelski had done: what better ideas had *they* got? Tanks, blood, economic mayhem and political defeat were the only alternative. And the international pay-off for not intervening, Gorbachev could reasonably expect, would be considerable.

Looked at that way – as the Soviet leader must have done, again and again – there was no contest. Admittedly, Soviet Communism, to which Gorbachev still proclaimed his loyalty, was doomed to lose either way. The East European revolutions were certain to feed back into the Soviet Union and destroy the system itself, which was already crumbling from within. But the retreat was braver, and more noble, if Gorbachev chose the second way out. Gorbachev was always a realist, and was never keen to spill blood. Combined, those two factors made the retreat much easier. Perhaps, too, he avoided thinking too hard about the implications of his retreat – or hoped that he could still keep the Soviet ship afloat, now that this commitments were slimmed down. The Soviet media sought to play down the dramas, so that nobody in Moscow would get subversive ideas. On the day that Solidarity so humiliated the Communists at the polls in June 1989, *Vremya* on Soviet TV gave the news thirty seconds of airtime, almost half an hour into the programme. (Nor was the news overshadowed by the enormity of events in Peking at that time: a report on the Tiananmen massacre was buried even further down than the Communists' humiliation in Poland.)

In July, in a speech in Strasbourg, Gorbachev abandoned, more explicitly than ever before, the Brezhnev doctrine, which had argued that it was legitimate to use tanks in order to 'protect socialism' in fraternal countries. Gorbachev said that there must be 'no use or threat of force ... within alliances'. At the same time, he warned the West against too sharp an ideological shift, saying that there would be negative consequences for all Europe if the West attempted to divert countries from the paths they had 'chosen'. In October, Gennady Gerasimov, chief Soviet supplier of crisp one-liners, set the official seal on it by declaring that, instead of the Brezhnev doctrine, 'We now have the Frank Sinatra doctrine.' In other words, from now on, the East Europeans could do it Their Way. The Sinatra doctrine was an acceptance of change, not an unleashing of it – the East Europeans were already doing it Their Way. By any measure, however, the new acceptance was a momentous turnaround.

Even through the summer of 1989, Gorbachev continued to cherish the hope that he could contain the changes that were taking place. By now, it was clear that the revolutions in Poland and Hungary were beginning to affect East Germany, too. On 2 May, Hungary snipped a hole in the barbed-wire Iron Curtain. They dreamed it up as little more than a good public-relations photo-opportunity, to show that they were opening up to the West; Hungarians were in any case allowed to travel almost freely. But the dismantling of physical barriers, together with relaxed Hungarian attitudes, made it possible for an increasing number of East Germans to find an escape hatch through to the outside world. Throughout July and August, they fled in ever increasing numbers. The Hungarians sometimes turned them back, but often turned a blind eye. Then, after a milestone decision by Hungary in September, the East Germans were allowed to go, officially – they did not even need to avoid the border guards. There were scenes of ecstasy among the East Germans who were encamped in the West German embassy in Budapest and who got into their Trabants and headed straight for the border that night. For the East Germans, locked up inside the Soviet bloc, an impossible dream now became real. Tass and Soviet television complained of the 'tendentious campaign' against East Germany in connection with the 'illegal departure abroad' of East German citizens. But this was all Canute-speak. Nothing could now stop the East German tidal wave of change.

The unceasing exodus led to increasing political pressure on the East German authorities at home. A popular slogan among the ever-growing demonstrations in the city of Leipzig was: '*Wir bleiben hier*! We're staying here!' The implication was: we are staying, because we are determined to force change. It was a moot point, which caused more political difficulties for the East German authorities – those who were determined to leave or those who were determined to stay. By October 1989, the East German authorities were already on the ropes, although both they and the Soviet leadership carried on as if everything was fine.

In one of the many historical ironies of 1989, the East German state, a child of the Cold War, effectively gave its last gasp on the very weekend of its triumphal fortieth birthday celebrations, attended by Mikhail Gorbachev himself. Indeed, the firework display on 7 October 1989, celebrating the achievements of forty years of what went under the name of socialism (poorly stocked shops, widespread fear and meaningless rhetoric) lit up the largest opposition demonstration that the capital had seen since the workers' uprising of 1953. Some of the crowds sang a mocking version of Happy Birthday as they marched. As the Stasi secret police and their assistants – pimply youths in windcheaters – attempted to clear the troublemakers off the streets, one old man was bundled into the back of a lorry. He had time to shout, before the lorry drove off: 'They've invited us to the birthday celebrations, don't you see!'

Gorbachev had flown in the previous day and delivered the traditional comradely kiss to Erich Honecker, the East German leader who had been especially shameless in his rejection of change. It was a killer of a kiss: there was little doubt that Gorbachev would much rather have been dealing with somebody like the Communist reformer, Hans Modrow, the Dresden party boss, who would be better equipped to help the Communist system adapt and survive. Still, Gorbachev's conversations with East German leaders were almost friendly. He issued sharp public warnings against a disturbance of the status quo and against questioning the existence of the Berlin Wall. He emphasized: 'It is precisely the recognition of post-war realities [i.e., the division of Germany] that ensures peace in Europe.'

During that fateful weekend, Gorbachev told the East German leader: 'Those who delay are punished by life itself.' But perhaps even Gorbachev did not guess quite how swift the punishment for the unrelenting Honecker would be. Before Gorbachev had finished waving goodbye from the steps of the plane that took him back to Moscow, the demonstrators were already on the streets of East Berlin. 'Gorby! Gorby!' they chanted – knowing that the very name of the reformist Soviet leader was a red rag to the Stasi. They sang the Internationale. And – the simplest, most provocative and most winning of all the slogans of eastern Europe in 1989 – they chanted '*Wir sind das Volk!* We are the people,' as the people's security forces bashed them over the head and carted them off to jail.

Even during that demonstration, as the Stasi lashed out, there was a mood of exhilaration among the crowd. At last, a nation had lost its fear. Soviet television was struck dumb. In its upbeat report on the birthday celebrations and on Gorbachev's visit, it failed to mention the pro-democracy demonstrations at all, let alone the violent suppression of the protests by police.

Meanwhile, the revolutionary snowball continued to roll. Two days after the East Berlin demonstration came the moment at which the East German regime, faced with the growing lack of fear of its citizens, finally lost its nerve. On 9 October, the authorities threw a cordon sanitaire around Leipzig: they told journalists in East Berlin that they should not go to Leipzig, intercepted correspondents who headed for the city and threw out those who arrived. With luck, it was possible to slip through the net. But the reason for the precautions was clear: there were widespread reports that weapons would be used at a protest to be held that night (it was later confirmed that a decision to use weapons had indeed been taken); the authorities did not want such events to be broadcast to the world. The *Chinalosung*, as East Germans had taken to calling it – the China solution – was close to being real.

In the event, the order to use weapons was rescinded at the last moment (politicians later quarrelled over who was to take the credit). But the demonstrators' courage was real enough. People knew that the hospital wards had been cleared for expected casualties. They could see the military vehicles standing in the sidestreets. In one street alone, there were sixteen trucks full of the armed workers' militias, who only three days before had publicly pledged the use of weapons, 'if need be', in an ominous letter to a Leipzig newspaper. I was present that afternoon when a pastor who was active in the opposition had a stand-up row with his young daughter: she wanted to go on that night's demonstration and he refused to let her, reasoning that he was allowed to die but he would not allow her to risk her life. And as I sat with others in the Nikolai-kirche in the heart of Leipzig that Monday evening, during the church service that always preceded the demonstrations, I heard the local bishop beg his congregation – and the tens of thousands more who stood outside – to be cautious: 'Remember, freedom is important. But nothing can be more important than life itself.'

Outside, when the service was over and the march began, there came the gradual realization: tonight, there would be no shooting. Astonishingly, there would not even be beatings or arrests. The lorries still stood in the sidestreets with their armed militias, but the occupants finished up in animated discussion with the demonstrators instead of shooting them. The end had come. Faced with the possibility of a Tiananmen in Europe, the East German leaders had finally lost their nerve.

For − and this was what counted − it was not a matter of what Moscow or anybody else had permitted. It was the people who decided. Tens of thousands went out on the streets of Leipzig that night in the clear understanding that they might be shot. They were right: the original decision had been that guns should be used. Presumably, some of those waiting inside the Nikolaikirche that evening and among the packed crowds outside felt − as I did − the occasional heaviness in the stomach that marked the dread of the unknown, the fear of bullets and of dying. Statistically, I worked out that even if there was a massacre in which fifty people died, the chances against it being me were 1000 to 1, which seemed comfortingly small. Perhaps others in the crowds made a similar calculation that night. Not all of them could win such a game of Leipzig roulette. And yet that did not change their determination to walk out and demand change. They were calm and even happy. And when there was no shooting, they knew it was *their* victory.

Thus it was, too, in the weeks to come. When the authorities had taken a tough line, people protested more at the obvious injustice. And when they took a soft line, people protested more, because they were no longer frightened. For the hardliners, it was an unhappy non-choice. In September, the East Germans had clamped down on travel to Hungary − and the protests got bigger. They beat up demonstrators − and the protests got bigger still. They closed the border to Czechoslovakia (where the embassy also began to fill up with refugees), and the protests were bigger still. Never before had East Germans not only been banned from travel to the West, but were also cooped up within their own country. Then the authorities planned (and publicly hinted at) a Tiananmen-style massacre in Leipzig − and the crowds again grew. It was at that point that the retreats finally began. From now on, the East German regime would never wield the same power again. Its death throes had already begun.

After the demonstration in Leipzig, I was not surprised to receive a late-night knock on the door and to be detained by the Stasi for a couple of hours before they threw me out of the country. (I was relieved that they had been so slow to catch up; I had filed my story from the post office, for that night's *Independent*, and was in any case due to leave for Berlin next day.) But, despite the secret police, the atmosphere of fear was already broken. As I paid my bill, before being driven away, the receptionist asked why I was leaving so suddenly, so late at night. I explained. With real anger, she said — within earshot of the waiting Stasi — 'It's a disgrace.' Only a few weeks earlier, it would have been impossible to say something like that out loud. But defiance was growing as the days of the *ancien régime* were so clearly numbered.

The decision not to use weapons was the first of many surrenders, each more extraordinary than the last. But, as the authorities changed tack and tried to offer more and more concessions, the policy of conciliation proved equally useless. The Monday-night marches in Leipzig continued to double in size every week. Honecker was sacked and replaced by his close comrade, Egon Krenz. Then, at the end of October, the authorities reopened the border to Czechoslovakia in an attempt to reduce the pressure at home. Immediately, the West German embassy in Prague — an eighteenth-century palace turned refugee camp — again filled to overflowing. Four thousand people were packed into the ornately decorated rooms, sleeping on multiple bunks, on floors, on the stairs, and — despite the cold and rain — in the open air. They were allowed out to West Germany, but only a handful at a time. This, too, was a makeshift solution that could not last. Finally, in the penultimate surrender, the East German authorities agreed on 3 November that East Germans no longer even needed to receive a piece of paper in Prague, nor to go to the embassy, in order to leave for the West. All that they needed to do was to go through Czechoslovak territory — a few miles was enough — on the way.

In was a most extraordinary surrender, as if a prison guard were to announce that the main gates of the prison would remain locked, but a side-door would, from now on, be permanently open. As of that night, the Wall served no purpose even for the East German authorities themselves. It was a focus of hatred — and yet it was not keeping anybody in. Clearly, the ultimate surrender — the removal of the Wall itself — had to be just around the corner.

From Prague that night, it was possible to draw the obvious implication: 'It is difficult to see this latest retreat by the East German leadership as anything other than the beginning of the end for the East Berlin regime — and perhaps the beginning of the final act for East Germany itself.' The Krenzes of this world sustained themselves with the illusion that they still held power and that their Politburo decisions were shaping history. But Krenz and his comrades were, by now, little more than bobbing flotsam caught up in the waves of change. They might give in a day or a month earlier or later. But they *would* give in. All the other avenues had been tried. Tightening the screws did not work; and partial loosening of the screws did not work. The dilemma had only one solution. And sure enough, on 9 November, came the ultimate miracle: by order of the powerless Politburo, the Wall broke open. The world as we knew it came to an end.

Yet again, the world praised Mikhail Gorbachev, as though he had dreamed up the fall of the Berlin Wall while having a late-night Kremlin bath. Certainly, it was magnificent that Gorbachev accepted the breach in the Wall – an option that he had rejected, so sternly, just a month earlier. But the East German leadership – and therefore Moscow, too – literally had no options left. Krenz was the man who had praised the Peking leadership for its resolute approach, after the Tiananmen massacre in June. And yet he allowed the Berlin Wall to be breached. It was pragmatism, of the right kind, that had again won the day: Krenz knew when he was beaten. Gorbachev, too – immeasurably more humane than Krenz – was intelligent enough to see that if the East German Communists had played all their cards, there was no point expecting them to win any more tricks. Equally, whipping out a pistol and shooting the true winners of the game would give the Communists a temporary, and less than useless kind of victory. Gorbachev's permission was useful, but not essential, for East Germany's final surrender.

In Czechoslovakia, too, it was clear that change was on the way. Opposition demonstrations began, in earnest, on the twentieth anniversary of the Soviet invasion in August 1988. In 1989, tens of thousands signed the most important opposition document for more than a decade. The opposition leader, Vaclav Havel, wrote in July: 'This society, for so long run down, silenced and atomized, is beginning to lose patience . . . People are beginning to interest themselves more in public affairs, to seek out truthful information, and to lose their fear.'

At the end of October 1989, as the revolutions elsewhere began to take off, the slogans in Prague, with their talk of the achievement of the masses and eternal friendship with the Soviet Union, were curiously dissonant with the changes that were taking place to the north, west and south. But everybody knew that, in the words of one opposition figure, 'a huge loosening has to come – we are the last island'. Jiri Dienstbier, who was forced at that time to work as a stoker (and who a few weeks later was metamorphosed into foreign minister, as part of the fairy story that was Prague), said that there were obvious reasons why the Communists were frightened of reform. 'The leadership knows that once it starts, in one or two weeks every government official who's not directly responsible for what has happened will move across to the other side.' Vaclav Havel, chainsmoking and drinking beer in his favourite restaurant by the river Vltava, talked of his country as a pressure cooker waiting to explode. Even the government spokesman let slip an obvious truth when explaining why the government did not want to introduce reform. 'We don't want to jump into the river when we don't know how deep the water is.' He was right: when the floodwaters broke through, the Communists would drown in democracy.

A clutch of conspiracy theories subsequently sought to prove that the Prague revolution was caused by Mikhail the Liberator, or by the KGB, or both. The main conspiracy theory was based on the fact that the secret police faked the death of a student during a demonstration. An ambulance removed what appeared to be a corpse – in fact, the body of an alive-and-well secret policeman – in what some later saw as a deliberate ploy to trigger more anti-government demonstrations. The idea was that the revolution could not, or would not, have happened of its own accord. In fact, there was a much simpler explanation for the secret-police ruse. It was later confirmed that the authorities wanted to discredit two journalists who ran an opposition news agency and whose reports were generally trusted in the West. The secret-police stunt successfully duped the agency into reporting the alleged death (an allegation that made headlines worldwide); the authorities were then able to accuse the opposition journalists of deliberately concocting stories. It was the kind of provocation that the Soviet-bloc secret police frequently engineered.

Some Czechs themselves later came to be persuaded that they had merely been accessories to their own revolution. In reality, though, the pressure was already irresistible, as opposition leaders themselves had emphasized. As became clear throughout eastern Europe – and as would eventually be seen in Moscow, too – even totalitarian regimes are sometimes much more unstable than might at first appear. The East European revolutions happened not just despite the forces ranged against them, but also because of those forces. The more violence the authorities used, the more support the protesters gained. After the official violence in Prague, people did not become more afraid. They only became more defiant, just as protesters had done in Leipzig. After the revolution in Prague, posters – black-edged, in the style of central

European death announcements – went up on street corners announcing the death of 'Soudruh Strach' – Comrade Fear. Date of death: 17 November 1989, when the beating up of demonstrators persuaded thousands to take to the streets who had never been on a protest demonstration before. Simon, a telephone engineer, said after the revolution was over: 'I laboured under a burden of guilt for twelve years because I didn't sign [the dissident document] Charter 77. On 17 November, as I lay on the ground and the police beat me . . . I felt free.'

By the end of November 1989, it was clear to all that the world would never be the same again. To see the revolutionary process gain momentum was an extraordinary experience, like watching a speeded-up film where a magnificent flower unfolds before your eyes. The unbelievable was fast becoming everyday. At last, an old paradox was beginning to find its resolution. In much of eastern Europe, there had long been a fear and cynicism on the part of both the rulers and the ruled. The nation feared its leaders and was sceptical of every victory that was won, believing that such victories would always, eventually, be followed by defeat. That was the message contained in Andrzej Wajda's 1981 film about Solidarity, *Man of Iron*, where the last words go to the secret-policeman character. He emerges from the Gdansk shipyard, promising that the agreements with the Solidarity strikers will be ignored: 'It's only a piece of paper. It means nothing!' Wajda's half-pessimism – a knowledge that the regime would eventually try to fight back – was widely shared in Poland at that time.

Yet the popular pessimism could also be mixed with a long-term optimism. An earlier Wajda film, with some of the same characters, was called *Man of Marble* and showed how people could be shaped – and broken – by the Communist regime. By 1980, however, as the new film title suggested, people could no longer be worked at will.

The Communists in the 1980s – simultaneously powerful and paranoid, like the defenders of apartheid in South Africa during the same period – suffered from a constant fear of the people whom they kicked around and believed that it was *they*, the rulers, who were doomed to lose. Both the rulers and the ruled were right to believe that power lay with the other side. In the short term, the hardliners held all the cards. But each time they used violence to secure victory, they increased the resentment and weakened their position for the next time. Eventually, they were forced to give up. It was only a matter of when the defeat would come. In eastern Europe, the final surrender came in 1989 – though nobody could be certain, even during 1989, that this was the final surrender. Until after the revolutions were over, the possibility remained of one last, vain crackdown, one last flick of the tail.

The final proof of the irreversibility of history — if proof was still needed — came in Romania, in December 1989. If nothing else, the megalomaniac cruelty of the Romanian leader, Nicolae Ceausescu, showed one thing clearly. Even tanks cannot stop the process of change once it has got under way. It all began in the western town of Timisoara, where a random spark — the eviction of a Hungarian pastor — lit the touchpaper, with small protests. It was here that the worst pro-Ceausescu killings took place, as the revolution began. But it was here, too, that victory was won. Not until three days after the revolution had succeeded in Timisoara did the rebellion take hold in the Romanian capital, Bucharest. On 21 December, Ceausescu could be seen, flapping his arms like a tormented crow, on the balcony overlooking Bucharest's largest square, as the crowds at a staged pro-Ceausescu rally started chanting slogans against the dictator. They knew what had already been achieved in Timisoara and they knew that they were no longer alone. The live television transmission was cut; but it was too late. The viewers already knew that the game was up, and so did the crowds. Like the East Germans and the Czechs before them, Romanians at last felt the loss of fear. And perhaps even Ceausescu, despite everything, half-understood that his time was up. At this point, the National Salvation Front — a Communist-dominated group of reformers — moved in and effectively hijacked the revolution. But the victory itself — first in Timisoara, then in Bucharest — was real enough.

The fate of Nicolae and Elena Ceausescu — two dead bodies, lying on the ground, after an execution on Christmas Day — contained a crucial lesson for the Soviet Union, if only the hardliners were ready to heed it. Certainly others in Russia noticed the implication. It soon became clear that the main message of East Europe in 1989 — that, in the last resort, no regime need be for ever and that no violence can halt the inevitable — would leave a subversive, buried trace in the Soviet Union, too. Once that realization began to grow, the Communist Party leaders in Moscow were powerless as never before.

7 What About the Workers?

In Lenin Square in the city of Donetsk, there was almost a holiday atmosphere. Thousands of miners sat in the sunshine in their coal-smeared working clothes and helmets, playing chess and dominoes, or just chatted, listening to the occasional speeches and public-service announcements. Marshals with red armbands ensured that nobody damaged the municipal rose-beds. There was no mistaking it: the revolution had at last begun. In eastern Europe, the system was already falling apart. Now, in July 1989, equally extraordinary events were beginning to take place in the Soviet Union, too.

The miners in Donetsk, at the centre of one of the two most important coalmining regions in the Soviet Union, were just some of the hundreds of thousands who, together, had created the most serious peacetime political crisis that the Soviet system had ever faced. During a few weeks in summer 1989, the miners said, 'Enough.' The scenes in Lenin Square were officially deemed to be impossible in a workers' state. But the spirit of rebellion had finally taken hold. Gorbachev may have ruefully reflected during those weeks that the televised sessions of the new Soviet parliament − only six weeks old − had a lot to answer for. The virus of half-democracy had begun to infect the Soviet body politic. Theoretically, that was just what he wanted. But *perestroika*'s original, Communist leaders began to be overwhelmed by the pressures which were now growing.

Living standards had fallen rapidly: Gorbachev's early hints of a quick turnaround had come to nothing. The first public mutterings of discontent, heard during Gorbachev's walkabouts in Siberia in September 1988, had become steadily louder in the past year. With *glasnost* more outspoken than ever, fear was diminishing and resentment growing. The daily revelations about the Stalin and the Brezhnev era did little for the popularity of the new, more civilized leadership. Far from being impressed by the less mendacious version of history, people were angry when they realized how much they had been lied to in past decades. Now, with radical voices being heard in the Soviet Congress of People's Deputies — on tens of millions of television screens every night — it was only a matter of when, and where, the tension would break.

The answer was Mezhdurechensk ('Between-the-Rivers'), in western Siberia, on 10 July 1989. Within a few days, 100,000 miners were on strike in the region, known as the Kuznetsk basin — abbreviated to the Kuzbass. From the Kuzbass, the Soviet Union's most important coal-producing region, the industrial unrest quickly spread. Strikes began in the Karaganda region in Kazakhstan; in Vorkuta, in northern Siberia; and in Donetsk, in the Russian-majority area of eastern Ukraine. There had been a number of small, isolated strikes in the previous two years, but this was by far the biggest industrial action that the Soviet Union had ever seen.

The Soviet authorities seemed unable to decide how they should react. Were these strikers to be condemned? Or should they be co-opted, as supporters of 'perestroika', whatever that might now mean? The Kremlin, confused, followed both approaches simultaneously. Gorbachev insisted that he was inspired by the strikes, which he said were in favour of perestroika. But he also warned that they could ruin the cause of perestroika and renewal. Many grievances, he insisted, had already been solved, or were about to be. He blamed the local Communist Party leaderships, who did not want to introduce radical change. But he also complained that people hostile to the socialist system were trying to manipulate the strike to their advantage. He singled out emissaries of the Democratic Union for blame, saying that the situation 'should not be underestimated'.

Despite Gorbachev's rebukes about political manipulators, the miners, at this time, were still keen to persuade others — and themselves — that this was only an economic strike. Political strikes were, for the moment, still beyond the pale. In the town of Makeyevka, near Donetsk, it was necessary only to approach a group of miners, as they sat playing cards or chatting by their tents, for the cry to go up: — 'It's an economic strike!' The phrase was used as a protective mantra. Economic strikes, after all, were safe — or safe-ish. Political strikes, emphatically, were not.

In a sense, the insistence that this was an economic strike was accurate. Again and again, the small basics of human life were quoted as triggers for the strike. The shortage of soap caused particular resentment, since the miners needed to scrub themselves clean of the caked coaldust after every shift. Never, they said, had they faced such difficulties before. The miners had previously received soap as part of their work allowance. Now, that had stopped – but there was no soap in the shops to buy. The wages, though much higher than the Soviet average, scarcely compensated for the difficulty and danger of the job: 10,000 working miners had died in the previous ten years. Several hundred people were killed every year in accidents in the Donbass region alone.

But it was not the danger that put people off. It was a growing sense that they had been deceived by those they had trusted. Certainly, the conditions were bad enough. The paid shift did not take into account more than an hour's walk (or crawl) underground, at the beginning and end of the working day, in order to reach the coalface. 'Of course, they should transport us. But they can't be bothered. We go everywhere on foot – and even the boots they give us are uncomfortable.' And always, the same refrain: they don't care. 'They tell us what to do. But we know what we *can* do.' For many, this was at the heart of what the strike was about. 'We are trying to make them see that we are people. They just see us as a way of fulfilling the plan.' The question of privileges was especially offensive. 'All the people at the party headquarters have special food. There are "diet" shops in town. But you won't see people with special "diets" going in there. It's for the regional party committee, the town party committee, those kind of people.' A group of strikers pointed to the huge Communist Party headquarters that loomed over the square, which had cost £30 million to build. 'It's a disgrace for Donetsk. *They* don't have the problems with soap. It's *us* who have all the problems.'

The mood of defiance was new. As one miner noted: 'People showed their strength. When the strike first began, they said: "Whoever leaves work now is on strike, and will be sacked." But people went out anyway.' And, meanwhile, despite the protestations, it was the political climate, not just economics, that underpinned the dispute. *Moscow News*, putting a toe into radical waters, pointed out: 'Direct analogies are a delicate matter in politics. But let us remember that events in Poland at the beginning of the 1980s began with purely economic demands from the strikers.' The comparison was accurate – dangerously accurate, from the Kremlin's point of view. The wave of Polish strikes in 1980, which culminated in the most triumphantly political victory for people's power that the Communist bloc had ever seen, began with something much more mundane: the re-pricing, on 1 July 1980, of a small number of meat cuts. For the Soviet authorities, it was an unhappy precedent.

Explicit politicization was yet to come. But even in 1989, it was easy to find the unresolved contradictions. In Makeyevka, one miner delivered the obligatory catchphrase about the economic strike. Then, as we continued talking, I asked what, for him, was at the heart of the strike. He paused for a moment, then replied: 'It's like Marx said, isn't it? You have nothing to lose but your chains.' The miner apparently sensed no contradiction between his Marxian talk of losing chains (with echoes of the slogan at the Lenin shipyard in Gdansk in 1980: 'Proletarians of all workplaces – unite!') and his insistence that this was a purely economic strike. There were other confusions, too. One miner declared: 'Naturally, I support Gorbachev completely.' Yet a few minutes earlier, the same miners had said that the strikes had happened because 'everybody is fed up of seventy years of Soviet power'. The first phrase would be heard less and less in the months to come; the second phrase, more and more.

This was not eastern Europe, not by a long way. People did not know what they wanted to get rid of, let alone what they wanted to put in its place. There was none of the light magic of Poland in August 1980 nor of Czechoslovakia in November 1989, when a nation rejoiced in its power to win impossible victories against an unwanted regime. None the less, there were startling similarities with eastern Europe, too. There was a revolutionary discipline, which – in a country which had always appeared either apathetic or anarchic, or both – seemed unbelievable. Even the strikers' presence in the town centre was organized with unheard of efficiency. The miners in Lenin Square – with their mining helmets and dressed in their working clothes – were, in effect, working out their daily shift. Miners turned up daily for work, as normal, and got changed. The only difference was that, instead of going down into the mine, they were then taken by bus to the centre of Donetsk, or to the equivalent rallying points in other towns, where they would work out their shift on the square. As one shift arrived, another would be summoned by megaphone back to the bus, and would go back to the mine and change into their ordinary clothes before returning for another day on strike the next day. Thus it was, day in, day out, for the entire duration of the strike.

Every last detail was catered for. Everybody knew that the official press would be looking for *huligani* to blame – hence the men with the red armbands to look after even the flowerbeds. All alcohol, too, was banned in Donetsk – and in Siberian mining cities, too – for the duration of the strike. In the Soviet Union, as in Poland, many people regarded vodka as part of their compulsory diet. And yet the Russians now pulled off the same trick which the strike committee had successfully used in Gdansk nine years earlier. Vodka meant drunks; drunks meant trouble; and trouble meant an excuse for the authorities to crack down. Therefore, no vodka. As far as the strike committees were concerned, the logic was simple. The strongest beverage being drunk on the square was kvass, the popular, thirst-quenching rye-beer. In some Siberian cities, the overnight drying-out cells that exist in every Russian town were reported to be empty for the first time in living memory.

At the mines themselves, the strike committees ensured almost military discipline. There were twenty-four-hour patrols to prevent damage to the mines – damage which, the strikers were convinced, would officially be blamed on the strikers themselves. Nor was that necessarily paranoia. One miner on patrol at a mine near Donetsk said that three times in as many days, persons unknown had tossed petrol-soaked rags on the pile of dry timber in one corner of the mine premises, during the night. The fires had been extinguished before they could do much damage. But the suspicion of Them, the nameless and faceless ones who wanted to make trouble for the workers, ran deep.

On the square in Donetsk, meanwhile, the atmosphere was amiable and relaxed. The only moment when it hardened was when one man, who claimed to represent the strike committee, told the crowd: 'Go to work, and everything will be done. I give you my honest word as a Communist.' He was greeted with boos, catcalls and derisive laughter. In the Soviet Union, there had been a time when lines like that would have been well received, but the respect for such pieties was slipping away, fast.

None of this pleased the authorities. *Pravda*, using a tried and tested method, published a letter – allegedly written by collective farm workers – which accused the miners of seeking 'artificially to create a famine, as in 1933 or 1947'. On the main television news, a telegram was read out which claimed to be from veterans of the Great Patriotic War. The message, which lasted for several minutes, talked of how the veterans had conquered fascism and asked the miners not to allow chaos in the country.

But the signals were mixed. Initially, Soviet television news did not allow the strikers themselves to have a voice; instead, pro-government voiceovers emphasized the huge losses to the economy. Soon, however, that changed. One evening, the television camera showed a Siberian mine director who complained about how unreasonable the strikers were being. So far, so normal. Then, suddenly, the camera swung round to focus on a member of the strike committee standing next to him, who shot down the mine director's claims. Such a right of reply was, at that time, unheard of and hardliners probably suffered apoplexies all across the country. A process was now under way that could not be reversed. One old man in Donetsk emphasized that this was the beginning, not the end. 'The miners started − but others will come. People are no longer afraid.' Or, as a miner in Makeyevka declared: 'This is just a little flower. The fruit will come later.'

The return to work was provisional at best. Nikolai Slyunkov, the Politburo member charged with persuading Siberian miners to return to work, offered sweeteners, literal and metaphorical. He signed one agreement in which he offered 10,000 tonnes of extra sugar, 3000 tonnes of washing powder and soap, 6000 tonnes of meat, five million tins of milk, 1000 tonnes of tea and 100 tonnes of coffee and cocoa. But there was no indication where this largesse was to come from, in a country where none of these items was to be found in abundance. Certainly, there was no suggestion that the elite, who had access to such products, would give them up. If the message was, 'To them that strike shall be given; from those that continue working shall be taken away,' then the implications were clear: everybody should down tools if they wanted a share of the goodies.

Gorbachev talked of a £10 billion injection of foreign imports into the Soviet economy. It was a startling suggestion, which could be interpreted in two ways. On the one hand, if the offer was serious, it spelt catastrophe for the Soviet economy even greater than the ruin which was already upon it. The Soviet Union did not have a spare £10 billion of hard currency to buy off its workers. Gorbachev appeared to be dreaming of a repeat of the economic policy that Poland had introduced during the 1970s. If so, he needed to look again at his briefing notes. After a workers' rebellion against Communist rule in Gdansk in December 1970, the Polish government introduced an official spend-spend-spend policy. Western imports, bought with Western credits, were used to fend off domestic discontent, as Edward Gierek created what he called a second Poland. The policy was temporarily successful, but left nothing over for long-term investment. That policy of living on the never-never was an important reason for the subsequent complete collapse of the Polish economy in the late 1970s when the crippling foreign debt came due; the growing economic crisis, in turn, was a key factor in triggering the unrest and strikes which led to the birth of Solidarity.

Alternatively, Gorbachev may have offered such promises without any intention of fulfilling them, in the hope that he could persuade the miners back to work, at least in the short term. Certainly, as the miners trickled back to work, they were suspicious rather than triumphant – despite endless pieces of paper, with important signatures, which promised that everything would now change. The strikers made clear that if the promises were not fulfilled, they were prepared to renew their strikes.

By now, the spirit of defiance was visibly beginning to grow in the Soviet capital, too. Arbat Street in central Moscow – where KGB men used to scuffle with demonstrators in the early Gorbachev years – became an unofficial centre of *glasnost*, with a strong pride in its we-don't-give-a-fig atmosphere. In the summer months, the area became a Russian Montmartre, with dozens of charcoal-portrait artists plying their trade and finding an almost lucrative way of making ends meet. Jazz bands played throughout the day, as the crowds filled what was now a pedestrian precinct, wandering at leisure, munching on kebab sticks or sitting at cafe tables with large portions of Russian ice-cream. It was touristy and the pavements were full of onion-dome artistic kitsch. But, like Pushkin Square – home for alternative demonstrations and alternative political pamphlets – the Arbat became a focus for a kind of Otherness, which would be difficult to stamp out.

An outfit called the Arbat Poets – a kind of Speakers' Corner in verse – declaimed poems to the passers-by, who gathered in crowds large or small. Part of the subject matter of the Arbat Poets was pure romance and existential angst. Mostly, though, they liked to break taboos. Lev Zaikov – who had replaced Yeltsin as party leader in Moscow – complained that, on the Arbat, 'Under the flag of democracy, banalities have blossomed, and sometimes overt anti-Soviet propaganda.' Zaikov was right; but his tirade had little effect. The anti-Soviet propaganda was one reason why the Arbat was so popular. One poem parodied the first line of the Communist Manifesto ('A spectre is going round Europe – the spectre of Communism'), declaring: 'The spectre of Communism is at a standstill.' Other subjects of attack included the 'party princes' of the central committee, the powers of the KGB – and Gorbachev himself. In some respects, the Arbat was untypical. But it was representative, in a different kind of way, of the changes and the disrespect for officialdom that could yet be in store. There was a quiet satisfaction on the Arbat, too, at the implications of what had begun to happen both in Siberia and in the Ukraine. As one man commented in the Arbat crowds: 'The working class has gained a weapon – which it had forgotten it had for seventy years.'

Only a few months earlier, police were still bundling people into police vans if they explicitly rejected the hymns to Communist restructuring and to the Communist Party leader, which remained the staple diet of *Pravda* and the *Vremya* evening news. But, by summer 1989, that repressive version of *perestroika* was already beginning to crumble. There was much that was (officially) not yet allowed. But there was much that was no longer forbidden, too. In the underpass on Pushkin Square, they were openly selling *Express-Khronika*, the dissident account of KGB dirty tricks and official horrors that had existed underground for many years. It was theoretically illegal, but for most of the time, nobody could be bothered to intervene.

Not surprisingly, the defenders of the *ancien régime* were worried. At the end of August, Vladimir Kryuchkov, head of the KGB – not generally thought of as a dyed-in-the-wool liberal – declared airily that the USSR need not worry about the appointment in Poland of Tadeusz Mazowiecki, eastern Europe's first non-Communist prime minister for four decades. Yet at the same time as Kryuchkov's insouciance about eastern Europe, there was considerable worry about the knock-on effect of such heresies at home. *Pravda* called for a crackdown on unofficial publications which criticized the Soviet Communist Party and singled out the illegal *Glasnost*. Two Siberian journalists were jailed and the unofficial bulletin that they worked on was confiscated (like much of the political material that was banned in Russia, the bulletin itself was printed in the Baltic republics and then flown 2000 miles to Novosibirsk). Later in the year, a journalist in Sverdlovsk, Sergei Kuznetsov, was sentenced to three years in a labour camp for slandering the KGB – even as the Berlin Wall came down.

But despite these attempts to put the brakes on, there was a new spirit of rebellion in the air. What had begun as a permitting from on high – 'Go on, Comrade Editor, tell the Soviet newspaper reader about some of the terrible things that Stalin and Brezhnev did to our party and our country!' – had now come of age and was beginning to turn rebellious. Gorbachev, the chief author of *glasnost* mark 1 (1985–88) was not always best pleased by *glasnost* mark 2 (1989 onwards). In October 1989, he called a meeting at which he lambasted the liberal press and demanded the sacking of the editor of the hugely popular weekly *Argumenty i Fakty*. Vladislav Starkov's offence had been to publish a survey of 15,000 readers' letters which indicated that the most popular parliamentary deputies were Andrei Sakharov, Boris Yeltsin and other radicals, including the economist Gavriil Popov and the historian Yuri Afanasiev. Gorbachev was not mentioned at all. Gorbachev's anger was even greater when he learned that the reason for his omission was that his rating was so embarrassingly low.

In many respects, even more remarkable than Gorbachev's demand that Starkov should go was Starkov's own response to the threats against him. He refused to go – and his colleagues stood by him, threatening to go on strike if he was sacked. Starkov declared: 'The paper's authority among the population at all levels is too high: that is exactly what frightens the party apparat.' Only a year earlier, it would have been quite unthinkable for any editor to indulge in such public defiance of the Soviet Communist Party leader, let alone to win the battle. Now, however, the new openness was gaining a life of its own. *Glasnost* had turned Frankenstein and threatened the comfort of its own creator. These small rebellions hinted at the much greater rebellions that were yet to come.

The battles over *Argumenty i Fakty* were of interest to more than just a small coterie of the chattering classes in Leningrad and Moscow. The Soviet Union had always been a country of avid readers; the average Russian was much better read than his British counterpart. Now, Soviet readers were also interested in the brave new world of political drama, for the first time. *Arguments and Facts*, with its brisk, statistics-packed style, gained a remarkable circulation of 30 million – proportionate to population, four times more than the circulation of the *Guardian*, *Times* and *Independent* combined. The paper received 10,000 letters a week. Meanwhile, Soviet readers began to vote with their almost-empty wallets and the circulation of the pro-establishment papers dropped sharply. *Pravda*, for example, lost almost half its ten million readers.

By now, Gorbachev was almost permanently at odds with the radicals. In a twenty-five-minute address on Soviet television, he complained of ultra-leftists (i.e. Yeltsin and his supporters) and of anti-socialists (i.e. the Democratic Union and the Popular Front organizations in the Baltic). He also criticized Yuri Afanasiev, rector of the Institute of Historical Archives and a leading radical, for his 'anti-socialist' statements and suggested that, with views like that, he should leave the Communist Party. (Later, when the leading radicals *did* start leaving the party, Gorbachev criticized them for that, too.) Following Gorbachev's attack on Afanasiev, *Pravda* and other pro-establishment papers took their cue to weigh in against him, too. The radicals became increasingly critical. Sakharov warned that Gorbachev was threatened by his hesitation between right and left; Yeltsin warned that if he did not speed up his reforms, he might face revolution, from below.

On the streets of Moscow came the first serious signs of rebellion, with unprecedented counter-demonstrations on the anniversary of the October Revolution on 7 November – the most sacred date in the Soviet calendar. (Because of the differences between the pre-Revolutionary and the modern calendar, Russian historical dates are confusing: the October Revolution has its anniversary in November; the revolution of February 1917 is remembered in March; and Christmas Day comes after the New Year.) Posters in the crowds on the day of the Great October Revolution (to give it its official title) declared; 'Down with the CPSU' and 'Workers of the World – we're sorry.' As East European Communism was swept away, the suppressed bitterness of decades began to spill into the open. One placard bore an epitaph for the era, with a phrase that later became a leitmotif: 'Seventy-two years on the road to nowhere.'

Meanwhile, Gorbachev came under sharp attack from the party hardliners, who were angry that he had 'lost' eastern Europe. At a closed-door central committee meeting in December, there was an onslaught from the regional party bosses who knew that their positions were under threat. Gorbachev threatened to resign, which (as on so many occasions before) called the hardliners' bluff, forcing them to back down. The hardliners barked loudly. They wanted to bite. But things were no longer going the hardliners' way.

In the international arena, Gorbachev was more beloved than ever before. In June 1989, when he visited West Germany, the wild enthusiasm had already been remarkable. 'Gorby, Gorby!' the crowds chanted, in adoration, as the brass bands played. Polls showed that Gorbachev was, for West Germans, the most popular politician in the world. He was trusted by 90 per cent of West Germans – almost twice as many as trusted George Bush or Helmut Kohl. Now, on 2 December, Gorbachev and Bush began a two-day summit on the Soviet liner *Maxim Gorky*, off the coast of Malta. The meeting took place in such a fierce Mediterranean storm that many of the logistical arrangements had to be abandoned. None the less, this was a moment when the international friendships were sealed. Both sides talked of entering a new era and of lasting peace. It was here, amid the December gales, that Bush and Gorbachev – again, in the words of phrasemaker Gerasimov – officially agreed to end the Cold War.

In the West, Gorbachev was now perceived as the man who had set out to liberate eastern Europe, single-handed. He was nominated Man of the Year many times over and *Time* magazine made him their Man of the Decade. Despite the international plaudits, however, there was already an increasing resentment, at home, at Gorbachev's failure to move faster towards change. In November, Sakharov argued that the abolition of Article 6, guaranteeing the Communist Party's leading role, should be debated in the Supreme Soviet. Gorbachev rejected the idea, saying that such discussion would be an attempt, under cover of criticism, to debase the role of the party. This, he said, would be an error that would cause unnecessary worry in the public mind. Soon, Gorbachev would be forced to back down on this, as on so many other issues. But for the moment he seemed determined to stand firm. Then the radicals demanded that Article 6 should be discussed in the full parliament, the Congress of People's Deputies, whose new session began on 12 December. Again, Gorbachev spoke fiercely against the idea.

It was at this moment that Russia's uncertain, lumbering moves towards democracy suffered a severe blow. As the country groped its way forward, it was important for Russia – resentful, unstable Russia – to have one man whose moral leadership was acknowledged by the entire nation. Somebody whose courage and integrity were unquestioned; who did not resort to demagogy; whose love of Russia had nothing in common with chauvinism or love of empire; and who did not count Communist hardliners among his close colleagues. In Russia, there was one such man. He died of a heart attack, late in the evening of 14 December 1989.

Andrei Sakharov – who in the months before his death topped the popularity polls – might have played an invaluable role in helping the country peacefully to pass through the dangerous bridging period between the Communist past and the unknown future. But Russia was not to be blessed in this way and the loss of Sakharov would leave a gaping wound. Like Vaclav Havel in Czechoslovakia – in jail a few months earlier and about to become president of his country – Sakharov, the soft-spoken fighter, had never compromised, never bent with the wind. Like Havel, he had come to represent the conscience of the nation – a nation that knew that it could, during the darkest years, have done much more. Now, Russians were grateful to him for having kept the flame burning through all those years.

In the hours before he died, he had been planning another attack on the Communist Party's leading role. He told a friend: 'There'll be a hard fight tomorrow.' Now that he was gone, everybody found it appropriate to praise him. Gorbachev, who had constantly been at odds with him — but who had, after all, brought him back from the long exile in Gorky — described his death as a great loss. Kryuchkov, head of the KGB, said that the banishment of Sakharov to Gorky in 1980 had been a flagrant error and an injustice.

Even Kryuchkov's tribute, sickeningly hypocritical though it was, gave an idea of how far the goalposts had moved. It was extraordinary that the head of the KGB, a known hardliner, thought it was necessary to declare his devotion to the memory of Sakharov. Equally important, too, was the popular reaction. The man who had once been spurned by his compatriots was now a national hero. Much of Moscow came to a standstill as 100,000 people gathered to pay a final tribute to him and joined in the funeral procession through the grey slushy snow, before his burial at the Vostryakovskoe Cemetery on the south-western edge of Moscow.

As one of the speakers at a rally in his memory declared: 'We were passive in his defence. As we take our leave, we can only say "Forgive us".' The democratic movement would never again have a single patron whose moral strength was so universally recognized. That would be a problem in the years to come. None the less, the emotional farewell for Sakharov was also a sign that Soviet society, unchanging for so many decades, had begun to be transformed. As a final requiem ended, thousands of clenched fists punched into the air. A new society was already being born.

8 The Unbreakable Breaks Up

Indissoluble union of free republics,
Brought together by Great Russia, for all eternity.
Long live the single, powerful Soviet Union,
By the will of the peoples created.

Be renowned, our free fatherland,
Firm bulwark of the friendship of peoples.
The party of Lenin, the popular force,
To the victory of Communism leads us on.

Even by the standards of national anthems, the words of the Soviet hymn seemed especially inappropriate by 1989. The very structure of the Soviet Union was beginning to crack. Almost every one of the Soviet Union's fifteen republics was straining at the leash, or was plagued by ethnic violence, as the old order began to collapse, with nothing to take its place. Yet in 1986, Gorbachev had felt able to make upbeat claims to the Communist Party congress in Moscow:

National oppression and inequality of all types and forms have been done away with once and for all. The indissoluble friendship among nations and respect for national cultures and for the dignity of all peoples have been established and have taken firm root in the minds of tens of millions of people. The Soviet people is a qualitatively new social and international community, cemented by the same economic interests, ideology and political goals.

A year later, Gorbachev was still talking of the USSR as a truly unique example in the history of human civilization. The Russian nation, he said, had played an outstanding role in the solution of the nationality question. In Estonia, he informed his hosts that the flourishing of nations and nationalities had been ensured because of the Leninist nationalities policy. It was all Walter Mitty stuff, but Gorbachev himself did not appear to realize this. At no time did he show any sign of understanding the aspirations of non-Russians in the republics, millions of whom felt that the relationship between Moscow and the republics was colonial at best, occupation at worst. As Sakharov put it, the Soviet Union was 'the last empire on the planet'. Sakharov argued that a better sobriquet for the USSR would be 'The country of the enmity of peoples'.

Barely eighteen months after Gorbachev's arrival in the Kremlin, there were already the first serious hints of the troubles to come. In December 1986, there were demonstrations in Alma-Ata, capital of the huge republic of Kazakhstan, in protest at the sacking of the local party leader, Dinmukhamed Kunayev. The crowds were little bothered about Kunayev himself, a Brezhnevite placeman who had done little to endear himself to the population, but there was widespread resentment that Kunayev's successor was an ethnic Russian. Two hundred people were injured and 1000 were jailed, following the unrest. Sparse details were published in the Soviet press, with accusations only against the 'extreme nationalists' who had caused the trouble.

But it was the huge demonstrations in Armenia which marked the first great eruption of the Gorbachev era, and made international head-lines, in 1988. Trouble had begun in late 1987, with demands on the environment. There were calls to close a rubber factory in the Armenian capital, Yerevan. But, as in the Baltic republics and elsewhere in the Communist bloc, grievances over the environment ended up providing flimsy cover for the political conflict that soon began to emerge.

In Yerevan, protesters started to demand the return of Nagorny Karabakh – an enclave in neighbouring Azerbaijan with an 80 per cent Armenian population. The Armenians argued that Karabakh should never have belonged to Azerbaijan in the first place. They blamed Stalin for handing it over after an independent Azerbaijan had officially ceded the territory to Armenia in 1920. Moscow, keen to be on good terms with Turkey – Armenia's worst enemy and Azerbaijan's best friend – reversed that decision and Karabakh was formally incorporated into Azerbaijan in 1923. Then, on 20 February 1988, the parliament in Karabakh – officially, an autonomous region within Azerbaijan – voted for the region to be transferred to Armenian jurisdiction.

That vote, which was rejected by the Azerbaijani authorities, was the trigger for the huge pro-Karabakh rallies that followed in Yerevan. They were by far the largest unofficial demonstrations that the Soviet Union had seen: within days, the numbers of protesters had risen from just a few thousand to around half a million. It was a dramatic early indication of just how explosive ethnic issues in the Soviet Union would prove to be. Initially, the demonstrations were not anti-Soviet in character. Banners claimed: 'Karabakh is a test case for *perestroika*!' Some people even carried pictures of Gorbachev. The peaceful mood did not, however, last for long. Moscow rejected the call for the transfer of Karabakh – but promised that the matter would be looked into. But there was not even a breathing space. On 28 February, Azeris in the town of Sumgait went on an anti-Armenian riot, partly as a kind of violent revenge for the Karabakh parliamentary vote. According to the official figures, thirty-two people were killed. This was the day that the smouldering Caucasus was set alight. The fire proved almost impossible to extinguish.

The issue of Karabakh had been a lingering source of bitterness for Armenians for six decades. *Glasnost* had given it the chance to explode. Now, through 1988, the Karabakh issue showed how dramatically events were beginning to run out of Gorbachev's control. He sought to buy himself a little time by promising Armenians a 'just' solution and suggested that some money would be thrown at the problem, in order to improve living standards in the impoverished Karabakh region. But that all meant little. In June, there was a pro-Karabakh general strike in Armenia, just ahead of a parliamentary session which was to discuss the issue. On the day of the session, hundreds of thousands crowded into Opera Square. The Armenian parliament bowed to the popular pressure and asked the Soviet parliament in Moscow to accede to the Armenian demands.

But Gorbachev now slapped the Armenians down, hard. In a move that had not been used against troublemakers since the Brezhnev days, an Armenian nationalist, Paruir Airikian, was expelled from the Soviet Union, without right of appeal. This, it was clear, was not a time for listening. In September 1988, ethnic violence again flared up: by the end of the year, more than 100 people had died. Meanwhile, the tension continued to grow. Foreign correspondents were banned from travelling to the region – allegedly, for their own safety – in an attempt to keep the turmoil under wraps.

Soon, it was not just a political crisis that Armenia faced. On 7 December 1988, Gorbachev gave a wide-ranging speech at the United Nations in New York. But the speech was entirely overshadowed by the horror of events in the Soviet Union that day. As Gorbachev left the United Nations in his presidential Zil, the prime minister, Nikolai Ryzhkov, telephoned him from Moscow. Human tragedy had struck at home. Armenia had suffered an earthquake the like of which the country had not seen. Spitak, a town of 15,000, was – in the words of Soviet television, which was freer to report the disaster than ever before – wiped off the face of the earth. Only a few hundred people survived. The earthquake caused huge damage to the city of Leninakan, too, with a population of a quarter of a million. Altogether, almost 30,000 people died. Not since the Turkish killing of tens of thousands of Armenians in 1915 had Armenia suffered such a national disaster. Gorbachev flew down to the earthquake zone to see the devastation for himself and talk to people there.

Even now, though, the subject of Karabakh scarcely slipped from people's minds. Gorbachev was indignant that this could be so. When ordinary Armenians raised the question of Karabakh with the Soviet leader, he complained bitterly that Armenians were being exploited by unscrupulous people, demagogues, adventurists and black-shirts. A furious Gorbachev left for Moscow and members of the Karabakh committee were arrested and later jailed. Sakharov argued that the arrest of the Karabakh committee 'flies in the face' of everything that Gorbachev was trying to do – but his pleas were to no avail.

The return of Karabakh would not improve any Armenians' lot – not even, necessarily, the Armenians in the poverty-stricken enclave itself, though they felt they had suffered, disproportionately, under Azeri rule. Above all, however, the return of Karabakh was seen as a way of regaining national dignity. It was the kind of issue which, negotiated bilaterally between the two disputing owners, might eventually be settled to the near satisfaction of both sides. But Moscow was, at this time, not seen by either side as an honest broker. The resentments merely got worse. Martial law was declared and armoured personnel carriers moved on to the streets of Yerevan. In January 1989, Nagorny Karabakh was placed under direct rule from Moscow.

In the spring sunshine on Opera Square, two months later, the troops and the APCs were still on twenty-four-hour guard, to prevent a recurrence of the protests of 1988. Armenia had always had a reputation as one of the most relaxed and attractive parts of the Soviet Union – with good entrepreneurs, good food and good brandy. Now, it was a country that was waiting for another explosion. 'All to the polls in the name of *perestroika*!' said one slogan in the centre of Yerevan. But everybody knew that the polls of the Soviet elections of March 1989 were, for Armenia, meaningless: the most popular candidates – including the oriental philologist, Levon Ter-Petrossian – were all behind bars in

Moscow. Ethnic clashes between Azeris and Armenians continued to get worse. In Moscow, they occasionally showed television pictures of Soviet soldiers in tanks, or of a single incident in the spectacular mountainous landscape, a short item on the news. But it scarcely impinged: the war continued. By the end of 1989, hundreds of thousands had fled from one republic to the other and the casualties continued to rise.

Meanwhile, in other corners of the Union, explicit rebellion against the Kremlin was beginning — and was beginning to be lethally suppressed. In the southern republic of Georgia, the pressure for change began in 1988. In November, crowds of 200,000 gathered, chanting slogans for independence. In February 1989, protest meetings were held on the anniversary of the incorporation of independent Georgia into the Soviet Union in 1921.

But 9 April 1989 was the lethal landmark. Demonstrations in the Georgian capital, Tbilisi, began five days earlier, with demands for independence. On Saturday 8 April, there were calls from the Communist leadership for the demonstrators to disperse. But that evening huge crowds again gathered on Rustaveli Avenue, in the centre of the Georgian capital. In defiance of the orders for them to return home, they stayed there, peacefully defiant. Until the tanks came. At four in the morning, the bloody nightmare began. An official massacre was carried out by Soviet troops, who used sharp-ended sapper's spades and gas against the crowds. Exit streets were blocked off, making it difficult to escape. Twenty-one people died. The victims were those who were unable to run away quickly and who were therefore easier to stab to death. Sixteen of the dead were women, including a pregnant mother, a seventy-year-old woman and a sixteen-year-old girl. Gorbachev, who was away in London when the decision to use force was taken — he returned to Moscow shortly before the massacre itself took place — appealed for calm.

In reality, it was now impossible for Georgia to become calm. The republic was inflamed and angered as never before. The Tbilisi massacre proved a watershed in the process of change in the Soviet Union. In a pattern that repeated itself, again and again, the effect of the violence was to radicalize opinion to an extraordinary extent. Troops and tanks moved on to the streets and a curfew was declared. But Tbilisi announced a general strike and protest meetings continued despite an official ban. A cavalcade of cars moved through the city in a column, horns hooting and headlights on; residents wore black armbands and declared a day of mourning.

Eduard Shevardnadze, himself a Georgian, condemned the killings and later revealed that he had come close to resigning as foreign minister. But his unambiguous reaction was the exception, not the rule, among his Kremlin comrades. *Pravda* complained that extremists and nationalists were hiding their true face behind a mask of commitment to *perestroika*. Gorbachev said that the Soviet government had a duty to defend the policy of democratization and *perestroika* – apparently, from the demonstrators. Morally, as Shevardnadze made plain, the violence was a clearcut issue. Despite *Pravda* and Gorbachev's seeming difficulty in allocating blame, there could, in reality, be no confusing the guilty and the innocent in Tbilisi that night.

But not all the violence of 1989 involved such morally simple divisions. Ethnic conflicts broke out in every corner of the Soviet Union, where the rights and wrongs depended entirely on who you were talking to. In July, there were clashes between Georgians and the Abkhazians, a minority within Georgia with an autonomous region of their own on the Black Sea. More than twenty people died in clashes which involved firearms as well as knives, sticks and stones. There were Georgian calls for the regional party leadership in Abkhazia to resign, for their alleged part in stirring up the ethnic trouble and for failing to bring to justice those who committed the initial killings.

The trigger for the unrest in Abkhazia was connected with the status of the university in the Abkhazian capital, Sukhumi, over whether it should be an independent Abkhazian university or a branch of the main Georgian university in Tbilisi. But this was no more than a starting point, a symbol that brought the old resentments into the open. Georgians argued that the Abkhazians were being incited by the Soviet authorities in Moscow. Certainly, declarations such as 'We Abkhazians want to remain part of the great Leninist family' were a reminder that declarations of nationalism often had as much to do with politics as with nationalities. None the less, the grouses were real, in Abkhazia and elsewhere. In South Ossetia, too – another corner of Georgia where the local population was disaffected with 'Great Georgian' rule – ethnic discontent (and ethnic violence) seemed inextricably interwoven with the politics of power.

Still, many Georgians were determined not to let the ethnic disputes distract them from what they still saw as their main aim: independence from Moscow. Every evening, tens of thousands gathered in the centre of Tbilisi. The protesters continued to concentrate on the one basic demand: separation from the Communist state. Even as the first great wave of miners' strikes began to spread, the Soviet Union was visibly crumbling at the edges.

There was little obvious tension. The atmosphere was almost that of a Mediterranean sea-front stroll − a chance to relax after a hot, sticky day, as people wandered chatting up and down Rustaveli Avenue or moved from group to group between their friends. But the aims of the gatherings were serious enough. Protesters waved the long-banned national flag and applauded speeches calling for independence from the Soviet Union. Posters declared: 'Freedom to Georgia' and 'Invaders, go home.' A middle-aged man on Rustaveli Avenue expressed a view so frequently repeated that it was difficult not to think of it as a kind of unofficial party line. 'Georgia has always been a multi-national country and there have never been any problems. I think the whole problem is that we've only got one party here. We must have an independent Georgia. We must get rid of the Bolsheviks.'

But even in self-confident, friendly Georgia − internationally renowned for its imaginative theatre productions and renowned in the other Soviet republics for its fine wines and shady businessmen − there were many contradictions. Despite all the rebelliousness against Soviet Communist power, there was still a lingering loyalty to Georgia's most notorious son. On top of Mtatsminda Hill, with panoramic views across the city, the plinth that bore his statue now stood empty at the end of an avenue of trees. But the park in which the statue had previously stood was still called the J.V. Stalin Central Park of Culture and Leisure. One of the city's busiest roads, along the river Kura, was the Stalin Embankment. Until a few years earlier, many Georgians still had pictures of the moustachioed dictator placed reverently on the dashboard of their vehicles and people had pictures of Stalin in their homes.

Gradually, that legacy was fading. The powerful opposition in Georgia rejected Stalin and emphasized its solidarity with opposition movements elsewhere in the Soviet Union. Groups with names like the Rustaveli Society (named after Georgia's national poet) and the Ilya Chavchavadze Society (founder of Georgia's nineteenth-century national liberation movement) came together in the single aim of pressing for independence. Georgia, an ancient kingdom, which never lost its sense of national identity, had briefly been free of Russian rule after the collapse of the tsarist empire in 1917: there was an independent social democratic government for three years. In May 1920, Lenin formally renounced all claims to Georgian territory and the right to interfere in Georgian affairs. But that did not last long: Russian tanks moved in, in February of the following year. Six weeks later, independence was finished.

Finished, but not forgotten. By 1989, even the Intourist office — a setting that traditionally represented the very embodiment of Soviet bureaucracy — had a poster commemorating Georgia's brief independence on the walls. In Georgia, as elsewhere in the republics, scepticism about Moscow's intentions ran deep. In the office of the Popular Front, on one wall hung a poster from the Baltic republics captioned '*Perestroika?*'. The picture was of an elephant trying to repaint itself with zebra's stripes.

Elsewhere, there was no simple rejection of Communism and Soviet rule. Rather, there was a bloody explosion of bottled-up resentments, whose existence the Soviet Union had denied for so long. All across the republics of Soviet Central Asia, the violence continued to spread. In Uzbekistan, violence broke out in June 1989 between Uzbeks and Meskhetian Turks in the Fergana region, in the east of the republic. More than 100 people, mostly Meskhetians, were killed and thousands of Soviet troops were sent in. During the clashes between Uzbeks and Meskhetians, whole settlements were burnt to the ground, as economic and ethnic chaos merged. Tens of thousands of Meskhetian Turks fled the republic — though they themselves now had nowhere to go. Like the Tatars from Crimea in Uzbekistan, they had been deported from elsewhere in the Stalin era — in the case of the Meskhetians, from Georgia. Georgia, in the meantime, did not want them back. The Fergana clashes barely began to die down before violence began in the town of Novy Uzen, in Kazakhstan, where at least five people were killed. And so it went on.

Throughout Central Asia, democratic opposition groups like Birlik ('Unity') — in Uzbekistan and elsewhere — failed to gain the mass momentum that they so envied among the Popular Fronts, which would soon oust the Communists in the Baltic republics. The leaders of the Central Asian republics were the most Brezhnevite, and the most resistant to change. Corruption, endemic in the Soviet Union, was especially strong in Central Asia. Communist barons retained their close links with Moscow and kept a tight hold on power. Opposition leaders were frequently harassed. Thus, politics remained in a Communist straitjacket, while ethnic politics were allowed to run wild. It was an unhappy mix.

By mid-1989, every corner of the Union was beginning to stir. Moldavia, a tiny republic in the south-west of the Soviet Union, had been Leonid Brezhnev's fiefdom in the 1950s. Like Georgia, the republic was famous for its wines (Intourist offered special wine-tasting tours); but it was also famous for its no-change policies. Even here, however, the old structures could not last for ever. Moldavia shared with the Baltic republics the unhappy distinction of having been annexed under the terms of the protocols of the 1939 Molotov-Ribbentrop pact. Before the war, it had been Bessarabia, a province of Romania.

After the Soviet annexation, everything was done to pretend that there was no connection between the Soviet Socialist Republic of Moldavia and the foreign country called Romania, the other side of the border. A language called 'Moldavian' was invented – in reality, Romanian written in a different alphabet. Romanian is part of the same group of languages as French and Italian: the Romanian (or 'Moldavian') for street is *strada*, the word for square is pronounced *piazza*, the world for light is *lumina*; and so on. In thousands of words, the close connection between Romanian and its linguistic cousins is clear and, not surprisingly, like all the other languages in the same group, Romanian is traditionally written in the Latin script.

Stalin, however, ordered that the Russian, Cyrillic alphabet be used in Moldavia – in order to suggest that Russian and 'Moldavian' were somehow related. Selected Romanian books were therefore 'translated' into Moldavian – i.e. republished with the same words but using different letters. All of this was in order to justify the Sovietization of the territory that had been detached from Romania because of a deal with Hitler. It was Sovietly surreal. But the effect of these convoluted games was serious enough. In the past forty years, Moldavia had been de-Romanized. Now, it was waking up to the possibility that things need not stay the same for ever. Demonstrations began in late 1988 and became increasingly frequent through 1989.

Small details took on a disproportionate importance, since everybody understood the larger implications that were at stake. Nicolae Dabija, editor of the literary weekly *Literatura si arta*, had begun publishing his paper in the Latin script – in other words, in Romanian. So shocked was the official distribution network that they initially refused to handle the paper. But the circulation of the paper rose more than tenfold. When I saw him, his most recent offence had been to publish, on the forty-ninth anniversary of the 'liberation' of Moldavia by Soviet forces on 28 June 1940, a commemorative poem of mourning rather than the required celebration of the establishment of Soviet power. Not surprisingly, the authorities were unimpressed.

In the shops, material in red, yellow and blue was withdrawn to make it difficult for protesters to sew themselves the flag that would within months be familiar to television viewers the world over – the Romanian colours, lifted high by the cheering demonstrators in Timisoara and Bucharest. The ultimate question, even then, was how and when those in Moldavia would start talking about rejoining Romania. For the moment, the subject was off the public agenda. Partly that was because Ceausescu was still in power in Romania. Nobody even contemplated being reunited with a country like his. Partly, though, it was simply a matter of self-protection. Moldavians knew that to challenge international borders at that time would be suicidal. In due course, however, this began to change. The nationalists became bolder: language laws were changed, so that Romanian became the first language of the republic instead of Russian. The republic even officially changed its name to Moldova. (This was primarily intended to make Moscow eat linguistic humble pie: in Romanian, the area had always been called Moldova and it was thus as if Finland suddenly announced that it was now called Suomi or Florence announced a name-change to Firenze.)

One certainty was that Moldavian independence, if or when it came, would be immensely complicated. Moldavia could not stay as part of the Soviet Union; but nor could it easily leave. One problem was that the borders of Soviet Moldavia were not identical with the Bessarabian territory which Stalin had hacked off from Romania fifty years earlier. Moldavia had lost two chunks to the Ukraine; and it had also gained a slice, to the east of the river Dniester, including the Russian-majority town of Tiraspol. Huge protests began in summer 1989 in Tiraspol and elsewhere against the pressure for Moldavian language rights. Later, Tiraspol – on the other side of the river Dniester from the rest of Moldavia – declared itself to be the capital of an independent republic, the Trans-Dniester Republic, which remained loyal to Soviet Communist power. Another area of Soviet Moldavia that had not originally formed part of Romania was inhabited by a Christian Turkic people, the Gagauz. Many of them, too, wanted no part of a non-Soviet Moldavia. The scope for both legal and ethnic complications was endless: by what right could Moldavia leave part of its territory behind? But by what right could Romania gain territory which had not been Romanian before 1940?

If the complications were severe in tiny Moldavia, the implications of change in the Soviet Union's second most populous republic, the huge and conservative Ukraine, were breathtaking. Here, the pressure did not begin with a rush, as it had in the Baltic. Through the early years of the

Gorbachev era, the hardline Vladimir Shcherbitsky remained in power. Ukrainians said of their republic: 'In Ukraine, you can take a holiday from *perestroika*.' None the less, even here, some changes began early – and then spread, slowly and surely, through the rest of the republic. The pressure for change began in western Ukraine, an attractive outpost of the Austro-Hungarian empire which had been a Polish university town (though always with a Ukrainian majority, in the countryside) before its occupation by Soviet forces in 1939. Lvov was annexed by the Soviet Union (or, as the official Soviet guidebook described it, 'began to breathe the air of freedom') under the terms of the same secret protocols of the Nazi-Soviet pact which paved the way for the annexation of Moldavia and the Baltic states. Stalin's territorial acquisition (also known as 'the campaign of liberation by the Red Army') was then formalized, under the post-war division of Europe at Yalta. In the western Ukraine, the memory of a non-Communist life was therefore relatively fresh. *Homo sovieticus* was not so dominant in Lvov as elsewhere in the Soviet Union.

Despite the fond dreams of many Poles, Ukrainians in Lvov had no desire to be part of Poland for a second time. But they had even less desire to be part of the Soviet Union. In this respect, Stalin's imperial greed backfired, many decades later: Lvov's restlessness played a crucial role in changing the mentality of the rest of the huge Ukraine, just as the revolutions in the tiny Baltic republics played an essential part in the collapse of Communism across the Soviet Union. If Lvov and the Baltic states had been left outside the Soviet Union, and had thus been unable to exercise their subversive influence from within the Soviet borders, it might have taken much longer for the nationwide rebellions to occur.

As early as February 1989, there were signs of unrest. When Gorbachev visited the city, he accused some people of using *perestroika* 'for their own ends'. A number of activists were arrested. But the first signs of resistance were already there – and not only in western Ukraine. In the same month, leading figures in the Ukrainian literary establishment threatened a showdown when the authorities tried to prevent even the publication of the electoral programme for the embryo Popular Front, which later came to be known as Rukh.

By the time of the Soviet elections in March 1989, Rukh was still, in effect, a banned organization. One of the most important opposition leaders spent election day in jail. But, despite the best efforts of the authorities, the movement continued to grow. Tens of thousands gathered for an unauthorized rally in Lvov on the fiftieth anniversary of the occupation of the city by Soviet forces, on 17 September 1939, waving the still-banned blue and yellow flags of the Ukraine. The same month, even though Shcherbitsky was still in power (some Ukrainians claimed that Gorbachev found it useful to have him there in order to put a brake on change in at least one corner of the empire), Rukh held its founding congress in Kiev. Rukh's name, like Sajudis in Lithuania, translated as 'Movement'. Like Sajudis, it was officially a 'movement in support of *perestroika*'. And, like Sajudis – though Rukh was not yet nearly so radical as its bold Lithuanian brother – the alleged support for Communist 'restructuring' would prove to be little more than a camouflage for the radical activities yet to come.

By the end of 1989, the rebellion in the Ukraine was only just getting under way. In the southern republic of Azerbaijan, it was beginning to reach a climax, which would end in a crackdown more bloody than all the pro-Kremlin violence in the rest of the country put together. Here, too, the pressure had been building gradually. In November 1988, there had been demonstrations by hundreds of thousands in the main square in the Azerbaijani capital, Baku, a port on the Caspian Sea and one of the most important centres for the oil industry in the Soviet Union.

Ethnic grievances initially topped the bill. As in Armenia, bitterness over the issue of Nagorny Karabakh was widespread. If the Armenians believed that Moscow was siding with Azerbaijan, the Azeris were convinced that the opposite was true. But, as had already happened elsewhere, ethnic complaints soon gave way to purely political demands, connected with workers' rights. The authorities eventually moved tanks on to the square and arrested the leaders of the protests. But the suppression of the protests did not mean the suppression of the discontent. The opposition continued to grow. Huge meetings took place in August and September 1989, when hundreds of thousands again attended rallies in Baku's main square – overlooked by a massive statue of Lenin, whose legacy was now being so clearly rejected. At the end of December, protesters virtually seized power in the provincial town of Djalilabad.

Soon, even more extraordinary events were to take place. In Nakhichevan, an enclave of Azeri territory in Armenia, on the Iranian border, thousands of Azeris destroyed frontier posts and cut barbed wire in a Caucasus-style re-run of the breaching of the Berlin Wall just two months earlier. Azeris live on both sides of the Soviet-Iranian border and some swam across the river Araks in order to reach Iran and fraternize with their fellow-Azeris, including relatives. For several days in January

1990, Moscow entirely lost control. (Tehran and Moscow were almost equally unenthusiastic about the new outbreak of Azeri brotherhood – the last thing the Iranian authorities wanted was a strengthening of the aspirations of their own, large Azeri population.)

During the same month, renewed ethnic killings began, this time in Baku. There were anti-Armenian pogroms, in which dozens died. Spokesmen for the Azerbaijani Popular Front condemned the violence, but to little or no effect. Thousands of Armenians fled. It was an appalling few days. If Soviet forces had intervened at this time, they could undoubtedly have saved innocent lives. They chose not to. But, as the ethnic violence subsided – not least, because almost all Armenians in the city had fled – Baku turned to rebellion against the Kremlin itself. On 18 January, tens of thousands gathered in the city centre and called for the resignation of the republican government and an end to Communist power. A general strike was called and huge crowds erected barricades in order to seal off the city centre from tanks. It was *then* – not while civilians were being murdered in previous days – that the Kremlin's patience snapped. An unprecedented warning from the Kremlin leadership was printed on the front page of *Pravda* that all necessary measures would be taken to stop 'today's tragedy turning into tomorrow's national catastrophe'. In the event, those necessary measuress were themselves the national catastrophe.

On the same day that the Kremlin warning was published, Soviet military might was again used – as it had been in Georgia nine months earlier – to crush rebellion against Communist power. Late in the evening of 19 January 1990, the tanks moved into Baku. Thousands of Soviet troops were involved in the assault. They crushed or shot everything in their path. Apartment blocks were spattered with gunfire. More than 100 people were killed in a single night.

After the Soviet attack, the city remained under a kind of military rule. The signs of protest were everywhere: black flags hung from many buildings and black ribbons were tied to most cars as a sign of respect for the dead. But troops were posted throughout the city, including in front of the offices of the now-banned Popular Front. Armoured personnel carriers stood on guard against the people in Parliament Square. Many of the dead lay in a cemetery above the old town centre, looking out across the Caspian Sea. On visiting the Avenue of Martyrs, as the row of graves soon became known, it seemed impossible to imagine that so many flowers could have been gathered together in one place. For several hundred yards, the carnations formed a scarlet wall, piled several feet high. There must have been hundreds of thousands, probably millions of flowers. Behind the flowers were dozens of freshly dug graves, each with a name and many with a photograph. The faces gazed out – young and old, smiling and serious, blurred and elegantly posed – as a stream of people shuffled by, paying their respect to the dead. Some of the graves contained children, whose plastic toys and scraps of clothing had been left on top – mementoes of those who had died. This was a crime that none in Baku was likely to forget. The killings brought a new revulsion against the Kremlin. Thousands of Communist Party members handed in or burnt their party cards. Portraits of Lenin and Gorbachev, too, were set ablaze.

Embarrassingly for the Kremlin, the military intervention was condemned not just by the Popular Front, but also by the speaker of the parliament. Worse, it was attacked even by the Armenian Popular Front, thus emphasizing that the military action had nothing to do with saving innocent Armenian lives. Indeed, Dmitry Yazov, the defence minister, said as much. He made it clear that the main purpose of the action was to get rid of the powerful Popular Front and to restore the Communist Party to power. 'Our task is ... to destroy the structure of power that has formed at all enterprises and offices. This is not a slip of the tongue – I mean power.'

Gorbachev seemed unrepentant about the civilian killings. Instead, he denounced extremists, vandals and criminals in Baku (and there had been all of those in the early days of the violence, unhampered by Soviet troops). Gorbachev said that it had been necessary to use arms against the instigators of disorder. Others saw it differently. Gary Kasparov, the chess player, was born in Baku and was in the city at the time; his family was forced to flee during the ethnic violence. But Kasparov argued:

> Gorbachev affirms that the troops were sent in to save people's lives. But ... why is such an action – the deployment of 20,000 armed troops – necessary to save people? There were three columns of tanks. What for? It's obvious those who died when the troops went in weren't those who had conducted the pogroms – they had already taken over the Armenians' apartments and weren't going to venture out. Those who died were the patriots who had demonstrated for Azerbaijan's independence.

The radicals in Moscow, too, sharply criticized the military action. And yet the West stayed aloof. Partly, perhaps, this was because the

Kremlin violence took place not in the European Baltic republics, nor in the Christian republic of Armenia, but in the Muslim republic of Azerbaijan. Partly, the West accepted the interesting official explanation that the military slaughter of civilians was necessary in order to prevent bloodshed. But, above all, the West remained convinced that Gorbachev was the only hope and was determined not to embarrass him, come what may. So keen was George Bush not to rock the Gorbachev boat that his reaction to the Baku killings was a message of support for the man who had ordered the troops in. 'I hope that he not only survives but stays strong.'

In much of the Soviet Union, however, the killings created increased bitterness that the Communist Party was still prepared to use lethal violence to hold on to power. Even the anti-Armenian violence, before the tanks moved in, was seen by some as a direct result of Kremlin policy. A Georgian newspaper compared the situation in the Soviet south to that of a group of unjustly imprisoned people who argue about their places in the cell rather than fighting together to escape. 'And then, imagine the self-satisfied expression of the prison guard, who is just looking for an excuse to go into the cell and beat up some bold prisoners. That is what Big Brother taught the Armenians and Azeris in Baku — and taught us, the Georgians, on 9 April.'

But blaming the Kremlin for worsening the problems was almost the only point on which it was possible to find agreement on all sides. For, like the disputes over territory between Serbs and Croats in Yugoslavia, the dispute over the ownership of Nagorny Karabakh was insoluble, unless there were huge reserves of goodwill and a readiness to compromise on both sides. As in Yugoslavia, each side had historical arguments which seemed compelling — until you heard the equally convincing arguments put by the other side. Compromise was what was needed; but there was no sign of it. Divide and rule had been the old imperial watchword. Now, the Communist rulers of the Soviet Union had the worst of both worlds. Many nations were violently divided — but they were no longer prepared to be ruled.

9 Going for Broke

One week before the Soviet tanks went into Baku, Gorbachev was facing yet another no-win situation, in another corner of the Union. On 11 January 1990, he arrived in the Lithuanian capital, Vilnius. His task was to persuade or bludgeon the Balts into line. The Lithuanians, when he arrived, were blithely unhelpful. One slogan in Vilnius especially riled Gorbachev by declaring: 'We welcome the head of a neighbouring state.' Gorbachev complained angrily, but with no effect. By now, there could be no question: the Lithuanians wanted out.

Gorbachev's crisis visit had been triggered not by the actions of the nationalist opposition, Sajudis — their turn was soon to come — but by the irreverence of the Lithuanian Communist Party. A few days before Christmas 1989 — while Ceausescu was being dramatically over-thrown in Bucharest — the Lithuanian Communist Party declared by a vote of 855 to 160 that it would, from now on, be an administratively separate entity from the Soviet Communist Party, the CPSU, of which it had until now formed a part. That might sound like a piece of obscure procedural etiquette, but, as Moscow's reaction made clear, this was much more than a breach of Communist good manners. In a real sense, the Lithuanian Communists, keen to establish their credentials for the republican elections which were about to take place, were deliberately defying the very essence of Soviet power.

The Lithuanian Communists declared the aim of the party to be 'an independent democratic Lithuanian state ... and the creation of normal living conditions for the Lithuanian nation and all the inhabitants of Lithuania'. The mischief-making journalist and Communist Party member, Algimantas Cekuolis, insisted that the Lithuanian party was not breaking off relations with the CPSU, but 'merely separating from it — to be like the Bulgarian Communist Party, or the French one'. But, as Cekuolis and his fellow-Lithuanians knew very well, the suggestion that Lithuanian Communists had the right to behave as independently as if they were on the *rive gauche* was certain to cause outrage in the Kremlin. Which it did.

An emergency session of the Soviet Communist Party central committee was called in Moscow for 25 and 26 December (Lithuania was, at the time, celebrating Christmas as an official holiday, for the first time for four decades). Gorbachev described the Lithuanian Communists' decision as a Trojan horse and angrily told the party leader, Algirdas Brazauskas: 'You have left the CPSU. Others will do the same. Let's think logically – what is left? . . . If everyone leaves the CPSU, that will be the end of the Communist Party.' Brazauskas retorted: 'We are small. We are just one per cent,' as though that solved the problem. But, as he knew, the answer was disingenuous. Like Imre Pozsgay in Hungary a year earlier, the thuggish-looking and popular Brazauskas had conspired to blow up the foundations of the existing one-party state. The Lithuanian Communists were, by now, explicitly committed to a multi-party system, a subject that Gorbachev had refused to even to allow parliamentary discussion of a month earlier.

Yegor Ligachev declared bluntly (and accurately): 'The last obstacle in the way of the separatists has been removed. What kind of *perestroika* is it, Comrade Brazauskas, if you announce that the main aim of your party is to set up an independent state?' Ligachev's attack on Brazauskas was applauded by his party comrades. So was Gorbachev, when he declared, with reference to the pro-independence activists: 'We must get rid of these adventurers – those who ignore reality.'

Even before the Lithuanian Communists had given their compatriots their best Christmas present for fifty years, Gorbachev phoned Brazauskas, demanding that the Lithuanians back down with publicly touted plans. Then, in the Soviet parliament on 23 December, Gorbachev warned, in response to the Lithuanian decision, that supporters of secession sowed 'discord, bloodshed and death'. But the dramatic words were to no avail. Now, after the special central committee session in Moscow, it was agreed that Gorbachev himself should go down to Vilnius to sort the Lithuanians out. At the party plenum, Gorbachev warned that there were clear limits to Moscow's patience and attacked the Communist Party for its 'endless concessions' to Sajudis (given that the Communists would soon be involved in a straight electoral fight with Sajudis, Brazauskas would no doubt have argued that the change of tack was not just morally justified, but electorally prudent, too).

In Vilnius, Gorbachev first went to lay flowers at the foot of a huge Lenin statue, on what had until recently been known as Lenin Avenue (now called Gediminas Avenue, after a medieval Lithuanian ruler). The

Lenin statue was little beloved by Lithuanians, but they let that pass. For the moment, the reception for Gorbachev was almost courteous, if somewhat suspicious. Banners at a huge rally emphasized that Lenin himself had guaranteed Lithuania its independence back in 1920. Quoting Lenin seemed as good a way as any to blunt the force of Gorbachev's attacks. There were parodies, too, of Soviet-speak. Echoing a favourite Soviet slogan – 'Lenin was, is, and will be' – a Lithuanian banner declared: 'Occupation and genocide – was. Mistrust – is. Independence – will be.'

Even here in Vilnius, Gorbachev showed his love of direct contact with the crowds. On Gediminas Avenue, he dived into the throng, ignoring the concerns of his security men, He argued and argued, telling the Lithuanians why they were wrong to want to leave. He appeared to hint at the possibility of compromise, declaring, 'We shall decide everything together.' As he got back into the Zil limousine, there was even scattered applause – unbelievable though that would seem only a year later. One Lithuanian standing nearby said he was glad that Gorbachev had come to Vilnius. 'He should have come a long time ago. It's always better for people to see for themselves.' For the moment he, like some of his compatriots, still believed that Gorbachev's own conversations and meetings would convince him of the justice of the Lithuanians' cause.

Huge crowds gathered on the main square, near the cathedral (which had reopened less than a year earlier; before that it was an art gallery and before that it was used as a garage). First came the speeches, where the Communists, too, made it clear that there was no turning back. Justas Paleckis, head of ideology of the newly independent Lithuanian party, told the meeting: 'Lithuania is on the road to independence – and nobody can stop it.' Then, after the speechifying was over, candles were lit. There were several minutes of almost complete silence; the only sound came from the flags that flapped noisily in the wind and rain. Red, green and yellow gleamed in the light of thousands of candles that were lit, and re-lit. Finally, the silence was broken by bells ringing out from the cathedral – which, in turn, gave the cue for church bells to ring all across Lithuania. Lithuania was consciously removing itself to another country – to Europe. In Prague, six weeks earlier, demonstrators jangled small bells for the end of an era; in Leipzig, they spilled out of packed churches chanting 'We are the people!'; in Bucharest, they ripped the Communist heart out of the Romanian flag. And now, in Vilnius, too, with church bells and silence, they revelled in the theatrical qualities of a European revolution, late twentieth-century style.

Here, as in eastern Europe, the Communist certainties had almost vanished. The published tourist maps were no longer accurate. Lenin Avenue was just one of a series of references to Soviet rule which had disappeared. The KGB headquarters, for example, was still in place. But it no longer stood on 21 July Street — named after the day in 1940 when the Soviet Republic of Lithuania was declared — it was now in 16 February Street, named after the date of Lithuanian independence in 1918. Red Army Street was now Volunteers Street, after the volunteer army which Lithuania had between the wars. And so it went on.

None of this did much to change people's lives. If you were looking at empty shops, the name of the street in which you were standing did not matter. But the name-changes did have a significance, inasmuch as they represented the nation's clear intention to take power back into its own hands. As in eastern Europe, where Gerasimov had proclaimed the Sinatra doctrine two months earlier, so here, too, they were singing their own tunes. Nor were they ready to let things change back. One woman in Vilnius, during Gorbachev's visit, expressed the widely held fear that hardliners could step in to prevent Baltic moves towards independence. But when I asked if it was possible to turn the clock back, she suddenly lost all her doubts. 'It can't be stopped. It would be Romania. I'm a woman — but I, too, would go out.'

Gorbachev still seemed, however, to have little understanding of Lithuanian aspirations. In one encounter, he saw a man with a placard demanding Lithuanian independence and demanded: 'Who told you to write that banner?' 'Nobody,' replied the man. 'I wrote it myself.' The exchange was shown on Lithuanian television that night; Gorbachev's question caused a ripple of laughter and disbelief among a group of Lithuanians who were watching. But Gorbachev was not amused, especially when the man added: 'Lithuania had a hard currency before the war. You took it all away in 1940. And do you know how many Lithuanians were sent to Siberia in the 1940s and how many died?' Gorbachev was not having this. 'I don't want to talk with this man any more. If people in Lithuania have attitudes and slogans like this, they can expect hard times. I don't want to talk to you any more.'

Gorbachev genuinely appeared to believe that the Lithuanian would not care about independence unless some group with evil intentions — fascist émigrés? the CIA? anarchist hooligans? — had put him up to it. It showed a remarkable misunderstanding of what the Baltic republics were all about. It was as if he had asked a Pole in June 1989, 'Who paid you to vote against the Communists and to vote for Solidarity?', or asked a Czech in November 1989: 'Who forced you to come into Wenceslas Square?' The misplaced question reinforced the Lithuanian view that Gorbachev lived not just in another country, but in another world.

When Gorbachev left Vilnius after his three-day visit, he was impatient, but not yet hated. Meanwhile, though, the independence train was gathering speed. In the parliamentary election on 24 February – just six weeks after Gorbachev's visit – Sajudis, with its pro-independence platform, swept the board. The Balts had always made it clear that it was these republican elections which would hold the key to the future. Elections to the Supreme Soviet in Moscow allowed their voices to be heard by Russians, and nationwide, because of the televised coverage of the parliament. But only the republican parliaments in the Baltic republics could make decisions about their own future. And so it proved.

When the new parliament was formed, it moved faster even than the Lithuanians had expected. As was to be the pattern again and again, the heavy threats from Moscow served only to speed up the process that was already under way. In Moscow, Gorbachev talked of increased presidential powers. In response, the Lithuanians brought forward the second round of their elections, in order to pip Gorbachev to the post. They were keen, too, to take the opportunity of breaking away while Article 72 of the constitution was still valid, which (in theory) allowed them 'freely to secede'. They were convinced that a proposed new secession law, announced during Gorbachev's trip to Vilnius – and which purported to be liberal – was only intended to keep them behind.

Drama followed drama, with bluff and counter-bluff. Then, only a fortnight after the Sajudis victory in the elections and two months after Gorbachev's 'Who-told-you-to-write-that?' visit, Lithuania made the final break. On 11 March 1990, by 124 votes to 0, with 6 abstentions, the Lithuanian parliament passed the Act of the Supreme Council on the Restoration of the Independent Lithuanian State. 'The Supreme Council solemnly declares the existence of the sovereign power of the Lithuanian state, annulled by an alien state in 1940. From this moment, Lithuania becomes, once again, an independent state.' A huge Lithuanian flag was unfurled and raised behind the dais. The deputies began cheering and sang the Lithuanian national anthem. Outside the parliament building, a crowd surged forward and tore down the hammer and sickle shield above the main doors. It was replaced by a cloth with an old Lithuanian symbol of a knight on horseback. Soviet Lithuania was no more.

This spring day marked Mikhail Gorbachev's fifth anniversary in power. He could hardly have imagined a less welcome anniversary present. For this was also the moment when the Soviet Union could be seen to have ended. Everything that came later was merely an attempt to deny the *fait accompli*, or a natural consequence and recognition of what had already happened. As one observer in Vilnius noted that day, the parliamentary vote in tiny Lithuania (population: 3.7 million) marked 'the beginning of the greatest transformation of the world map since the end of the British empire'.

Gorbachev condemned the move and gave Lithuania a three-day ultimatum to return to the Soviet fold. But the bluster could get nowhere. After a series of threats, and an order from Gorbachev that Lithuanians should surrender all weapons (it was an odd command, since the Lithuanians had not used any weapons in their battle for independence), came the first serious show of force, when a convoy of tanks rolled through Vilnius on 22 March. Then five days later, Soviet troops occupied a number of buildings, including the headquarters of the rebel Communist Party. They seized and beat up young Lithuanians who – with the encouragement of their government, which provided alternative service – had evaded the Soviet draft. Gorbachev had earlier said that force would not be used, but then authorized the military occupation of the buildings. Now, he said that force would not be used 'unless lives were threatened'. The Lithuanians were not impressed.

The West was unenthusiastic about the Lithuanians' attempt to make a run for it. They had put Gorbachev on the spot, which was unwelcome. The response of Margaret Thatcher was not untypical. She praised Gorbachev's foresight, skill and dominance, and, in effect, told the Lithuanians that they should pipe down, saying that people should not be provocative 'on either side'. She stated: 'This is a very difficult position for both President Gorbachev and for the people of Lithuania.' She did not comment on the kidnapping of young Lithuanians, nor on the seizure by troops of public buildings, and even claimed that the 1975 Helsinki accords legitimized the existing Soviet borders (in reality, the Helsinki accords said only that borders should not be changed by force; theoretically, Britain had never accepted the annexation of the Baltic states in 1940). Smaller countries, which were closer to the scene of the action and felt that the needs of small countries counted for as much as those of the Great Powers, gave a tougher response. Norway accused Moscow of brutal actions and of embarking on a destructive course. In Poland, Lech Walesa warned against violating the sovereignty of Lithuania.

When the Lithuanians declared their independence, even they did not really believe their own rhetoric. Vytautas Landsbergis, Lithuania's new president, was – though he might not have wished to admit it – making a declaration of intent, not a statement of new realities. Still, even the declaration of intent was enough to wrongfoot the Soviet authorities, as one small incident showed. Moscow forbade foreign correspondents to travel to Vilnius, on pain of expulsion. Nor were visas for Vilnius issued at Soviet embassies abroad. Gorbachev insisted that the declaration of independence was invalid and illegal. But, if the Lithuanians said they were independent, why not take them at their word and ask them for entry to non-Soviet Lithuania? It seemed that there was nothing to lose by calling the bluff of both sides: on the one hand the Lithuanians, who said they were 'independent'; and, on the other hand, the Soviet KGB border guards, who until now had always had unchallenged control.

From London, I telephoned the Lithuanian foreign ministry in Vilnius (each Soviet republic had always had its own foreign ministry – tame, meaningless institutions, created as a Stalinist fiction; only now did they take on much greater meaning than Moscow had ever intended). Initially, the Lithuanians said they were unable to admit anybody into their republic – despite the declaration of independence a fortnight earlier. Finally, though, they decided that they could not miss this opportunity to cock a snook at the still all-powerful Moscow. There was thus a remarkable scene at Vilnius airport that afternoon, when Edward Lucas – the *Independent*'s correspondent in Prague, who had just arrived on a flight from East Berlin, without a Soviet visa – was grilled by the KGB guard, who, in accordance with Soviet law, wanted to expel him instantly.

At that point, a group of Lithuanians turned up. 'Who are you, then?' asked the indignant Soviet border guard. 'The foreign minister of Lithuania,' came the reply from Algirdas Saudargas, former research biophysicist. The KGB officer declared: 'This man hasn't got a visa.' 'I know. We're going to give him one.' 'How?' 'Now.' Whereupon a newly minted rubber stamp and ink pad were produced from a manila envelope. 'Congratulations on the first Lithuanian visa,' said the foreign minister, as the KGB officer glowered down at the purple stamp – valid for entry to the Republic of Lithuania – with no mention of either Soviet or Socialist.

All of this was sheer bluff on the Lithuanians' part. The visa had no reality, beyond that of willpower. None the less, after a number of phone calls, referring upwards to the KGB in Vilnius and Moscow, the Soviet authorities allowed their bluff to be called. A year earlier, Moscow could not possibly have backed down on such a clearcut issue. No Soviet visa would have meant: next plane home. Now, after an hour's delay, the unexpected visitor was admitted to the newly 'independent' Baltic state, with no other document except Lithuanian visa number 0001 (the pre-war ministry files had been destroyed, so the numbering had to start again from scratch), dated 28 March 1990.

In a sense, this was a readjustment for both sides. Despite all their brave talk, the Lithuanians had not really believed that they controlled their own border-points (nor would they fully control them for another eighteen months). Equally, however, the confidence of Moscow that its orders would always be obeyed was wavering for the first time. It was an important change. The Soviet foreign ministry subsequently expressed its indignation that Moscow had, by its public acceptance of the Lithuanian purple visa-stamp, lost face so badly. It ensured that there was no repetition. But the tiny surrender had already taken place and could not be entirely erased. Dozens of more serious diplomatic minuets between Moscow and Vilnius – a surrender, followed by a reassertion of will, followed by another surrender – would take place in the months to come.

A game of bluff and counter-bluff was now being played. Moscow imposed an economic blockade of the republic and on 18 April announced a cut-off of oil and gas supplies to the republic, including the oil for a large refinery in the north of the republic. To some extent, this was liable to backfire on Moscow: the oil refinery at Mazeikiai supplied much of its refined oil to the rest of the Soviet Union; and, if Lithuania's gas supplies were cut off, then so would the supplies be to the Kaliningrad region, an enclave of territory on the Baltic Sea which formed part of the Russian republic, but which was surrounded on all sides by Lithuania. Moscow was in danger of cutting off its nose to spite its face. None the less, the intention was clear enough. Then, two days later, there was a renewed show of Soviet force, when paratroopers forced their way into a Lithuanian printing plant. They beat up some of the civilians who had been on guard there for weeks.

Even now, the West was loath to speak out. Speaking of Lithuania a few days after the beatings up and the imposition of the blockade, George Bush said, 'Let's have it done in a way that is not egregious to the Soviet Union.' The choice of words was confusing. But the general idea was as clear as ever: Gorbachev comes first. In Moscow, there was greater scepticism. One portrait of the Soviet leader on sale on the Arbat had as its caption: 'No gas, no oil for Lithuania,' and asked 'Have *you* restructured youself?'

By now Vilnius was not alone in its acts of defiance. Once Lithuania had forced the pace, the two other Baltic republics – where the Popular Fronts had also gained clear majorities in republican elections in March – made it a point of honour to join in. The harsher the threats against Lithuania, the more Latvia and Estonia felt obliged to show solidarity. One Estonian leader described the Baltic moves towards independence as a kind of bicycle race, where teams change leaders to keep up the pace. To start with, Estonia was in front. Now, Lithuania raced ahead, while Latvia and Estonia came gasping up behind. On 30 March, Estonia, too, declared: 'The occupation of the Republic of Estonia by the Soviet Union on 17 June 1940 has not disrupted the continuity of the republic of Estonia *de jure*.' The parliamentary resolution declared 'the state supremacy of the Soviet Union in Estonia to be illegal from the moment of its enforcement, and proclaims restoration of the Republic of Estonia'. It allowed for a period of transition, but even that was of little comfort to Moscow. Gorbachev telephoned the Estonian president, Arnold Ruutel, and threatened Estonia with Lithuania-style punishment. Ruutel was unmoved and replied simply: 'Estonia understands the consequences of its actions.'

Finally, on 4 May, Latvia became the last of the three to make the break. And, like the other two Baltic republics, Latvia was duly condemned by Gorbachev. He telephoned Alfred Rubiks, the hardline local party leader, and instructed him to make it plain that Moscow was prepared to take 'political, economic and administrative measures' against the republic.

Many in the West urged caution upon the Balts at this time, suggesting that they should closely examine the new secession law, which theoretically provided the possibility of being able to leave after five years, if a host of complicated conditions were met. But the Balts were convinced that the secession law – the 'divorce law', as Gerasimov dubbed it – was only intended to prevent them from seceding. In any case, they said, they had never asked to be part of the Soviet Union, so needed nobody's permission to leave. The Balts argued by use of a harsh analogy: 'Divorce is only possible between married partners. But we weren't married – we were raped.'

As one East European country after another voted the Communists into oblivion, and said goodbye to the Soviet bloc for ever, the Balts began what were described as 'negotiations' with Moscow on their future. The Lithuanian parliament even declared, on 29 June 1990, that it was prepared to freeze its declaration of independence for 100 days, from the beginning of official talks. But the compromise was more apparent than real. Moscow was not interested in concessions and Lithuania – though it did not say so openly – was not very interested either. It soon started talking about setting up its own army units.

In truth, there was no compromise that could still be made. With their dramatic declaration on 11 March, the Lithuanians blew a hole in the walls of the Soviet state – a country that had been brought together by force and was held together by one-party rule. There was no way back. Instead, many other republics were beginning to follow the Lithuanian lead. At the same time, extraordinary changes began to take place in Russia itself. That was the most important change of all, for, once Russia began to be transformed, Soviet power would cease to have any meaning at all.

10 Russia Rises

'Mikhail Sergeyevich, no right turn!' warned one placard, with the appropriate traffic sign painted on it, as the crowds poured into Manege Square in the centre of Moscow. There were more protesters on that day, 4 February 1990, than Soviet Russia had ever seen. One of the main demands was the abolition of Article 6, which guaranteed the Communist Party's leading role – a demand which Gorbachev had, until now, consistently rejected. Many placards simply had a figure 6 crossed out. In Lithuania and the other Baltic republics, Soviet-style Communism had been completely abandoned. Here in Russia, though, things were not yet so clearcut. The crowds still needed to press for change. The police in Moscow no longer beat up demonstrators as they had done a year earlier. But thousands of police and interior ministry troops lined up – first in Gorky Street and then at the entrance to Red Square – in order to stop the crowds, with their heretical demands, getting too close to the nation's rulers.

The rebellious mood marked a dramatic change. Already, the effect of the East European revolutions in previous months had begun to seep through to the heart of the empire. Many in Manege Square – officially, the Square of 50 Years of the October Revolution, but few bothered to call it that – believed that the changes in eastern Europe were a clear example to follow. One speaker said: 'We know of other meetings that there have been in Bucharest, in Warsaw. Our meeting stands alongside those.' A poster mimicked Soviet small ads, with the declaration: 'I will swap an old-style Bureau for a Czech-model round table.' Certainly, for many Russians, the comparison – between the still powerful Soviet Politburo and the round-table talks that helped to dismantle the old regimes in eastern Europe – was not to the Politburo's advantage.

On Manege Square that day, there were no more taboos. Calls were made for the resignation of the Communist Party central committee and the Politburo. 'V ot-stav-ku! V ot-stav-ku!' – 'Resign! Resign!' – chanted the crowds, loud enough to be heard inside the Kremlin walls. For many, the disillusion was now total. After seeing what had happened in eastern Europe, the early Russian fear had almost vanished. 'Down with the KGB!' said one slogan. Another declared: 'The time has come for the political repentance of the party, before the people.' There was a growing mood of confidence. One man on the square declared: 'Today it's clear to all that the moment of power of the Communist Party is coming to an end.' Another man nearby added that it was obvious that Article 6 must be abolished: 'Of course I'm in favour. To have only one party is unnatural.'

It was not only in the capital that the Russian mood was becoming more radical. A few days before the huge demonstration on Manege Square, I visited the city of Novokuznetsk in western Siberia, at the heart of the Kuzbass region where the 'economic' strikes had begun in 1989. It was unseasonably mild. Instead of the crisp cold of the Russian winter, there was a grey dampness on the streets, matching the greyness of the ever-emptier shops. The mood of the miners was simultaneously depressed and angry. After the return to work following the strikes the previous summer, it soon became clear that the official promises they had received bore about as much relation to reality as a Brezhnev speech. One miners' leader remarked: 'Last year we rejected all political points. But then we understood: the economy does not exist without politics.' Now, the demand for the removal of Article 6 topped the agenda — and there were threats of further strikes if the article was not abandoned.

Nor was it only at the grassroots that the unhappiness about the continued strength of the Communist Party could be heard. Ivan Khamin, an ex-miner who was now a mine director, complained of the baleful influence of the Communist Party on his work — even as he sat in his office, in front of bookshelves weighed down by dozens of compulsory Lenin tomes. Like almost everywhere else in Siberia, Novokuznetsk had played its part in the nationwide network, the 'archipelago', of the Gulag (whose name is an acronym for 'state camp administration'). The camps were now empty of political prisoners, but the inheritors of the Gulag mentality — mindless representatives of a mindless regime — remained in place. Khamin complained of the useless party meetings that he was constantly summoned to, instead of doing his work. Khamin's sidekick was visibly disconcerted by his boss's disrespect, especially in front of a foreigner, and tried to speak up on the party's behalf. But Khamin was unabashed. If anybody wanted to sack him, he said, then that was fine by him. He would return to being an ordinary miner. The party's authority, he continued without a pause, was falling apart. East European Communism a few months earlier had happened on a distant stage. None the less, Khamin argued proudly, events there were seen by many of his workers as a call to arms.

Khamin's complaints about the party meetings were a reminder of how the party was still seeking to cling to its old powers. At the same time, though, the fact that he was able to make such abusive remarks emphasized how far changes had already gone. A year earlier, it would have been unthinkable for a Soviet manager to be so unashamedly rude about the organization that was supposed to be the brains, honour and conscience of the motherland. Now, anything went.

There were other hints in Novokuznetsk, too, of the curious way in which the new openness and the old habits were out of joint. In my hotel, I chatted to the *dezhurnaya* – the floor-lady, one of the famously formidable breed who always played such an important role in the Soviet hotel regime. The *dezhurnaya*, literally 'the duty woman', was the keeper of your room key; she sold tea, biscuits and mineral water for a few kopecks at any time of the day or night; and, most importantly in the traditional scheme of things, she kept an eagle eye on guests' movements. No foreigner could leave his hotel room without being spotted; it was one of the *dezhurnaya*'s duties to keep the *vlasti*, the powers that be, informed.

From the *dezhurnaya*, I ordered a taxi for early the next morning. She took the order. Then, a few minutes later, she rang through to my room, apologetic. Could she check which country I was from and where would my taxi be taking me? I told her, and she apologized again for disturbing me. She explained: 'We need the information for the *gosbezopasnost*, you know.' (*Gozbezopasnost* was an abbreviation for the State Security Committee – in other words, the KGB.) Giving the information to *gosbezopasnost* was, her tone implied, one of those tedious chores that hotel staff the world over need to carry out. Almost five years into *perestroika*, the floor-lady was still required to let the KGB know of the planned movements of the foreign guest staying on her floor, and thought it perfectly natural that she should do so.

But, despite the still obligatory calls to the secret police, an era was already drawing to a close. Now that the powerful weapon of fear was destroyed, the party itself was doomed. There were still many who were reluctant to accept that fact – and who would try desperately to prevent the changes from taking place. But time had moved on. At an election meeting in Novokuznetsk for forthcoming republican elections to the

Russian parliament, the loudest applause was for those who spoke out on two subjects. On the one hand, there was the environment, a subject that aroused passion among the hundreds of thousands of people who were daily poisoned by the clouds that billowed from the chimneys of the huge Stalin-era factories in Novokuznetsk. *Glasnost* had taught people the horrifying statistics of the disease and death that was caused by those rainbow-coloured clouds, and anger was running high. But a close-run second to the environment – and closely linked in some people's minds – was, as with the miners, the demand for the abolition of Article 6. Speaker after speaker demanded it, to loud cheers.

This was a people which had lost its patience. There was anger over the state of the economy, and anger over living conditions. Many of the small one-storey houses in Novokuznetsk had no hot water; some had no running water at all. On one house, a slogan declared bitterly: 'Welcome to the Stone Age.' The slogan on another house proclaimed that these were the 'slums of socialism'. I was with a group of miners when we passed one of the propaganda posters that had long been a familiar feature of every Soviet town, large and small. 'The good of the people – that is the supreme goal of the CPSU,' it said. The miners – traditional heroes of countless posters and slogans about the building of Communism – pointed to the uplifting slogan and laughed. For them, the Communist Party's concern for the good of the people was no more than a sick joke. Nor was there much respect for the man who led that party. Much less, certainly, than only a year earlier. Gennady Grabko, a former miner and an opposition journalist, spoke for many of his comrades when he insisted: 'Gorbachev is the last authoritarian figure. Society grows, like a human body. We need more freedom – a bigger shirt.'

Yet again, Gorbachev showed that he was not oblivious to the growing pressures from below. He resisted the pressures. But he did not want the shirt to rip apart. Gorbachev met miners' leaders in Moscow and heard them demand the abolition of Article 6 and threaten a renewal of strikes. Then, that weekend, came the huge radical demonstration in Moscow, with the same demand. Finally, the following Monday, Gorbachev proposed the most dramatic retreat that there had yet been: Article 6, he suggested to the Communist Party central committee, should indeed be abandoned. Forget everything that he had previously said on the subject. Where he had said 'no', read 'yes'. And where he had said 'yes', read 'no'. The central committee obediently accepted the proposed change, with a 99 per cent vote in favour. Less

The newly appointed Mikhail Gorbachev, visiting the Zil car factory in Moscow in 1985. There was considerable enthusiasm for a leader who, for the first time, was interested in talking to people.

A funeral in the Armenian-majority region of Nagorny Karabakh, disputed between Armenia and Azerbaijan. Ethnic clashes began in early 1988. Four years later, more than 1,000 people had died in what had become a continuous, low-level war.

Popular resistance, combined with the incompetence of the plotters, led to the speedy collapse of the coup in August 1991. The crowds chanted Yeltsin's name as he acknowledged their cheers.

Gorbachev, on being rescued from the Crimea, initially proclaimed his loyalty to the Communist Party. But he later acknowledged that he had 'returned to a different country'.

Outside the KGB headquarters, only three days after the coup had been declared, crowds gathered to pull down the huge statue of Felix Dzerzhinsky, founder of the Soviet secret police, which dominated the centre of Lubyanka Square.

The collapse of Communism did not mean easy pickings. Widespread poverty was real, and there were bread riots in some cities. This woman said she was lucky to have found discarded loaves of bread on a rubbish tip.

By the end of the year the Union was dead. On 25 December 1991, Gorbachev appeared on television to resign. Minutes later, the red hammer and sickle flag that had flown over the Kremlin for seven decades was down, to be replaced by the Russian tricolour.

than two months after Sakharov's death, the concession that Sakharov had fought so hard for had at last become real. The lynchpin of the system had been removed — and the system itself was now ready for collapse.

Theoretically, Article 6 was not crucial to the Communists' hold on power. The party's guaranteed leading role had only been introduced into the constitution by Brezhnev in 1977, and the party had done very nicely before that. But the fact that the rulers of the Soviet Union now felt forced to jettison Article 6 was a move whose importance it was impossible to overstate. Internationally, the action was hailed as an extraordinarily courageous act — which, in a sense, it was. Certainly, it was a milestone in the collapse of Communist power. But Gorbachev was not politically deaf. As the visit to Novokuznetsk made so clear, he would have faced an explosion of discontent if he had failed to move. This dramatic moment was yet another of Gorbachev's bold retreats.

Gorbachev was not alone among international leaders in announcing a stunning retreat from power at this time. In one of the neat symmetries with which history now seemed replete, his abandonment of Article 6 came during the same days that President F. W. de Klerk of South Africa announced the unbanning of the African National Congress and allowed Nelson Mandela to walk free. Like Gorbachev, de Klerk was internationally praised. But it was also widely agreed that the first prize for courage and vision did not go to de Klerk. Rather, the victory was perceived as belonging to Mandela himself — and, by extension, to South Africa's disenfranchised majority. Most observers believed that de Klerk's great virtue was in recognizing and accepting the inevitable.

Mandela subsequently struck up a good working relationship with de Klerk — just as Andrei Sakharov achieved a good relationship with Gorbachev. Both men gave credit to their respective liberators for unlocking the door. Both acknowledged, too, that the pressures from the hardliners were very real. De Klerk, like Gorbachev, clearly deserved admiration for the radical change which he introduced. And yet both Sakharov and Mandela were wary of attempts by the undemocratically appointed presidents of their respective countries to dodge half-commitments to democracy. Of politicians it could be said that some are born democrats, some achieve democracy and some have democracy thrust upon them. Presidents de Klerk and Gorbachev hovered in limbo between the second and third categories. Their track records meant that neither leader even made it on to the shortlist for category one. The pressures from below on de Klerk were obvious, and widely acknowledged. The pressures from below on Gorbachev were equally clear – but often ignored.

Meanwhile, if South Africa's hardliners felt betrayed by de Klerk and felt sure that there must be a way of preventing the minority from losing its God-given right to rule, so, too, hardliners in Moscow could not quite believe what was happening and attempted to blame it all on Gorbachev. Vladimir Brovikov, Soviet ambassador to Poland, complained: 'Reactionaries of every hue are slandering Communists and singing a requiem for the CPSU, for Leninism and socialism.' He added: 'It is said that the people back *perestroika*. But what *perestroika*? The one that for the past five years has brought us into crisis, anarchy and economic decay?' Ligachev complained that nobody should take too much notice of the anti-Communist demonstrations in Moscow. 'A mob is not the entire people. And a rally in Moscow is not the whole of Moscow – far less the entire country.'

There was some truth in Ligachev's words, though less than he might have wished. Certainly, apathy was widespread. It was also true that many Russians felt nostalgia for the Brezhnevite past – when everything seemed stable, the shops were less empty and the future held no surprises. But Ligachev ignored the upward curve of rebellion, which eastern Europe had seen in 1988 and 1989, and which the Soviet Union was beginning to experience now. Not everybody was rebelling against the system, by any means. Probably, the rebels were not even the majority. But the number of those who rejected the system continued to increase, month by month, and even week by week. The implications of that, for the hardliners, were more worrying than anything else could be.

Nor was it just in Moscow, or among the miners, that rebelliousness was growing. At the beginning of 1990, there were rebellions throughout the immense Russian republic – all of which made it clear that Russians were losing their fear, as never before. The coverage of the East European revolutions in the Soviet media had been eccentric or downright misleading, but the basic facts were inescapable. Russians knew, in short, that people power was real. Now, they wanted to try it for themselves.

A whole string of rebellions took place in the early months of 1990, which had in common only a belief that ordinary people should now be allowed their say, for the first time. One typical mini-revolution was in the *oblast*, or administrative region, of Volgograd (formerly Stalingrad), an area almost the size of England. First, there was a grassroots rebellion within the Communist Party at corruption among the local party leadership and at nepotism in the allocation of housing. Vladimir Kalashnikov, the local party leader, was unrepentant. But the protests grew: tens of thousands gathered along the banks of the river Volga in order to demand the resignation of the entire local party leadership – which they quickly achieved. Kalashnikov talked of dark forces, causing the leadership's unpopularity. But these rebellions were a crucial turning-point in terms of the Russians' ability to force the leadership to back down.

There were similar resignations in a dozen other cities. Sometimes, small incidents caused the flare-up. In Chernigov, the rebellion was triggered by a car crash. One of the cars belonged to the *oblast* Communist Party committee; both driver and passenger were drunk. The boot of the car was found to contain a hoard of luxury foods such as ordinary citizens were unlikely to see from one end of the year to the next. That, for many in Chernigov, proved to be the last straw. Huge demonstrations followed at which people demanded the abolition of party privileges, the resignation of the *oblast* party leadership and the conversion of Communist Party buildings into hospitals and schools. All in all, a politically expensive car crash. The *oblast* revolutions, as they soon became known, were yet more proof that it was no longer a handful of men – let alone one man – in the Kremlin who controlled the pace of change. Soviet society itself had begun to stir.

If the *oblast* revolutions and the protests in Manege Square seemed to provide encouraging indications of a society on the move, other changes were less heartening. One of the main reasons for calling the demonstration on 4 February had been to protest against the anti-Semitic threats and violence, which were encouraged or sponsored by the neo-fascist fringe group known as Pamyat, or Memory. Anti-Semitism, traditionally strong in Russia, grew, even as the economy got worse. A Jewish restaurant was daubed with swastikas, its staff (both Jewish and non-Jewish) were threatened and windows smashed. On Pushkin Square, where a hundred leaflets now bloomed, you could buy not just the unofficial liberal press, but also, for a few roubles, *The Protocols of the Elders of Zion*, an anti-Jewish forgery which was concocted by the tsarist secret police at the beginning of the century and gained popularity in Nazi Germany. In Leningrad especially, there were many attacks and several apparently racially motivated murders. In Moscow, a writers' meeting in January 1990 was interrupted by a group shouting slogans like 'Kill the Yids' and demanding that 'Comrade Jews' should leave the hall.

The fact that many Soviet Jews were now at last able to leave for Israel — which, with its well-stocked shops, abundant food and decent clothes, seemed a Promised Land for Jews and non-Jews alike — only worsened the already existing resentments. If large numbers of Jews were able to leave, that was simultaneously a reason for envy and blame. Jews and non-Jews who spoke out against the anti-Semitism received abuse in almost equal measure. *Sovietskaya Rossiya* blamed blatant Zionists for the talk of anti-Semitic violence and asked: 'Who benefits from these baseless rumours? Is it not clear?' Even Yuli Vorontsov, the deputy foreign minister, said it was all the fault of sources close to Israel. The authorities seemed determined to do nothing. *Ogonyok* pointed out that police at the meeting in the Writers' Union building were keener to arrest those who were being attacked than to arrest what one officer described as the 'comrades from Pamyat'. *Ogonyok* asked bitterly, in connection with the anti-Semitic abuse: 'What slogans did they need to shout in order to be considered guilty of a criminal action?'

Pamyat itself, which was theoretically concerned with the preservation of Russia's heritage, was not necessarily as powerful as it wished or believed. But popular intolerance was real, as was the need to find a scapegoat for the fact that everything had gone so badly wrong. Sometimes, it was clear that the authorities worked closely with the anti-Semitic groups, even though the latter usually claimed to be 'anti-Bolshevik', and there were clear links between Pamyat and the KGB.

There were, though, some reasons for optimism. Pamyat did not become a mass movement and many Russians turned out for a demonstration *against* the violence, with slogans like 'No to pogroms!' But, despite the voices pleading for reason, the resentment and hatred continued to grow. Always, somebody else had to be to blame. That was a worrying element, for the future, once the system came to break down entirely.

In the Caucasus and Central Asia, meanwhile, the mournful list of ethnic flashpoints grew. In February 1990, violence broke out in the Central Asian republic of Tajikistan. It was triggered by resentments over the allegedly favourable treatment for Armenian refugees who had arrived in the Tajik capital, Dushanbe, but it quickly became more generalized. Non-Tajiks — including many Russians — were the main target of the attacks. They held important government posts and the resentment of Tajiks at being second-class citizens in their own country was, as in Kazakhstan, an important contributing factor to the explosions that took place. There were reports that women whose hair was not covered, or who were wearing Western clothes, were attacked by groups of Tajiks who went on the rampage through the streets of Dushanbe. Radio Moscow described the clashes as round-the-clock riots. Tanks were brought into the city and in confrontations between the rioters and security forces, several dozen died.

At the same time, ethnic clashes in Samarkand, in the republic of Uzbekistan, led to a curfew being imposed. There were violent demonstrations in Frunze, the capital of the small Central Asian republic of Kirghizia, on the border with China. The clashes between Armenia and Azerbaijan continued, too. Within the next few months, the violence became worse. In June, there were renewed clashes in Kirghizia. More than 300 people died in fighting between Uzbeks and Kirghiz in the region of Osh, near the border with Uzbekistan, in the worst violence that had yet been seen. The fighting flared after a dispute over the allocation of land, in an area where homelessness and unemployment were high. In Moldavia, too, there were fierce clashes between the Romanian-Moldavians (who wanted to break away from Moscow) and the Gagauz (who declared that they were setting up their own republic: they wanted to break away from Moldavia and to stay loyal to Moscow).

Those outbreaks of violence did not take place till June but by spring 1990, it was clear that almost every corner of the Union was on the edge of political, economic or ethnic chaos. The violence in February gave Gorbachev a powerful argument for giving himself increased powers. He argued in favour of a new presidential system (until now his official title had been 'Chairman of the Supreme Soviet', an unofficial equivalent of president), in which the new president would be able to mobilize the army, declare a state of emergency and control the country's constitution. He said that the powers were necessary in order to prevent the initiative being seized by those who had nothing in common with 'the requirements of socialist society's revolutionary reform'.

The radicals were sceptical that the new powers would help to curb the spiralling ethnic violence and forced a delay in the vote. On 25 February, there was another huge radical demonstration – held partly in connection with the proposed presidential powers. Only three weeks after the almost gentle 'no-right-turn' slogans, the attitudes to Gorbachev were sharply critical. But perhaps even more important than the tone of the slogans was the note of defiance sounded by the demonstration against the powers that be. *Vremya*, the television news, created an extraordinary climate of fear in the days leading up to the 25 February demonstration. There were repeated warnings of unspecified dangers – alarmingly reminiscent of the threats that had been heard in eastern Europe as the Communists fought off defeat. So severe were the warnings that a demonstration in Leningrad, planned on the same day, was cancelled for fear of bloodshed. In Moscow, many who attended the demonstration believed that the chances of official violence – beatings-up, arrests and perhaps even shooting – were high. Some stayed at home because of the fear. But many others went out despite everything.

The authorities did not, in the end, use violence. The sidestreets were full of troops – but they stayed, stony-faced, in their trucks. That, too, was a kind of victory for the protesters. Crucially, as in Leipzig in October 1989, the demonstrators consciously defied the threat of violence in order to make their voices heard. For the first time, the Soviet capital was beginning to get a taste of what people power – defy the authorities and never mind the consequences – might one day be like.

Meanwhile, central Communist power continued to collapse. The party leadership attempted to stave off defeat. Eager to please an increasingly sceptical population, it offered 'humane, democratic socialism' in its new draft platform. But the party's promises of a new approach – reminiscent of the insistent claims by East European Communist Parties that they were now reborn social democrats – were increasingly irrelevant. That was not just because of the pressure from the crowds. The party leadership was also outflanked by the pressure for genuinely democratic reform that was growing within the party itself. In January 1990, radical Communists banded together to form the Democratic Platform, spiritually closer to the non-Communist opposition than to the hardliners with whom the Democratic Platform shared a party leader. Gorbachev himself expressed his unhappiness with the Democratic Platform's moves and announced that the party had no time to obey the call of the Democratic Platform to turn itself into a 'run-of-the-mill parliamentary party'. Communists, he said, would be too busy solving the country's problems to have time for 'trivial parliamentary games'. None the less, despite this stern rebuff from the boss, the Democratic Platform attracted more and more of the best and brightest who had not yet given in the little red membership card.

The local elections in spring 1990 proved another unhappy watershed for Communist power. In the old days, it never really made any difference which local body took what decision. All the endless different committees and soviets (i.e. councils – the 'Soviet' Union was officially a union of workers' and peasants' councils) were, in effect, the same. *Obkom, raikom, profkom, Mossoviet, Lensoviet, gorsoviet.* Each ugly acronym stood for a single thing: one-party rule. The important decisions were in any case handed down, by telephone, in what was widely known as telephone law.

Now, all that suddenly changed. In the elections on 4 March, the powerful city councils in Moscow and Leningrad gained majorities from the Democratic Russia movement – broadly, the non-Communist opposition – which soon took delight in challenging the Communist Party on its own ground. The Russian federation's new parliament also gained many radical voices, including Boris Yeltsin, who – to nobody's surprise, but to the hardliners' dismay – gained a landslide victory in his home city, Sverdlovsk. Other embarrassments for the Kremlin included the defeat of the Soviet coal minister by a leader of the miners' strike committee in the Siberian city of Vorkuta.

Real battles began to take place, not just between Moscow ('the Centre') and the rebellious republics, but also between the Communist Party leadership, on the one hand, and Russia's elected political bodies, on the other. Such battles were a startling novelty. In the months to come, Gorbachev – who eventually succeeded in persuading parliament to elect him president, with somewhat smaller powers than he had first demanded – attempted to remove powers from the elected councils, including the right to authorize street demonstrations. But Gorbachev's moves against the councils only reinforced the popularity of the city councils in Leningrad and Moscow, and of their radical leaders, Anatoly Sobchak and Gavriil Popov. Both men floated in and out of tactical alliances with Gorbachev. But the councils' clear electoral legitimacy meant that it was difficult to emasculate them entirely – without a complete mockery of the *perestroika* and reform to which the Communist Party claimed it was now dedicated.

The heresies flowed thick and fast. Moscow city council decided to remove the statue of Lenin – compulsory in every public place – from the council chamber. It was a small indication of how they saw the founder of the Soviet state. Some, however, clung to the old certainties. In a speech on the occasion of Lenin's 120th birthday, Gorbachev attacked the hardliners, but turned angrily on those who were sceptical of Lenin himself. He told his audience that Lenin was the greatest thinker of the twentieth century and added:

As the historical impact and social essence of *perestroika* are being evaluated, destructive approaches to Lenin have come into the foreground. These trends are dangerous . . . They are aimed at identifying Lenin with Stalin, and can paint all Soviet history black, to portray the October Revolution and the ensuing events as errors and even worse, as crimes against the nation and humanity . . . But disrespect is out of place here. Philistine slander of Lenin as a man is immoral, and attempts to cast aspersions on his noble goals and aspirations are absurd.

In the speech, Gorbachev clearly identified himself strongly with Lenin. He embarked on a long description of Lenin's battles to force through the New Economic Policy, which had allowed a slight relaxation of the Communist economic rules – and which Gorbachev appeared to identify with the economic liberalization that he, too, had allowed. The Gorbachev philosophy was, on the one hand, anger with the hardliners for their obstinacy (and a barely coded attack on Andreyeva, Ligachev and their comrades):

Lenin not only had to struggle with himself and his political opponents but had to withstand strong pressure from his comrades in the party who reproached him for 'giving up the principles' of Marxism and even 'deviating' from it . . . For all his love for theory, Lenin changed his mind when life demanded, disregarded any postulates or dogmas which had seemed sacred, and relied on a specific analysis of a concrete situation, which he considered to be the living soul of Marxism . . .

On the other hand, he showed an apparently undiminished commitment to introduce a Leninist brave new world:

From time to time nowadays, we are asked whether the October Revolution was necessary at all, and whether it wouldn't have been better for Russia to stop after the February Revolution. In the political struggle of ideas, such deliberations, which are absurd with respect to the past, pursue demagogic goals . . .

Our society has no reasonable alternative to socialist *perestroika*, for it is a complicated, but inevitable way of tackling difficulties which will lead us to a real progress. Advancing along this way, we cannot do without Lenin's heritage, enriched with the experience and lessons of our own and world history.

There was no reason to disbelieve the sincerity of Gorbachev's proclaimed commitment to Leninism. The paeons of praise were passionately expressed – even while he delivered attacks on his hardline comrades. Nor could there be any doubt that Gorbachev was thinking of himself when he talked approvingly of Lenin changing his mind, 'when life demanded'. For here was the crux of the matter. Gorbachev, too, changed his mind when life demanded – and would do so again and again, in the months to come. His ability to do so was a strength, not a weakness; those who failed to adapt were much more dangerous. But that phrase from Lenin emphasized the reality that Gorbachev moved away from the Communist status quo only when he was forced to. Gorbachev wanted to avoid the fate of the intransigent Honecker, the East German leader whom he had warned, in October 1989, might soon be punished by life itself.

In many respects, it was no bad thing that so many of Gorbachev's retreats were so reluctant. It meant that each retreat, when it did come, was clearly irreversible. Hardliners might still dream of a what-if option, with fantasies of how they could have prevented Communism from collapsing, if they were in power. But there were no other options – Gorbachev, the self-proclaimed Lenin devotee, had tried them all.

On the streets, the pressures continued to grow. Ten days after Lenin's anniversary (traditionally, Russians had to perform a *subbotnik*, an extra day's 'voluntary' work, to mark the occasion of his birthday) came May Day, one of the most sacred events in the Communist calendar. Yet 1 May 1990 was, for Gorbachev, a humiliation. As the Soviet Communist Party leader stood on the Lenin mausoleum to watch the traditional May Day marchpast, a group of demonstrators jeered and catcalled. Slogans emphasized the message of the February demonstrations – that nothing was any longer taboo. 'Dictator = president without election', said one slogan. 'Down with the Red fascist empire,' said another. 'Gorbachev resign.' And, again, the now familiar slogan that so clearly summed up the sense of total disillusion: 'Seventy-two years on the road to nowhere.' Gorbachev drummed his fingers impatiently on the podium – and finally walked off.

Never had a Soviet leader been so humiliated before. The image was striking: in its way, it was as much a turning-point as those extraordinary few seconds less than five months earlier when Ceausescu was jeered by the crowd. Gorbachev was no Ceausescu. And yet – as the crowd knew well – his lack of electoral legitimacy was almost complete. The party leadership was not amused. Gorbachev complained of extremists and said that the demonstrators had embarked on a 'dangerous path'. There were warnings, too, of 'an avalanche of unforeseeable consequences'. Shortly after the May Day humiliation, 'slander of the president' was put on the statute books as a criminal offence. But the embarrassment remained.

Gorbachev's lack of legitimacy was especially glaring when one looked at the increasingly powerful position of his arch-rival. By spring 1990, the man who Gorbachev had consigned to the rubbish-bin of history in 1987 was not only the most popular politician in Russia, but was also fast regaining power. On 29 May, Yeltsin was elected chairman of the Russian parliament – in effect, Russian president. Gorbachev had backed a different candidate. But he was rebuffed. Yeltsin used his new power-base to attack the position, and credibility, of the Soviet leader himself.

Gorbachev accused Yeltsin of trying to excommunicate socialism, but the crowds only loved Yeltsin the more. Their adoration of him exceeded even the love for Gorbachev in the earliest days. Crowds held his picture high, as if it was an icon (indeed, some people seemed dangerously close to believing that Yeltsin was a miracle-working saint). Gorbachev and Yeltsin were constantly at odds over ideology. Yeltsin announced: 'Those who still believe in Communism are moving in the sphere of fantasy.' (The fact that he had changed his views mattered not at all to most Russians – after all, they, too, had once believed in the greatness and goodness of Communist power.) Gorbachev retorted: 'I am a Communist, a convinced Communist. For some, that may be fantasy. But for me, it is my main goal.' It was not a platform that could gain him support: by his continued declarations of loyalty to Communism, he lost the support of the radicals; and by allowing himself to be pushed into accepting radical change – at home and abroad – he lost his conservative supporters, who wanted him to Do Something to preserve the status quo. Western politicians supported him. But, in Moscow, that could change little.

The election of Yeltsin as Russian leader meant several more nails in the coffin of Soviet power. He was not only a powerful rival to Gorbachev, but, even more important, he was able to sabotage the very structure of Soviet power from within. Before Yeltsin's election, there had been jokes about the day that Russia would secede from the Soviet Union. Everybody knew that it was a contradiction in terms: If Russia seceded, then there was nothing left. Soon, however, the joke was close to becoming real. On 12 June 1990, Russia declared its 'sovereignty'.

From now on, Russian laws were deemed to have primacy over Soviet laws. This undermined the Kremlin's position, terminally. For, if even Russia refused to be subordinate to Soviet Communist law, then who *would* obey?

Russia's direct talks with the Baltic republics through the summer of 1990 – when both sides signed deals, as if between independent countries – were subversive, too. The agreements emphasized that when Gorbachev complained about the Balts' attempts to break away, he was speaking only for himself and the Communist Party leadership. Russia's elected leader, on the other hand – with mass support in the very republic which might have been expected to be most strongly against Baltic independence – supported the Balts at every turn. The new city council in Leningrad, the Russian city that was closest to the Baltic republics, also struck independent deals, to the Kremlin's indignation.

Increasingly, the Balts began to use a historically resonant phrase that harked back to the Polish and Lithuanian rebellions against tsarist rule in the nineteenth century. It was the same phrase that the brave handful of Russians used when protesting against the Soviet invasion of Prague in Red Square in 1968: 'For our and your freedom.' As time went on, and the pro-Kremlin violence increased, the connection became real.

Already, Gorbachev's power was beginning to crumble. Until now, Russia and the Soviet Union had loosely been used as synonyms. This had been, strictly speaking, incorrect: Russia was, after all, only one of fifteen Soviet republics. But in the broader sense, it had been accurate. Russia's policies, goals and philosophy were identical with those of the Soviet Union. There had been no separate 'Russian' politics, representing the Russian Soviet Federative Socialist Republic, with its 150 million inhabitants (more than half of the total population) and with more than three-quarters of the huge territory of the USSR. Unlike all the other republics, the Russian republic had never had its own Communist Party, its own television channel, or any of the rest of the trappings which every other Soviet republic could boast. It did not need to – it represented, after all, the centre of Soviet power. Now, all that was beginning to change. Russia itself was reborn – and challenged Communist power itself.

In the wake of the republican elections, many republics began to move. Barely a week after Russia's declaration of sovereignty, Georgia and Moldavia passed similar declarations. A month later, even huge Ukraine followed suit. Like so many political events in the previous year, the prospect of Ukraine breaking away was unthinkable for Moscow.

And like so many other unthinkable events, it was also becoming inevitable.

The pressure in Ukraine grew steadily after Shcherbitsky, the hardline party leader, was finally ditched in November 1989. On 21 January 1990, in commemoration of Ukraine's brief independence in 1918, millions of Ukrainians joined hands in a human chain that stretched from Lvov to the Ukrainian capital, Kiev — even as the Azeris buried their dead in Baku. In the elections in March, while Lithuania and the other Baltic republics declared their independence, Rukh swept the board in the western Ukraine: Lvov regional council was soon dominated by ex-political prisoners. The Communists still ruled in Kiev. In Lvov, however, the Soviet flag was hauled down and replaced by the blue and yellow national flag of Ukraine. Even elsewhere, in the traditionally conservative, Russian-majority parts of eastern Ukraine, and in Kiev, there were signs that not all was as it seemed; the support for Rukh continued to grow. It was clear that there were more shocks to come.

In Moscow, Communists gave up more and more of their dogmas in order to survive. But it never seemed to be enough. The party continued slipping down the precipice. On 2 July 1990, the fateful 28th Congress of the Communist Party of the Soviet Union opened in the huge glass-and-steel Palace of Congresses inside the Kremlin. Many observers expected that the party might split. On one side was the radical Democratic Platform. On the other, the hardliners, still led by Yegor Ligachev. Ligachev complained of thoughtless radicalism, and liberals were duly booed by the congress. Gorbachev found himself under attack by the conservatives, who blamed him for everything that had gone wrong. But Gorbachev gave at least as good as he got. As in his Lenin birthday speech, he complained of 'those who stubbornly cling to the past, who ... try to justify their conservative posture under the pretext of promoting the people's interests, the purity of ideological principles'. During the congress, Gorbachev even came out with his by-now-traditional threat to resign — a tactic which he had praised Lenin for successfully using and which he now used as a regular turn. He pointed out to the hardliners that their protests were in vain:

I have noticed in the atmosphere of the congress, in many speeches and in the manner in which some delegates conduct the discussion, that by no means everyone has understood. The party is living and working in a different society, and we need a different, renewed party, with a different style of work. We are not changing our line, our choice, our allegiance to socialist values. But believe you me, the party's success depends on its grasping that society has changed. Otherwise it will be pushed aside by other forces, and we will lose ground.

Gorbachev was right that society had changed. Paradoxically, however, he himself still seemed unwilling to grasp quite how much. He continued to talk of a vanguard role for the CPSU. He began to talk of a multi-party system. But, the next moment, he talked of *perestroika* as a peaceful revolution which could help the country to develop 'within the socialist choice'. This was a phrase which, in 1990, sounded absurd to independent Russian socialists and non-socialists alike. The most important feature of the Soviet political system was that it had never offered a choice of any kind. That was precisely where the problem lay.

Gorbachev acknowledged: 'Actual experience has proved to be far richer than we imagined it would be when we started our revolutionary change.' Even now, however, he seemed at a loss to understand the clear dynamics of change. He attacked the Communist Parties in the Baltic republics for breaking away from Moscow, and argued: 'As a result, the Communist movement has weakened sharply in those republics, and other political forces have come to power there.' *As a result?* It was a bizarre interpretation. The decision by Brazauskas, the Lithuanian party leader, to establish the Communists' political independence was a hugely popular move in Lithuania. Brazauskas could hardly be blamed if, despite the boost to the party's credibility, and despite his own personal popularity, four decades of Soviet Communism finally weighed too heavily in the balance and Lithuanians voted overwhelmingly for Sajudis.

Gorbachev hoped, perhaps, that his attacks on the hardliners would be the main event. Yet again, however, the radicals upstaged him. By far the most spectacular moment of the congress was a simple statement from Yeltsin. As the Russian leader himself later declared: 'I waited for the right moment. I didn't want to do it in writing. I wanted to make a real impact.' He succeeded. Yeltsin, who two years earlier had begged to be rehabilitated by the party, now announced, with a parting shot at President-cum-party-leader Gorbachev: 'As the leader of my republic, I must represent the will of the people. I announce my departure from the party, to be better able to govern my republic, and to work with all parties and organizations.' The party, once all-powerful, was fast becoming sidelined – together with its leader – by the swirling changes in the world outside. A number of radicals abandoned the sinking ship at the same time, including the powerful new council leaders in Leningrad and Moscow, Sobchak and Popov.

Yeltsin's show-stopping departure apart, the congress ended almost tamely: no split, just another stage in the slow death of the party. Disillusion was now almost total, and it was not just the big shots who were seeking to leave. Almost two million party members gave in their party cards in 1990. That was fifteen times more than the previous year. The 1989 figure had itself been seven times more than in 1988, the optimistic days of *perestroika*, when a mere 18,000 decided they had had enough. Joining the Soviet Communist Party would by now have been as eccentric as taking out East German citizenship in 1990, just before the country was abolished.

The congress adopted the new programme which talked of the party being loyal to the legacy of Marx, Engels and Lenin, freed from dogmatic interpretation. Such phrases meant nothing in particular but sounded simultaneously loyal and pioneering, which fitted the bill. The reality was that those who stayed behind in the party were, increasingly, the embattled and resentful hardline rump. Already at the end of 1989, an internal opinion poll had suggested that only 4 per cent of party members believed the party's authority was high; and a third of all Communist Party members believed their own party to be incapable of reform. That disillusion continued to deepen.

For the moment, the party still appeared to hold the reins of power – though less than before, with the creation of Gorbachev's Presidential Council, which was deemed to represent the new inner circle of power (Gorbachev later got rid of it). But the problem for the party was that its structures existed, above all, as a way of carrying out all-Soviet policies, co-ordinated from the centre. Yet Soviet domestic policies scarcely existed. As the historian Yuri Afanasiev wrote at this time:

> In official documents, we now see a remarkable paradox. They entirely ignore the obvious: the Soviet Union as a single state no longer exists. The Soviet President, the Soviet Council of Ministers and all the other 'Soviet' institutions no longer have any meaning. They hang in the air, a fairytale king's palace without a kingdom.

Afanasiev remarked, too, on the continued inability of Soviet leaders to see that the Soviet system itself had run its course:

Gorbachev-style *perestroika* has been just that: a 'restructuring' of society, without changing its fundamentals ... The Baltic states are leaving the USSR, and one after another, republics – including Russia and the Ukraine – have declared sovereignty and said that they will organize their own financial systems. This process should be seen as positive, but clearly it has been rejected both by the prime minister and, so far, by President Gorbachev.

Gorbachev, unwilling to accept the arguments of the radicals for starting completely from scratch, came up instead with his own idea for change, a new Treaty of the Union. The Balts had first suggested a new, looser union treaty back in 1988 and the idea had been enthusiastically endorsed by Sakharov. But Gorbachev had retorted: 'As is known, the treaty of 1922 is still valid and retains its juridical force to this day.' As late as September 1989, he was still insisting that the Baltic republics had become part of the Soviet Union at the wish of their own peoples.

But, like the much-quoted Lenin, the Soviet leader changed his mind when life demanded. Certainly, by summer 1990, life had begun to demand. When Gorbachev realized that not just the Lithuanians, but also Latvia and Estonia were heading for the Exit door as fast as they could; when he realized that anti-Kremlin feeling was growing fiercer, every month, in many other republics, and was backed up by parliamentary declarations; when he realized that even Russia's elected leaders were going along with the anti-Kremlin mood; when he realized, in short, that the Soviet Union was flying apart, even while he ordered it not to, then Gorbachev changed his mind.

Thus, the Union Treaty emerged, a child of necessity. Suddenly, all the talk was of the need for a renewed federation. In July, Gorbachev told the party congress: 'We must now, without delaying a single day, draft a new treaty of the union that will become the basis for deep-going transformations of our multinational state.' Gorbachev's hope was that he could dissuade the Balts, and other republics, from breaking away altogether. The message of the Union Treaty was essentially: 'Sign here on the dotted line – and we promise you that all will be well, and that you will no longer be constrained. But, if you fail to sign – woe betide you, for your punishment will be severe.' Not surprisingly, there was a marked reluctance among the republics to go along with this new voluntary-but-compulsory deal.

Soviet officials sought to portray the proposed Union Treaty as a kind of latter-day Treaty of Rome, the agreement which had led to the creation of the European Community. But they ignored one crucial point. Unlike Gorbachev's union treaty, the Treaty of Rome did not contain an implicit hidden agenda, of tanks on the streets if a country decided against signing up. Until the bitter end, Gorbachev appeared not to understand that the more he bullied and threatened force, the more impossible it became to secure any kind of general agreement.

In an apparent acknowledgement of the cause-and-effect relationship between the Baltic declarations of independence and the more liberal proposals now being proposed, Gorbachev added: 'What we lived through and reflected upon in recent times has caused us to realize that updating of the union cannot be confined to mere, even though considerable, extension of the rights of the republics and autonomies. What we need is a real union of sovereign states.' But the concessions had come too late — especially since the new proposals were still not accompanied by any apology for the brutal injustices of the past.

Meanwhile, the contrast between domestic chaos and international praise continued to grow. At a Bush–Gorbachev summit in Washington and at Camp David at the end of May, there were many mutual congratulations. And, in July, there was a historic meeting with the West German leader, Helmut Kohl, at a meeting on Gorbachev's home turf in Stavropol. The world watched as President Gorbachev and Chancellor Kohl set the seal on German unity, all wreathed in smiles. For Soviet viewers, it was just another international shindig, like the dozens in which Gorbachev had already been involved. Few Russians cared. German unity was neither good news nor bad, just something that happened in a faraway country which — unlike the Soviet Union — was at peace with itself. For many Russians, the approach of German unity, which would once have seemed so traumatic, was almost an irrelevance.

It was at Stavropol that Gorbachev finally assented to Nato membership for a united Germany. Only nine months earlier, in October 1989, he had sharply criticized those who called for the Wall to come down. Then after the Wall came down, he said that German unification was unacceptable. Then, in February, when it had become quite inevitable — by now the crowds had for months been chanting 'We are *one* people' — he accepted the principle of a united Germany. (Tass, brazenly ignoring its own past tirades on German unity, declared that the Soviet leadership 'did not in the past, and does not now' have any problems with the principle of self-determination.) Still, though, Gorbachev insisted in March that Nato membership was 'absolutely ruled out'. And sure enough: what he absolutely ruled out in March, he accepted with a broad smile in July. It was a classic victory, Gorbachev-style.

Gorbachev's acceptance of German unity, on Bonn's terms, was no doubt made easier by Helmut Kohl's jangling of deutschmarks, with the implicit promise of more to come. But this was not just cash-for-unity. More important was the fact that the Soviet leader had no more cards to play. How was he supposed to stop German unity? With tanks, which would roll through non-Communist Poland to Berlin? With a Warsaw Pact invasion, when the Warsaw Pact had already collapsed? By ordering a group of East German Communists to seize control? It was clearly futile, unless Gorbachev was prepared to unleash a full-scale revolution at home, and cataclysm in all Europe. By agreeing to German unity, he could at least turn to other, more pressing matters at home — where the problems only seemed to multiply.

11 In Search of a Miracle

One day, according to an early *perestroika*-era joke, the train that was reserved for the use of the general secretary of the Soviet Communist Party broke down. Inside the luxurious train carriage, three Soviet leaders, past and present, were gathered. Each had a different suggestion as to what they should do next. Stalin demanded: 'Shoot the driver!' Brezhnev ordered the curtains to be closed and declared: 'We are making magnificent progress!' But Gorbachev got out of the train, ran up and down several times and started shouting very loudly: 'Now, everybody – *push*!'

That popular anecdote was a remarkably accurate summary of Gorbachev's initial approach to repairing the Soviet system and the Soviet economy. He believed that extra effort was the key to solving all the problems. It was, in a sense, a philosophy that harked back to Alexei Stakhanov, the miner who was reputed to have overfulfilled his quota by 1400 per cent when he hewed 102 tonnes of coal in one day. Stakhanov's productivity launched a thousand propaganda films and slogans in the Stalin era. Gorbachev, it seemed, still had a sneaking respect for the Stakhanov style. He declared in *Perestroika* in 1987: 'I like this phrase: working an *extra bit harder* [Gorbachev's italics]. For me, it's not just a slogan but a habitual state of mind, a disposition.' Perhaps, in the circumstances, it was not surprising that he and Margaret Thatcher (who prided herself on needing only five hours' sleep a night) saw themselves as two of a kind – nor, conversely, that he and the snooze-loving Ronald Reagan never achieved a close rapport.

It was clear, back in 1985, that it was the economy by which everything would stand or fall. *Perestroika* – and *perestroika*'s pillion-rider, *glasnost* – had been launched in order to save the economy. There were endless promises that things were about to get better. Gorbachev made it clear that economic efficiency must be improved; the unceasing flow of central funding for economic un-productivity would, he suggested, eventually run dry.

Gorbachev had not, as the Russian phrase had it, sucked these ideas out of his finger. Radical economic thinking continued even through the Brezhnev years — though the radicals were always kept well out of harm's way. Professor Abel Aganbegyan, a physically and intellectually substantial Armenian, was director of the Institute of the Economics and Organization of Industrial Production, attached to the Siberian Department of the Academy of Sciences of the USSR, in the Siberian city of Novosibirsk. The title of his institute was conventionally Soviet, the work of the institute was heretical. It was here that research continued, emphasizing need for reform. In 1983, Tatyana Zaslavskaya, a sociologist and economist at Aganbegyan's institute, delivered to a closed seminar a paper that attacked the heart of Soviet complacency. In her paper — which became known simply as the Novosibirsk Manifesto — she called for a radical restructuring of the system of economic management. She argued, in effect, that the entire Soviet command economy had ceased to work and that something quite new was needed in its place. This was Gorbachevism, two years before Gorbachev.

At that time, although the semi-reformer Andropov was already in power, these were dangerous waters. The seminar buzzed with excitement. But the arguments of the Novosibirsk report were considered such political dynamite that all distribution was banned except for individual copies which had to be signed for. Zaslavskaya herself later described the manifesto as the first swallow of *perestroika*, flying high in the sky while the ground was still frozen. Despite the security precautions, the Novosibirsk report was leaked to the Western press, and caused uproar at home. For months, the institute was turned upside down by the KGB. According to Zaslavskaya herself, 'They scoured the country to find those missing documents.' None the less, despite the official disapproval, the Novosibirsk reformers continued to gain importance. And when Gorbachev came to power, Aganbegyan and Zaslavskaya were catapulted to prominence. Both were hauled back to Moscow, where they became members of Gorbachev's inner circle of reform. As Gorbachev himself emphasized, the new reforms were not intended to represent any kind of about-turn. He was indignant at the very idea:

Why should the Soviet people, who have grown and gained in strength under socialism, abandon that system? We will spare no effort to develop and strengthen socialism ... Just think: how can we agree that 1917 was a mistake, and all the seventy years of our life, work, effort and battles were also a complete mistake, that we were going in the 'wrong direction'?

Despite Gorbachev, there were some early attempts to question the nature of the status quo. As early as 1987, while the Soviet leader was talking airily of the socialist market, the economist Larisa Popkova pointed out in the magazine *Novy Mir*: 'You cannot be a little bit pregnant.' Other radical economists began to make themselves heard. Nikolai Shmelyov, also in *Novy Mir* (which had published Solzhenitsyn in the 1960s and was no stranger to heresies), declared that there was 'no more effective measure of work than profit'. But these declarations were intended to be shocking, and had little effect on policy-making at this time.

Nevertheless, a few economic reforms were introduced, within the existing system, which attempted to tidy up the worst anomalies. The cornerstone of the new economic reforms was the self-financing of factories, or cost accounting, known as *khozraschot*. The idea was that the central bureaucrats in Moscow no longer controlled every aspect of the factory's production. At last, reality was to get a look in. Vanya's complaint about the white and the black bread in Vitebsk in 1985 should – theoretically, at least – cease to exist. If people wanted black bread, they would get black bread; and if they wanted white, they would get white. Each factory would produce what it needed, and be responsible for making the books balance. That was the essence of the much-touted *khozraschot*. Gorbachev declared: 'We have laid the foundations for a full-scale offensive in every area of the process of accelerating and extending the restructuring.' Or, to quote Gorbachev's own words: 'Onward to full cost accounting!'

But, despite the fanfares, *khozraschot* made little difference to the overall health of the economy. It eradicated some of the grossest absurdities. But that was not the same as making the system work. The legalization of co-operative businesses in May 1988 changed the landscape somewhat. Certainly, they filled a market gap. The co-operative restaurants, for example, were invariably cleaner and the food was better. Sometimes, the service was downright courteous. But, though the co-operatives – small private businesses, by any other name – were useful, they were also expensive. They were resented almost as much as they were needed. Many regarded those in the co-operatives as 'speculators' – and there was nothing more hated than a *spekulyant*.

Partly, this was because of a real conservatism about the idea of paying more for a better product. *Homo sovieticus* had learned to think of that as a moral crime. But there was an understandable resentment, too, of what amounted to mafia law. So byzantine were the regulations governing the co-operatives that it was essential to bribe in order to get things sorted out. Pay-offs became a way of life, like it or not. Good relations with the authorities were essential. One Russian acquaintance, a member of a translators' co-operative, described how the members of the co-operative hired an expensive ex-KGB officer – not because he had any useful skills (the slashing of car tyres and the successful placing of microphones in a hotel-table vase were not generally regarded as essential qualities for a translator, nor even for an administrative accountant), but because he had the essential contacts to keep the co-op out of trouble.

For a price, the co-operatives offered services and products which were not available before. But the number of co-operative ventures – barely 2 per cent of the total economy – was not great enough to make the economy as a whole seem more efficient, let alone to bring prices down. The command economy lost its ability to command, but there was no market economy to fill the market. The queues were longer than ever, and the resentments grew.

There were other reasons for resentment, too. There was the increasing realization – courtesy of *glasnost* – of quite how badly Russians lived, by comparison with the rest of the developed world. The new opportunities for travel helped to destroy old illusions. In the 1970s, a trip to the West was, for all except a tiny, trusted minority, pure fantasy. But from 1988 onwards, passports became more freely available. Those who did travel to the West were often shocked by what they saw. As one Russian visitor to London remarked, with real sadness: 'I never realized that we were so poor.' It was a view that was echoed, again and again, as the official lies were stripped away and the disillusion grew. Once upon a time, official comparisons between East and West always sought to demonstrate that the Soviet system worked better than the West. Now, it was the other way round. Published comparisons between the West and the Soviet Union – health, housing, work safety, workers' rights, environment, diet, technology, travel, you-name-it – were invariably, and humiliatingly, to the disadvantage of the country that had once thought of itself as a superpower.

One aspect of the Soviet economy which began to change during the *perestroika* era was the greater involvement of Western firms. During the Brezhnev era, there had been a steady trickle of Western investment.

Now, however, joint ventures sprouted everywhere. Ice-cream parlours, an English pub, pizzerias, a golf course, a photocopying shop ... by 1988, there were all of these, each opened with a little flurry of publicity. Moscow seemed to be living in an entirely different world. The reality, however, was different. Many of the new businesses were available only to foreigners. As the ordinary shops, in the real Russian world, became ever emptier, so the number of hard-currency shops − the Finnish supermarket, the German supermarket, the Swiss-Soviet joint venture − grew in number, so that it was eventually possible to buy whatever you wanted, from fresh lettuce in winter to French champagne, as long as you possessed the right passport and therefore the right-coloured money. As the well-stocked (Irish joint venture) duty-free shop at Moscow's Sheremetievo Airport proclaimed, with apparently unconscious irony: 'All major international currencies accepted.' That did not, of course, include the rouble, the local currency of a failed superpower. In the Soviet capital, the Soviet rouble was less than worthless.

In Poland, after the Communists were ousted in 1989, one of the government's earliest aims was to get rid of the hard-currency shops, whose official title, all too accurately, was 'shops of internal export'. By introducing radical economic reform, the Poles succeeded: within little more than a year, Polish shops were well enough stocked for the hard-currency shops to be no different, and they sold their products for the local currency, the zloty. Other East European countries moved in the same direction. In the Soviet Union, however, more and more hard-currency shops opened − and, at the same time, the real Soviet economy continued to collapse.

In one crucial area, agriculture, nothing at all seemed to change. There was talk of reversing the 'de-peasantization' of the land, and, certainly, there was reason enough to introduce radical change. As in eastern Europe, the statistics indicated that private farming was infinitely more efficient. The 2 per cent of land which was accounted for by private plots provided a third of the country's vegetables, meat, eggs and milk, and more than half its potato crop. None the less, the collective and state farms continued overwhelmingly to dominate Soviet agriculture. Nor was there any pressure for change.

Stalin created the collective farms, with a policy of mass murder. In the 1930s, any peasant who was halfway efficient was judged to be a *kulak* − a 'fist', or rich, exploitative peasant − and was therefore shipped off to the camps. Millions were sent to Siberia; millions more died of the man-made famine, which was designed to break the peasants' will, at home. It was one of the grimmest episodes in the USSR's grim history. Now, five decades after their creation, the collective farms were no longer a source of fear, but they were still as inefficient as they had ever been. Typically, the farm chairmen were plump party loyalists, whose most conspicuous talent was the ability to spout propaganda for long periods without drawing breath and to deliver reams of false statistics when required (the second quality was now less in vogue than it had once been).

Gorbachev – who had studied agriculture and who had been responsible for Soviet agriculture – remained a loyal defender of the collective farms. 'I know how much fiction, speculation and malicious criticism of us go with this term, let alone the process itself. But even many of the objective students of this period of our history do not seem to be able to grasp the importance, need and inevitability of collectivization in our country,' he wrote in 1987. Gorbachev added: 'Without collectivization, we would not be producing as much per capita as we do, satisfying for the most part our vital requirements. And, of particular importance, the possibility of hunger and undernourishment has been eliminated for ever in our country.' The prospect of privatization worried him. In 1988, he told the presidium of the old Soviet parliament: 'The attempt to restore private property means to move backwards – and it is a deeply erroneous decision.'

There were proposals for modernizing the system somewhat, including the introduction of 'land-lease', which was supposed to open up new possibilities by allowing a peasant to take over temporary responsibility for a plot. In practice, it meant little. The collective farm chairman and other party worthies still controlled life in the countryside and the management of the land. The old structures were neither shaken nor stirred. Gorbachev remained loyal to the bigger-means-better Soviet way of thinking long after others had abandoned it. In 1989, he declared that critics of the collective farms had failed to think things through. 'It is precisely now that our big collective and state farms will be able to work in the right way.'

The disastrous situation in the shops and on the farms was just one aspect of the economic dead-end in which the Soviet Union found itself. As the boldness of the Soviet press continued to grow, the dire condition of all corners of the Soviet welfare state – which, in reality, did not exist – was laid bare for all to see. For years, the statistics had been massaged in order to contradict the visible reality and suggest that the Soviet

Union had a flourishing welfare state. Now, the appalling truth began to be revealed about many different aspects of Soviet society.

The figures for infant mortality, previously falsified, were now admitted to be more than twice as high in the Soviet Union as in Britain or the United States, with around 30 deaths per 1000 in the first year of life. It was admitted, too, that a third of district hospitals had no hot water and a quarter had no sewerage. The propaganda posters had once made great play of the fact that the Soviet Union had the largest number of doctors and dentists in the world. True, there were doctors and dentists, but, as was now acknowledged, there was no health care. Soviet patients took it for granted that they would be abused, neglected or misdiagnosed. They knew that, even with the best will in the world, the necessary drugs would not be available to treat them (unless, of course, they were part of the elite, who had special 'closed' hospitals where everything was available). And they knew that the only way they could expect to get even the basic minimum of treatment was by bribery of the (badly paid) doctors and nurses alike.

Housing was as bad. In 1986, Gorbachev undertook to ensure that every family would have its own flat or house by the year 2000. This, he said, was a tremendous but feasible undertaking. But, even among the most dreamy of Soviet citizens, the promise soon came to seem entirely unreal. Millions continued to live in the hated *komunalki*, the communal apartments where nothing was shared, but everything was jealously guarded (and stolen), where several families, strangers to each other, lived together in a single apartment for years or decades. In a country where the divorce rate was high, couples often continued to live, together with in-laws, under the same roof, because there was nowhere to move out to. Rents were tiny − £10 a month was the norm (counting at the old official rate, when an average salary was about £200 a month). But this was little comfort for those who would gladly have paid more − if they could only have found a decent home to rent.

The environment, too, suffered disastrously, because of the Stalinist economic philosophy and because of the conspiracy of silence. The Soviet philosophy had always been the bigger, the better. The knock-on effect, and the effect on people's health, were ignored − and when some of the effects were understood, they were kept as a state secret. Now, throughout the country, the horrendous environmental cost began to be counted.

One of the most notable examples was in Central Asia, where Soviet economic policies wreaked ecological havoc following the obsessive planting of cotton, or 'white gold'. Cotton came to dominate the economy to such an extent that all other factors were ignored – both the economic viability and the human and environmental cost. In order to irrigate the land, rivers were diverted in an overcoming of nature that led to the virtual extinction of the Aral Sea, into which the rivers flowed. On the official maps, the town of Aralsk was shown as a port. In the 1960s, Aralsk had indeed been on the edge of the Aral Sea, but twenty-five years later, the maps were wrong. Now, the town was forty miles away from the inland sea which gave it its name. A new desert had been created, and a death sentence pronounced. The rivers running into the sea were so polluted by chemical fertilizers draining off the land that the water was no longer drinkable – yet for many households there was no other water supply. The incidence of typhoid rose thirtyfold; that of hepatitis, sevenfold. Mothers were warned not to breastfeed, because it might harm their children. Tens of millions of tonnes of poisonous salty dust swirled up into the atmosphere every year from the new desert: rainwater thousands of miles away was affected by the destruction of the Aral region. In the words of the *Literary Gazette*, the Aral Sea became a catastrophe zone that was 'comparable with Chernobyl'.

In the past, the Aral basin had always been fertile. The sea provided rich fishing and the land was good pasture. The neighbouring Central Asian republics consisted partly of good land, used for growing fruit of all kinds, and partly of desert – the Kryzikum, or 'red sands', and the Karakum, or 'black sands'. The Soviet planners were undaunted. Where there was desert, let there be cotton. Where it was dry, bring in water, and more water, and let the sea run dry. It was *glasnost* which permitted the scale of the disaster to become known. But, if *glasnost* permitted the problem to be discussed, that was not the same as tackling the cure. At a time when the Soviet Union was already in the throes of an economic crisis, nobody wanted to take responsibility for abandoning the cotton-growing that had caused all the problems in the first place.

The same contradiction could be found across the Soviet Union. In almost every area, people were dying because of the pollution. Seventy million people lived in towns where pollution exceeded the maximum permissible levels five times over; and more than forty million lived in areas where the pollution was fifteen times greater than the permitted levels. Even when the dangers were known, little was done about them. After a gas leak in the town of Orenburg in January 1989, dozens went to hospital with gas poisoning and children had to go to school in gas masks. The ministry, it later turned out, had authorized the construction of the plant without a filtering system, because it would cost too much. After the leak, the gas-processing plant refused a demand by the health authorities to cut its output, arguing that it had to fulfil the plan.

The accident at Orenburg was not an isolated example. The inefficiency and lack of controls meant that such incidents were common. The only difference now was that people were allowed to hear about them. In Leningrad, diseases of the upper respiratory tract affected nearly one third of the population. In Magnitogorsk, a majority of the children suffered some serious illness. There were similarly worrying statistics in hundreds of cities across the Soviet Union. The Soviet population was gradually being killed by the Plan. And, because of the disastrous situation in the economy, there was no money to change that.

At the same time, the reality was defiantly ignored. In January 1989, the Communist Party's official platform repeated Gorbachev's earlier promises: greater industrial output, more apartments and improved food supplies. In fact, industrial output fell, millions continued to live in the depressing *komunalki* that seemed such a potent symbol of Soviet life, and the food queues were worse than they had ever been. By autumn 1989, there was little pretence, even among the country's rulers, that the economy was going anywhere but down. It was officially acknowledged: 'The dynamism of the economy in the current year has, in many of the most important directions, decreased month by month. Social tension has increased. And the balance of the national economy has weakened.' Despite the constant talk of 'radical reform', when push came to economic shove, the Soviet people always got more of the same. The reform package put forward by the prime minister, Nikolai Ryzhkov, in December 1989, avoided all the difficult questions and again assumed a reliance on traditional central planning, with a continued ban on private property. In the words of one leading radical, this was a government 'which still lays down in the plan how many eggs a hen should lay'.

By now, the crime rate was soaring. Five years earlier, Soviet cities had been safe. Admittedly, the newspapers covered up crime when it did occur, but it was not just a question of fiddled statistics. Violent crime was rare. Unaccompanied women could walk alone at night and even flagged down the informal 'taxis' – private cars whose drivers were looking for extra cash – without fear. By 1990, such cosiness was a thing of the past. The incidence of violent robbery and murder increased by leaps and bounds. Russians were understandably worried at the transformation of their country from one of the safest in the world to one of the most lawless in the space of just a few years. The soaring crime rate was just one aspect of a society that had lost its way.

In February 1990, great fanfares surrounded the opening of the world's largest McDonald's – almost fourteen years after discussions with the Soviet authorities first began. The queues were so long that they had to be controlled by policemen – even though each Big Mac cost more than half a day's wages. But the availability of astonishingly expensive hamburgers, and the development of a clutch of new hotels, did nothing to change the nature of the economy itself. There were shortages of many basic products, and some rationing was introduced, but the Soviet leadership seemed incapable of introducing serious change.

In May 1990, an emergency economic plan was produced, the latest in a long series, none of which got anywhere. Valentin Pavlov, the finance minister, proposed a raft of price rises – which, in turn, triggered a wave of panic buying across the country. Gorbachev made a fifty-minute appearance on television, urging people to 'evaluate the problem calmly'. Even now, however, as Soviet leaders talked about radical reform, they shied away from the phrase 'private property' and banned the 'exploitation of man by man'. In other words, except in limited circumstances, you were not allowed to employ anybody. In essence, the new plan amounted to two things: higher prices and an unchanged basic system. Again and again, the pattern was repeated: there was talk of radical reform, and then it vanished, like a will-o'-the-wisp, just before it was agreed and implemented.

Anguished about how to introduce the change that increasingly seemed so essential, Soviet leaders began talking about a referendum on reform, to give themselves the credibility that they craved. But they soon abandoned the idea when they realized that it was certain to backfire. Just as the East European Communists had done in the 1980s, Soviet officials began to complain about the immaturity of the people whom they were forced to rule and who refused to accept painful, but necessary economic reform. Certainly, price rises were much resented and little understood. But rarely did the Soviet officials wonder if part of the problem lay with themselves. Gorbachev complained: 'In politics, the public does not accept pluralism and has complexes about ideological concepts and cliches. In economics, it's a case of "you mustn't touch this, you mustn't touch that". Everywhere, we are being hindered by complexes.'

That was partly true, as later attempts at change would clearly show.

But talk of ideological hang-ups was also a convenient let-out. Life itself, as Lenin and Gorbachev liked to say, would show that Gorbachev and his close comrades had at least as many 'complexes about ideological concepts' as did millions of ordinary Russians, thoroughly disillusioned with ideology of any kind. Nor was it the people's fault if they did not understand the meaning of economic change.

The East European Communists had already faced such problems. In November 1987, as the Communist economy in Poland spiralled downwards, a government referendum asked Poles, in effect, whether they wished to live better in the future – and, if so, would they please vote for price reform? (The two questions promised economic changes which would produce 'a clear improvement in living standards' within two or three years, and talked of 'deep democratization of political life'.) Since the existing state of the economy was appalling, and was certain to get worse, the only sensible answer was yes. The Poles answered: no. 'Woe is us,' said the Communists, 'look what a mulish people we are obliged to rule.' Some in the West, it must be admitted, accepted the Communists' seductive line. As late as spring 1989, at a lunch at the Polish embassy in London – intended to soften up Western opinion in favour of the Communist authorities – one financial commentator opined that, if Solidarity gained power, Poland's credit rating would fall 'like a stone', because of Solidarity's unwillingness to accept reform.

The Polish officials purred with satisfaction. They had successfully turned reality upon its head. In fact, the Solidarity government, when it ousted the Communists a few months later, introduced painful economic change that the Communists could never have dreamed of. As the opposition leader Jacek Kuron pointed out at the time of the referendum in 1987, the no-vote did not mean a rejection of reform, as such. It merely indicated, in Kuron's words, that Poles had 'no confidence in those who are carrying the reforms out'. In effect, the Polish answer meant: 'We refuse to say yes, because that would give satisfaction and credibility to you, the Communist regime. And that, we refuse to do.'

Poland's 1987 no-vote contained an unwelcome message for the Soviet authorities three years later. Leonid Abalkin, the deputy prime minister in charge of economic reform, referred wistfully to Poland's privileged position, following the Communists' departure. 'Poland's government enjoys the people's trust and can bring in very unpopular measures with the support of society.' Whereas the Soviet Union did not, and therefore could not. Despite the Soviet envy of the Polish example, few of the Kremlin's leaders acknowledged the lessons of Poland from

1987, or accepted the logical next step: why not change the government, and the political system, as Poland had done, in order to give reform a chance?

Russia was very different from Poland, which had a much clearer idea of what it wanted, but what the two countries had in common was the need for a government which could gain popular trust. In the 1930s, many people had trusted Stalin. But times had changed. By now – after the collapse of eastern Europe, after the miners' strikes, after the mass protests in Moscow and after the Baltic declarations of independence – it was hopeless for the Kremlin's Communist leaders to think that they could somehow regain control. By summer 1990, the economy was falling apart as never before. There was panic buying in advance of price rises. And there were shortages that even the Soviet Union had not yet seen. Cigarettes ran out in some areas and in a country of heavy smokers, that was the last straw. In the city of Perm, in the Urals, tobacco rebels barricaded themselves in the city centre and even elected a protest committee. Interestingly, they combined their yearning for nicotine with political demands, including the abolition of Communist Party cells in the workplace. The rebellion was bought off when Soviet troops delivered a quarter of a million stockpiled cigarettes. But the shortages continued. Most shocking of all in a country where real hunger was still a live memory, there were even bread shortages. Bread was rationed in some areas to 500 grammes a day.

In 1990, Gorbachev continued to talk of the need for a 'regulated market economy', which appeared to be the equivalent of St Augustine's plea, 'Make me good, O Lord – but not yet.' He talked, too, of 'socialist democracy', a Soviet phrase that less hidebound Communist Parties had long since abandoned. (As one Hungarian official remarked in the months before the revolutions of eastern Europe got under way: 'Here in Hungary, we no longer talk of "socialist democracy". Either you have democracy – or you don't. It seems to us that it's as simple as that.')

Gradually, talk of the regulated market economy gave way to talk of the market economy, pure and simple. Still, however, it remained all talk. Gorbachev – as in politics, so in economics – seemed keen to have it both ways. At the Communist Party congress in July 1990, he insisted: 'By moving towards a market we are not swerving from the road to socialism, but are advancing towards a fuller realization of society's potential. It is this that underpins the conception of *perestroika*.' Still, his end-of-term report at the 28th Party Congress was forthright. He noted that the situation in the shops was worse than ever: the situation on the consumer market, he said, was intolerable. A critical point had been reached. Fundamental changes were now needed, he said: diverse forms of ownership and management, and with a modern market infrastructure. This would, in turn, create 'new and powerful motivations for fruitful work, for greater economic efficiency'. It was dramatic stuff. It seemed that the crunch had finally come. Now, it was a matter of attempting to put some flesh on the visionary words.

Already, genuinely radical programmes for economic recovery were being worked on. Grigory Yavlinsky, Boris Yeltsin's deputy prime minister (and himself an economist), came up with a radical crash programme for Russia to move to the market. Yeltsin, newly elected Russia's leader, was keen. Then, in August 1990 – two months after Yeltsin's election – a remarkable deal was struck: Gorbachev and Yeltsin agreed in effect to be co-sponsors of a souped-up version of the Russian plan, which could be implemented throughout the Soviet Union. Through the month of August, a team of economists held brainstorming sessions until late at night at a government dacha outside Moscow, led by the radical senior economist, Stanislav Shatalin, and Yavlinsky, his younger colleague.

Gorbachev remained in close touch with the team. He phoned several times a day from his holiday villa in the Crimea, and appeared enthusiastic. After his return, and after Yeltsin returned from his holiday in Latvia, the two men met for a long session of one-on-one talks in Moscow – for the first time in three years. Admittedly, none of the most serious questions about the future of the Soviet Union – the right of the republics to gain unconditional independence from Moscow, or the persistence of one-party rule – was being tackled. Nevertheless, if you closed your eyes and tried not to concentrate too hard, things at this point looked almost rosy.

But, as so often before, the dreams quickly evaporated. A rival government team, working for the prime minister, Nikolai Ryzhkov, came up with a much more cautious plan. Gorbachev suggested merging the two plans, in a version that would be '99 per cent Shatalin'. In reality, Gorbachev's own continuing queasiness about privatization (and especially private ownership of land), together with the insistence by Ryzhkov and Abalkin that radical change was out of the question, persuaded Gorbachev to abandon the pro-market plan that he had seemed so enthusiastic about. Yeltsin complained that merging the two plans was 'like trying to mate a hedgehog with a snake'. Shatalin, the soft-spoken professor of economics who was also chairman of Spartak football club, used an analogy to make his point: 'Imagine I am captain of Spartak and we are playing Dynamo. Can I really tell the opposing captain: "Let's do a deal and let both sides win?" I am not playing in this game.' But despite Shatalin's complaints, Gorbachev was determined to let both sides win – or, more accurately, to let both sides lose. When Yeltsin attacked the watering-down of the pro-market plan and complained that Russia's radical plan had been sabotaged, Gorbachev described his remarks as strange and immoral.

Meanwhile, mutterings of a threatened coup grew louder, especially after unexplained troop movements near Moscow in September. The rumours became so strong that the defence minister, Dimitry Yazov, appeared on Soviet television in order to insist that there was no cause for concern. At the same time, the constitutional quickstep continued. Gorbachev announced that his Presidential Council would now be abolished and that the Federation Council, consisting of the leaders of the republics, would rule supreme. But it was just another decree. The reality was a continuing drift towards chaos.

By now Gorbachev was the international superstar. In November 1990, at the pan-European Paris summit of the Conference on Security and Co-operation in Europe – the climax of fifteen years of the Helsinki process, linking arms talks and human rights – Gorbachev talked of how the Soviet Union was moving away from totalitarianism to freedom and democracy. His country, he said, was becoming a state anchored in the rule of law and political pluralism. It was good visionary stuff, and it went down well. Here in Paris, Gorbachev was among friends. He signed the treaty on Conventional Forces in Europe, a landmark arms agreement. He signed the Paris Charter, which committed the Soviet Union – at least in theory – to free and fair elections, to be held at 'reasonable intervals'. Georgy Shakhnazarov, a Gorbachev aide, when asked when such free elections might take place in the Soviet Union, replied that the grossly rigged 1989 elections had already been free. This made the Kremlin's understanding of the word 'free' somewhat questionable. Still, the commitment was, in theory, clear enough.

The summit was partly overshadowed by the domestic political dramas of one of its participants. Margaret Thatcher was in the process of being thrown to the electoral wolves after a revolt inside the Conservative Party. Thatcher insisted repeatedly that she would not resign – including a dramatic appearance on the steps of the British embassy in Paris. She finally bowed to the pressure and resigned the morning after the summit ended. But, if the extraordinary demise of

Britain's longest-serving prime minister was one reason for the summit's inclusion in the history books, it was important on its own account, too. All the political leaders reached for the thesaurus of superlatives. Francois Mitterrand said the signing of the Paris Charter was a moment without precedent. Helmut Kohl called the summit a watershed in the history of Europe. And Gorbachev himself said it was a crucial turning-point in our history, the effects of which were likely to be felt for centuries.

Just a month earlier, Gorbachev had been awarded the Nobel Peace Prize. Eastern Europe was free; and the West was deeply grateful to the Soviet leader for not causing problems in connection with United Nations sanctions against Iraq, after the invasion of Kuwait, three months earlier. But despite the lofty rhetoric at the Paris summit, the contradictions remained. Moscow demanded that the three foreign ministers from the Baltic republics who had been invited as 'guests' to the summit should have their passes withdrawn. The guest status had itself been a compromise; the Balts had wanted official observer status and had been denied it. But, in deference to Gorbachev, the French hosts hastily un-invited the Balts and banned them from the CSCE proceedings altogether. Denmark and Iceland protested, but the big players at the summit were unwilling to disturb the status quo.

In Paris, Gorbachev made the first of a series of requests for large dollops of international aid. In private meetings with Western leaders, he asked for emergency deliveries of food, with the promise of more to come. The shopping list included requests for pork, beef, flour, butter, powdered milk and vegetable oil. Within weeks, Moscow was publicly talking of a food crisis such as it had not seen for decades. There was much talk of *golod* – hunger, also translatable as famine. At the beginning of December, Yuli Kvitsinsky, a deputy foreign minister, flew to Brussels and pleaded for emergency assistance, including food and medical supplies. The European Community held an emergency meeting a few days later and quickly approved a billion-dollar food package for Moscow. Hans-Dietrich Genscher, the German foreign minister, said that he believed that more was needed.

Emergency aid could be useful. But the contradictions were many. For the reality was that the Soviet Union's problems still stemmed partly from a continued refusal to change the existing system. The 1990 harvest was one of the best that there had been for many years. The renewed food crisis was vivid proof of the collapse of the already moribund distribution network. It was officially estimated that 100 million tonnes of the 240-million tonne grain harvest was wasted because of bad storage and transport; 60 per cent of the fruit and vegetable harvest was said to have rotted. Despite this, Moscow had still hung back from radical change. Indeed, the resale for profit of that food, to prevent it rotting, would have been banned under the existing law.

Equally startling was that the flurry of official requests for food aid came even as Gorbachev flatly rejected the privatization of land in a meeting at the end of November. Thus, the one single measure which could so obviously improve food production was rejected as ideologically unacceptable — even as the lorryloads and planeloads of aid began to arrive. And the contradictions continued. Radio Moscow reported that stockpiles of food had been found in the warehouses of food stores whose shelves were empty; the implication was that the food had deliberately been withheld. Anatoly Sobchak, leader of Leningrad city council, even sought to argue that the authorities were deliberately making things worse in order to destroy people's belief in democratic change:

> After failing to crush the democratic and national independence movement, the Communist Party structures — including the state apparatus — tried to worsen the economy, to discredit the democratic choice which has been made ... That, it seems, is the only way to explain the acute food crisis, after one of the best harvests that Russia, during the era of Soviet power, has seen.

Gavriil Popov, the mayor of Moscow, blamed the acute shortages on poor distribution and on hoarding. He also criticized the collective and state farms for failing to sell their produce.

There were many paradoxes. The Soviet ambassador to London, Leonid Zamyatin — a former Brezhnev spokesman and Gorbachev appointee, later sacked for supporting the August coup — wrote to *The Times* asking for cash donations to the former superpower, to be paid into a special new Soviet bank account for the centralized distribution of aid. Yet Zamyatin's letter was published at the same time as a report in the now-liberal *Izvestia*, which pointed out that the defence budget had just been raised by more than £20 billion for the coming year, instead of being cut as originally planned.

To cap it all, the Kremlin announced that the KGB would be given responsibility for distributing aid, to ensure that it reached the right hands. Gorbachev issued a presidential decree whereby food distribution would now effectively be controlled by vigilante groups – 'workers' control committees', acting together with the secret police. Except for the fact that 300 million people were suffering the effects, it all seemed like part of a blackly surreal farce.

Certainly, the political omens were getting worse by the day. Before Gorbachev left for Paris, he appointed a hardliner, Leonid Kravchenko, as head of state television and radio, in what radicals saw as a worrying sign of things to come. Then, the hardline parliamentary group Soyuz (literally, 'Union') demanded the sacking of the liberal interior minister, Vadim Bakatin. Gorbachev obliged, replacing Bakatin with the much disliked Boris Pugo, former head of the Latvian KGB. As deputy to Pugo, Gorbachev appointed Boris Gromov, former head of the armed forces in Afghanistan.

Gorbachev also issued a presidential decree annulling republican laws which allowed young men to escape conscription. This was clearly aimed at the Baltic republics, where the local governments suggested that citizens should avoid call-up for the Soviet army. Accidentally or otherwise, Gorbachev's decree was an important building-block in preparing the subsequent Baltic crackdown, when the alleged need to find army 'deserters' played a key role. The threats grew ever louder. On 11 December, Kryuchkov, head of the KGB, complained that the country was now in the grip of 'extremist radical groups ... supported morally and politically from abroad'. By the time that the Congress of People's Deputies opened, on 17 December, there was no mistaking the dark clouds that were gathering.

Then, on 20 December, came a dramatic moment that confirmed everybody's worst fears. Eduard Shevardnadze, Soviet foreign minister and the most consistently liberal member of the Soviet leadership, delivered what he said was 'the shortest and most difficult speech of my life'. Certainly, it was the most devastating speech that the Soviet parliament had heard. Gorbachev sat expressionless and the hall went deathly quiet as Shevardnadze spoke:

Comrade democrats ... You have scattered. The reformers have gone to ground. Dictatorship is coming. No one knows what kind this dictatorship will be, and who will come – what kind of dictator, and what the regime will be like. I want to make the following statement. I am resigning. Let this be my contribution, if you like, my protest against the onset of dictatorship ... I cannot reconcile myself to the events which are taking place in our country, and to the trials which await our people. I nevertheless believe — I believe that dictatorship will not succeed.

Gorbachev was furious. He retorted: 'Shevardnadze's action must be condemned . . . To go now is unforgivable.' He claimed to Shevardnadze that he saw 'absolutely no threat of dictatorship'. Shevardnadze later made it clear that his resignation came after weeks and months of failure to gain support from Gorbachev for the radical line. 'The only thing I needed, wanted, and expected from the president was a clear delineation of his position, a direct rebuff to the right-wingers, and an open defence of our common position. I waited in vain.' Shevardnadze was bitter at what he regarded as Gorbachev's determination not to see what was happening. 'Everything, even resigning from the team, was in vain. The president always remained deaf to the advice of the people genuinely loyal to him . . . Did he not see it? Or did he not want to see it? Or was it something else? I don't know.'

The Shevardnadze resignation was the most politically charged event in Moscow since Gorbachev came to power almost six years earlier. If people had not yet focused on the dangers of an impending crackdown, they could now no longer fail to do so. Every indication was that the Soviet Union was spinning out of control. Whether Gorbachev was in league with the hardliners, or had become their pawn, or was merely unwilling to stand and fight against them, now hardly mattered. In each case, the disastrous effect would be the same.

12 Crackdown

'Owing to the aggressive behaviour of a group of militants, tear-gas grenades had to be used. In retaliation, stones were hurled and shots fired. An officer was killed. . . . Soldiers had to return fire.' Thus Soviet television, on 13 January 1991, reported a regrettable incident that had taken place in the Lithuanian capital, Vilnius, in the early hours of the same day.

The reality of Bloody Sunday — as the liberal Soviet press soon dubbed it — was grimly different. Thousands of demonstrators formed a human barrier to protect the Lithuanian television tower from attack by Soviet troops. The crowds that gathered included mothers with young babies and old-age pensioners. Men and women sang songs as the tanks began to rumble through the town. They linked arms as the Soviet troops used tear-gas and smoke bombs against them. Then, just after two in the morning, the shooting began. The gun turrets of the tanks swept backwards and forwards, and there was the crack of automatic weapon fire. Some were shot dead, some were crushed by the tanks, which crunched over cars and people alike. That night, thirteen Lithuanian civilians died.

This was the lethal flick of the dying monster's tail about which the Balts had been warning for two years. The lies and the deaths could not conceal the reality: the Communists had finally lost control. Even from the hardliners' point of view, the violence — which was intended to intimidate the population — was wasted. A teenage girl was unbowed: 'The soldiers started shooting right at us. We have no weapons. But I am more angry than afraid.'

Shevardnadze, with his spectacular resignation three weeks earlier, had done his best to raise the stakes. But Gorbachev had slapped him down — and the West was relieved that Gorbachev was still in place. If Gorbachev was still in charge, ran the argument, then all was well. In his New Year address, Gorbachev described the integrity of the Union as a 'sacred cause'. So sacred that the violence to keep it together had already begun, even as he spoke. Throughout December, there had been several unexplained bomb explosions in the Latvian capital, Riga, which damaged Communist Party buildings, but caused no injuries. The Balts – who had always scrupulously avoided violent resistance – feared that the explosions could provide a pretext for the army to move in.

Further violence came on 2 January, when interior ministry troops seized a printing house in Riga, on the pretext that it belonged to the Communist Party. Five days later, in accordance with the Gorbachev decree of the previous month, troops were sent to enforce conscription in the Baltic republics – where less than one in four had answered the Soviet call-up; the overwhelming majority were doing the alternative, civilian service introduced by their own republican governments. With the increasing threat of a Soviet crackdown, draft evaders were officially advised to go into hiding.

On 7 January, Gorbachev ordered airborne troops into the three Baltic republics. Meanwhile, protests against price rises in Lithuania, especially by the Russian and Polish minority, led to the resignation on 8 January of the Lithuanian prime minister, Kazimiera Prunskiene, which enabled Moscow to describe the situation as unstable. More and more troops arrived in Vilnius and Soviet military vehicles appeared in many parts of the city; the railway station was closed. With the atmosphere becoming more tense by the day, huge crowds filled the centre of the town.

The West, at that time, had understandably fixed its attention elsewhere. The countdown had begun for a war against Iraq that seemed inevitable. The world held its breath as UN Secretary-General Javier Perez de Cuellar continued his last-minute peace shuttles before the 15 January deadline for Saddam Hussein to pull out of Kuwait. Baltic leaders warned publicly that the Soviet leadership could be expected to launch a crackdown at exactly the same time as the Gulf War, in the expectation that the bloodshed in the Baltic would go unnoticed because of the bombs over Baghdad.

Certainly, all the signs of an impending crackdown were there. On 10 January, Gorbachev sent an ultimatum to the Lithuanian parliament – or, as he described it, the 'Supreme Soviet of the Lithuanian Soviet Socialist Republic' (which had voted itself out of existence ten months earlier). Gorbachev's message, read out on Soviet television, accused the Lithuanians of 'gross breaches of, and departures from, the constitution of the USSR and the constitution of the Lithuanian SSR'. In addition, he complained, the Lithuanian government had pursued 'a policy aimed at restoring the bourgeois system and ways that run counter to the interests of the people'. The tone was all too similar to the warnings in the Brezhnev era before the tanks came.

Gorbachev demanded that all acts that contradicted the Soviet constitution should be revoked. The following day, in apparent response to his televised statement, an ominously named National Salvation Committee was set up in Lithuania, demanding the imposition of presidential rule. The leaders of the Baltic republics called for a renunciation of further military force, but without much hope that their voices would be heard. Increasingly, it was clear that it was not a matter of if, but when.

The committee issued a statement declaring that it was taking over 'all powers in Lithuania'. The committee's statements were widely quoted by Tass and on Soviet television, although it remained a shadowy organization, without named leaders. The committee accused the Lithuanian government of bringing the republic 'to the brink of poverty, political reaction and national strife', and added: 'They claim that they are acting in the interests of the people, but this is a lie. They are struggling for money, property, foreign trips and power.'

On 11 January, the same day that the salvation committee announced that it was taking power, Soviet troops seized the main press building in Vilnius and stormed the defence council – in effect, Lithuania's defence ministry. Outside the Lithuanian parliament, a crowd of 10,000 linked arms. One demonstrator summed up the mood: 'If they want to take this building, they will have to drive their tanks through the crowds.' Which, not long after, they did.

The brutal attack entered the history books – as the crowds, who risked and lost their lives, knew that it must do. The killings in Vilnius increased the determination to resist and proved to be a key moment in accelerating the disintegration of the Soviet Communist state. After the killings, thousands of Lithuanians impaled their Soviet passports on the steel fences covering the barricades across the entrance to the parliament building, in a symbolic severing of all connections with the USSR. Awaiting further attacks, Lithuanians barricaded themselves inside the sandbagged parliament. There were some rifles and dozens of Molotov cocktails, but many of the volunteers in the parliament were armed with nothing more than sticks. It was a purely symbolic resistance: all those who came to the parliament were ready to lose their lives. It was intended to make the human and political cost, for the attacking forces, too high. It was clear that many people would die. Outside the Vilnius parliament, waiting for the next Soviet attack, a Western reporter confessed to feeling afraid. The response from a Lithuanian was almost envious: 'That's because you have something to lose.'

Gorbachev, who had not hidden his desire to be rid of the problems caused by the troublesome Balts, denied prior knowledge of the killings, as did the defence minister, Dmitry Yazov, and the new interior minister, Boris Pugo. Even now, however, Gorbachev — who was 'unable to come to the phone' when Landsbergis telephoned him as the attack on the television tower began — did not condemn what had happened. On the contrary, he insisted that it had been a defensive action, by the Soviet side. His anger against the Balts on Soviet television was clearly real.

In Riga, meanwhile, the killings were just getting under way. On 16 January, one man was shot dead by Omon, the hated Black Beret forces of the Soviet interior ministry. Barricades were erected all around Riga's Old Town, including the streets surrounding the republic's parliament. Night after night, huge crowds filled the city centre, in defence of the further violence that they expected and feared. Yet the atmosphere was almost one of celebration. Typical were Privite and her husband Janis, a forester, who had come specially by bus from the small town of Talsi, fifty miles west of Riga. When I met them, they were whirling round and round to the sound of Latvia's Isabella waltz, played by a brass band just near the Dom, the old cathedral. It was two in the morning on 20 January; Roberts Murnieks, the driver killed by the Black Berets, had been buried only the previous afternoon, at a funeral attended by thousands. And yet the city continued to party. The philosophy of Privite and Janis was, quite literally: let us dance and be merry, for tomorrow we may die. Privite — somewhat breathless from the dancing — said matter of factly: 'My children are all grown up. And I'm not afraid for myself. Why should I be?'

There was an almost unworldly innocence about the Balts' preparations. In Vilnius, they played classical music. In Riga, amid the wafting birch and pine-smoke of the fires at which Latvians gathered and chatted, there were jazz bands, rock bands, solo saxophones and guitars. The cinema showed free films all night (those who stuck it out until 5 am were treated to a showing of *Emmanuelle*). In the cathedral, people slept in the pews, or queued for the free tea and sandwiches which the local authorities had organized.

But, after the Lithuanian killings, everybody sensed that there was more to come. In one corner of Riga cathedral (reopened only recently, after decades as a museum), there was an improvised operating theatre. Near the entrance, stretchers stood against the wall, together with piles of gas masks. Doctors and nurses – Russians as well as Latvians – came here night after night, waiting for the moment when they would have to care for the victims of the violence that was to come. They were relaxed, as they chatted through the night. The threat of bloodshed was imminent and real – and seemed to frighten nobody. Lia, a sixty-seven-year-old cleaner, was one of those who spent the night in the cathedral. She said simply: 'We have lived through so much. All my family were in Siberia. Things will be bad now – but I think we will be independent. Even if I die, I want my children to see it.'

Latvia's turn came, just a week after the killings in Lithuania. On the night of 20 January, Black Berets stormed the Latvian interior ministry building in Riga. Five people died – two policemen defending the building and three civilians, including two Latvian cameramen, who were filming the attack from a park nearby. By the next morning, the places where they had been shot were miniature shrines, with candles and flowers. Small groups gathered, in silence. After the killings, an additional slogan appeared on one of the barricades, quoting the phrase that Primo Levi had used as the title for his story of Jewish partisans in the Second World War: 'If not we, who? If not now, when?' To resist the tanks was impossible; but not to resist was inconceivable. It was a message which would soon have direct relevance for Moscow, too.

A year earlier, when Gorbachev had visited Vilnius, attitudes towards him had merely been sceptical; now there was real hatred. Slogans compared Gorbachev to Saddam Hussein. In Kuwait, the war on Baghdad had just begun, which would soon oust Saddam from Kuwait. But the Balts felt that Gorbachev had been able to get away, literally, with murder. On the front page of one Riga paper, a photograph of Mikhail Gorbachev was seen hanging on barbed wire – with the caption, 'The Nobel prize-winner'.

Meanwhile, the mood was changing among Russians, too. Many Russians in the Baltic republics had long been wary of the loss of political and economic security that would come with independence. Some remained suspicious, even now. The pro-Moscow, pro-Communist movements like Inter-Front commanded support among those who felt that the Balts were trying to steal their birthright. Some Russians felt as strongly about living in a non-Soviet Estonia, Latvia or Lithuania as the *pieds-noirs* settlers in Algeria had felt about the loss of an *Algérie française*.

But fewer and fewer Russians now rejected the idea of Baltic independence entirely. Sergei Chernov, an Estonian government spokesman and himself an ethnic Russian, suggested just after the Vilnius massacre: 'The Russians here understand that the Soviet Union offers no food, no prospects, no freedom. Just the same Communist power. Our government gives them hope – which Gorbachev cannot do.' The Russian-language paper *Sovietskaya Estonia*, produced by ethnic Russians, now had an editorial line which was very clearly in favour of a non-Soviet Estonia. The paper compared the ultimatums of the pro-Kremlin faction to the Soviet ultimatums of 1940, when Stalin had annexed the Baltic states.

Russian disillusion, because of the pro-Kremlin violence, was growing all the time. In Riga, at an all-night flower stall near Freedom Avenue – formerly Lenin Avenue – one woman said: 'I'm a Russian. But what would you feel if you saw your country being terrorized? I support the Latvians. What's happening here in the Baltic is Red Terror, that's all.' In the Old Town, a group of workers erected a kind of Berlin Wall – a solid, ten-foot concrete barrier – to protect the parliament. The Russian builders insisted that Moscow was wrong to oppose Latvian independence. 'We're for independence. And sooner or later, it will happen,' said one. His colleagues said they were building the wall against the Communists – 'against the CPSU'.

Gorbachev continued to complain of Baltic extremism. Yet it was difficult for him to sustain his argument that Baltic independence was intrinsically anti-Russian when the most popular Russian politician in the country flatly condemned the violence – in the way that Gorbachev refused to do. Immediately after the shootings in Lithuania, Yeltsin flew to Estonia and signed a joint declaration, together with the three Baltic presidents, which protested at the killings and the use of Soviet troops. To Gorbachev's fury, Yeltsin suggested the creation of a non-Soviet (and, by implication, non-colonial) Russian army. He even encouraged mutiny, arguing that Russian soldiers should not allow themselves to be used 'against the rule of law, against the Baltic nation'. Gorbachev retorted that Yeltsin must be losing his mind.

Crucially, the unrest was now beginning to feed back into Russia itself. On Freedom Avenue, a Russian-language slogan showing the Soviet Communist Party with a swastika said: 'Today, Lithuania, Latvia and Estonia. Tomorrow: Leningrad? Moscow?' By now, this was seen as more than mere Baltic rhetoric. The threat was taken seriously in Russia, too. A week after the Lithuanian killings, and just hours before the Black Beret attack in Riga, came one of the biggest protest demonstrations that Moscow had ever seen. A quarter of a million people poured down Gorky Street – which was now Tverskaya Street once more, as it had been until 1932 – into Manege Square. In 1968, just eight people came on to Red Square and waved the slogan 'For your and our freedom', before being taken off to jail. Now, hundreds of thousands were prepared to come out on the street – believing that the freedom of the Russians and of others was indeed inextricably linked. Immediately after the killings, Sakharov's widow, Elena Bonner, called for Sakharov's name to be deleted from the list of Nobel prize-winners, saying that she did not wish it to stand alongside that of Gorbachev. Now, slogans in Moscow declared: 'Gorbachev – executioner', and showed pictures of the Soviet leader, his face as if smeared with blood. Such Russian solidarity with the Balts was, for the Kremlin, the most alarming development imaginable.

Not all Russians shared the pro-Baltic feeling, or were in favour of the mass demonstrations in Leningrad and Moscow. As Ligachev had reminded his comrades, a quarter of a million people did not represent the nine million inhabitants of Moscow, let alone the 150 million inhabitants of the Russian republic. Some passers-by were hostile and thought there should be more *poryadok* – order, or discipline. One grim-faced Muscovite declared: 'These people don't want democracy. They want anarchy.' None the less, the very fact that this huge demonstration was taking place was remarkable. Russia had already changed – and was continuing to do so.

One sign of the new shift in mentality – a sea-change whose importance would be proved in just a few months' time – was the Soviet newspaper coverage of the Baltic killings. Gone, now, was the early lickspittle version of *glasnost*, which hit out at permitted targets but implied that the Soviet leadership, in its new *perestroika* guise, was infinitely wise and entirely miraculous. Gone, too, was the cautiously critical tone of 1989 and early 1990, when liberal papers merely hinted at the taboo topics – including Lenin, or even (most daring of all) Gorbachev – with a nudge-nudge of disrespect. Now, no holds were barred.

The daily *Komsomolskaya Pravda* – theoretically, the paper of the Young Communist League – carried a front-page headline which asked simply: 'Tbilisi. Baku. Vilnius. What next?' A photograph from a pro-Baltic protest in Leningrad showed the slogan: 'The tragedy of Lithuania is our tragedy.' *Komsomolskaya Pravda* launched a bitter attack on the 'highly distorted' news coverage of Soviet television, commenting: 'In Lithuania blood was being spilt – and they showed us Walt Disney cartoons.' The new *Niezavisimaya Gazeta* (literally, 'The Independent Newspaper') carried a front-page cartoon showing a Soviet paratrooper stamping on Lithuania and declaring: 'With a fraternal greeting.'

The front-page headline in the armed forces daily, *Red Star*, sagely quoted a statement by Gorbachev that 'dialogue is necessary'. But other papers did not let the Soviet president off the hook so easily. *Komsomolskaya Pravda* quoted his more hardline remarks, before and after the killings. Under the mocking headline 'Official Versions', the paper quoted the catalogue of complaints from Gorbachev about the gross violations by Lithuania of the Soviet constitution. The weekly *Kommersant* (closed down in 1917, 'for reasons beyond its control', as the paper noted) said that the killings in Lithuania marked the attempt to 'replace a democratically elected government with a Moscow-backed puppet regime'. *Moscow News*, which had once been a tame Brezhnev paper and then became a semi-tame Gorbachev paper, now turned on the Soviet leader himself. It carried a headline that declared: 'Unwilling to go, the regime stoops to crime.' The paper criticized Gorbachev for trying to justify the military action in Lithuania, and asked: 'After Bloody Sunday in Vilnius, what is left of our President's favourite topics of "humane socialism", "new thinking" and the 'European home"? Virtually nothing.'

And so it went on. Gorbachev was furious and called for a suspension of the liberal new press law. But the papers remained undaunted and appeared to retort: 'Close us, if you dare.' Yuri Karyakin, in *Moscow News*, said he was 'flabbergasted' by Gorbachev's tone. But he added, in remarks that would have considerable relevance in the months to come:

> Hundreds and thousands of bottles were opened in the last six years, and their genies couldn't be enticed back inside or sealed up any more. How can that be done? Through censorship? By people like Kravchenko? By means of calling retired people like Ligachev back to work? By jamming foreign broadcasts? By reintroducing control over photocopying machines? Too much truth is out. Too many people can now know the pangs of conscience, and that cowardice is abject. In many people, courage has been reborn.

Rebellion was widespread: *Komsomolskaya Pravda* published an open letter from sixty leading actors, playwrights and producers in which they said they would refuse to work for Soviet television until the 'garrotte of censorship' was lifted. Poland saw such a boycott in 1982, after the declaration of martial law. Czechoslovak actors and musicians organized similar actions in 1989, as the pressure on the authorities grew. In Russia, though, this was new – even, though it seemed a dangerous word to use, revolutionary.

The Soviet leadership could no longer simply flick its fingers and get its undemocratic way. The popular television current affairs programme, *Vzglyad* – which had already run into trouble on several occasions in the past – was taken off the air after making a programme about the Shevardnadze resignation. Such commentaries the Kremlin did not need. But the *Vzglyad* team protested publicly – and, in a development unthinkable in the past, continued working, despite the ban that kept them off the screens.

There was an attempt, too, to silence a Moscow news agency whose coverage was sympathetic to the Balts. Interfax had begun life harmlessly enough, as a loyal, pro-Gorbachev offshoot of Radio Moscow. It brought in useful hard currency by offering its daily reports (distributed by fax, as its name suggested) to foreign correspondents and businesses in Moscow. By 1991, however, it was too independent-minded for its own good. But the decision to get rid of Interfax backfired when Yeltsin provided the agency with alternative premises; in practice, Interfax (no longer connected with Radio Moscow) continued its operations – after signing off, with a dramatic and defiant final burst – almost uninterrupted.

In another attempt to curb the rebellious spirit, Radio Russia – a new radio station for the Russian republic – was relegated to a wavelength where millions of Russians could no longer hear it. When the head of Russian broadcasting protested, he was told by Gorbachev's new man, Leonid Kravchenko, that the initiative came directly from the president. (On Kravchenko's desk at the Soviet television centre, there was a clutch of phones, including a Kremlin hotline, the so-called *kremlyovka*. This carried a scruffy piece of sticky tape, which declared simply – lest anybody should dare to forget – 'Gorbachev'.) Kravchenko complained that Radio Russia was a hostile station, with a 'vile' attitude. Its main crime was to have taken a clearly non-Communist line: it was sympathetic to the Balts and highly critical both of Gorbachev and of the CPSU.

Indications of the newly subversive mood could be found in the most surprising places. In a building just off Pushkin Square that had until recently been the House of the Old Bolsheviks, there was now a performance devoted to what a programme note called 'the cabaret show which had been the life of our country for the last seventy years'. The master of ceremonies gave a historical sketch of the situation before the then-fashionable Bat Cabaret, in its first incarnation, was forced into exile in 1917. 'Meetings, demonstrations, empty shelves, uprisings at the edge of the empire − and everybody expected a change of government ...' He added − to disbelieving laughter: '... I'm talking only of 1912.'

On stage, there was an abundance of scratchy violin music, to create the obligatory nostalgic mood, together with a sprinkling of singing-and-dancing frivolity. But there were plenty of hints of the serious threats, too. Assurances of complete freedom were given, even as a soldier leaped forward with riot shield. One man, speaking in Gorbachev's distinctive southern accent, proclaimed: 'There are two opinions. Mine. And the incorrect opinion.' He added: 'Only dictatorship can save the people from capitalism.' The audience, facing emptier shops than ever before, roared with delight. Truly, Russia − obedient, unquestioning Russia − had changed.

The Bat Cabaret was just one among many performances that marked the new disrespect for the very foundations of the Soviet state. In the early years of *perestroika*, the theatrical surprises were mostly confined to plays that slammed the bureaucrats, or mentioned Trotsky favourably. Now, even the most anti-Soviet work ever written was powerfully brought to life on stage − and nobody raised an eybrow. The director of the stage version of *Gulag Archipelago*, Vyacheslav Spetsivtsev, was eager to insist that *Gulag* should not be seen as mere history. 'Our society is the creation of the *Gulag*. Everything that we see today is the result of the *Gulag*.' He asked the audience to stand, before the performance began, in silent homage to those who had died in the Baltic a few weeks earlier. The message of the play − which used the relentlessly cheerful songs of the Stalin era to hammer home its point − was simple: the Soviet system that was created by Lenin, and developed by Stalin, had destroyed the freedoms that the Baltic republics and others might otherwise have enjoyed. And, in so doing, the system destroyed any hope for Russia itself, as it emerged blinking into the world from the collapse of the tsarist empire. One woman wrote in the comments book in the theatre foyer: 'When I heard that one worker in our factory had given up his party card after reading this book, I understood how much we are crushed, and how they have hidden the truth in vain. Such performances are necessary − for the truth, however bitter it is.'

Performances such as those at the Bat Cabaret or at Spetsivtsev's theatre were, in one sense, unimportant, for they were seen by a relatively small number of people. But they were symptomatic of the much greater changes that were taking place. The street protests brought a quarter of a million on to the streets. The liberal press had a circulation of tens of millions. And popular television programmes had viewing figures of more than 100 million. There was no corner of the country that was unaffected by the challenges to the status quo. It was a crucial change. In the weeks after the Lithuanian killings, the writer Alexander Kabakov reflected on the changes that had already taken place, even as the authorities tried to strangle radical voices and as some kind of attempted crackdown seemed increasingly inevitable:

> I don't feel like being afraid, and that's an end of the matter. We've drunk the antidote. Fear, which poisoned us all our life, slowly but surely — like an ancient venom — did its job. It killed people. But freedom, which we greedily fell upon, killed fear within a few years. We've become totally different, having discarded the principal specific symptom of *homo sovieticus* ...
>
> We have been given freedom in the same way that they now want to lease land — in word only, as attempts are now being made to turn leaseholders back into serfs. Yet freedom differs from property. It permeates the substances of whoever uses it, even temporarily. And we can't give it up, even if we wanted. It is not us who possess it, but it which possesses us. In the long run, what can they do to us? Suppose they kill us. But we've already become free. They can't rob us of that.

The next official turn of the screw came with a decree which took effect on 1 February, authorizing military vehicles to patrol the streets of Moscow and other cities. Theoretically, the patrols were in order to combat rising crime. Certainly, the crime rate had risen dramatically. Few believed, however, that the military vehicles had anything to do with reducing crime. Rather, it was assumed that the decision to put the army on the streets was connected with a possible crackdown on public unrest, if or when the authorities saw fit. One opinion poll suggested that only 15 per cent of people in Moscow and Leningrad were in favour of the new 'anti-crime' measures. When it came to an assessment of Gorbachev's role, the new spirit of rebellion was equally clear: a mere 15 per cent believed that his tough stance was helping to solve the problems in the Baltic republics; 70 per cent thought he was making things worse.

Many saw the new decree as a reason to be worried about what was still to come. Yet in a perverse way the new decree was also a tribute to the changes that had taken place. The fact that the Kremlin felt it necessary to have armoured personnel carriers available for use against the Russian people was an indication of how rebellious the mood had become; it was one more reminder of how desperate the Kremlin leaders had become, as they floundered in search of a way to save the dying system which had lasted for better or (mostly) for worse for seven decades. The authorities now feared the people as much as − perhaps more than − the people feared the authorities. No change of mentality would be more important in the months to come.

Beyond signing pieces of paper which authorized APCs on the streets, and beyond killing people in the Baltic republics, the leadership seemed bereft of a vision for the future. The government team got worse and worse. In December, Gorbachev had chosen as his vice-president Gennady Yanayev, a bureaucrat with a reputation as a dull hardliner. The Soviet parliament balked at appointing such a man to the heartbeat-away-from-the-Kremlin post. But Gorbachev became angry and used the familiar tactic − a threat to resign. 'If this leadership is to succeed, it must have the men it wants,' he told the Congress of People's Deputies. He forced the issue to a second vote, when the parliament, still piled high with Communists, did what it had been told.

Next came the new prime minister. Nikolai Ryzhkov, the Gorbachev loyalist who defended the military-industrial complex to the bitter end, resigned after suffering a heart attack at the end of December. The heart attack, though real (in itself unusual for a Communist resignation), was convenient: nobody wanted him in the job any longer and even Ryzhkov himself did not seem eager to stay. There was a clutch of politicians now waiting in the wings, with reformist economic credentials, who were ready to take his place. But Gorbachev's nominee provided yet another sign that all was rotten inside the Kremlin. Valentin Pavlov, the finance minister who had done his best to oppose market reforms and who was said by Gorbachev to be gifted with a profound knowledge of economics and finance, became Gorbachev's new prime minister, the day after the Vilnius killings.

With the appointment of Kravchenko as head of broadcasting, Pugo as interior minister and Yanayev as vice-president, Pavlov's appointment seemed to confirm the worst. One commentator asked why Gorbachev had not made the radical appointments that 'our society has been insistently demanding': 'What about farsightedness, advance thinking, or at least the instinct of self-preservation? Today, Gorbachev is surrounded by a quickly decreasing number of men capable of generating independent principled ideas ... Is he fully aware of the sort of game plan his new team is likely to offer?' But Gorbachev had no time for such talk – not from the press (which, he appeared to believe, should be grateful for the gift of *glasnost* and should know its place), nor from liberals in parliament, nor from former allies like Shevardnadze. Gorbachev had already stood by while his defence and interior ministers authorized civilian killings in the Baltic; now, he allowed his chosen prime minister to create further havoc with the already collapsing economy.

Pavlov's first important act as prime minister was to pop up on Soviet television news one January night, with the announcement that 50- and 100-rouble notes were no longer legal tender. The decree was supposed to mop up the surplus cash roubles that millions of Russians kept stashed away at home, literally under the bed or hidden at the back of a bookshelf. Theoretically, the measure was aimed at speculators and was intended to curb the black market. In practice, black marketeers (who used the US dollar or gold and diamonds as their main currency and scarcely bothered with useless roubles) had ways of circumventing the ban. It was therefore the ordinary Soviet citizen who was worst hit.

In a country where state bank accounts were (understandably) distrusted by a large proportion of the population, where cheques were almost unknown, and where even large purchases, like cars, were made with huge wads of cash, the cancellation of the banknotes had a devastating effect for the most vulnerable. A maximum of 1000 roubles – about three months' salary – could be officially exchanged. But the rest was, from now on, of use only for decorative or hygienic purposes. The cancellation of the banknotes might have made some sense if accompanied by other measures. Pavlov's decree was, however, carried out in isolation and therefore seemed unlikely to bring any benefits at all.

Pavlov subsequently claimed that (unnamed) Western banks had been planning an economic coup, which had been prevented by a matter of hours. According to Pavlov, roubles were to be smuggled from the West into the Soviet Union in order to create a financial war, depose Gorbachev and change the political system. Certainly, many people were involved in all sorts of shady deals, but as for deposing Gorbachev – most bankers and politicians in the West thought of little else but how to keep him in power. Soviet bankers and economists ridiculed Pavlov's claim; within a couple of months, embarrassed by the implausibility of it all, even Soviet officials tried to bury it.

There was more to come. A few days after the announcement that wiped out people's savings, Gorbachev signed a decree which gave the KGB sweeping new powers in the investigation of economic sabotage – a phrase which had an unhappy ring of the Stalinist era, when people were taken away and shot for sabotage, organized by Trotskyist and imperialist agents, and other assorted enemies of state. Under the new decree, KGB officials were allowed to enter buildings 'without hindrance' if they deemed it necessary. Theoretically, the decree was to improve the supply of consumer goods. In reality, it merely heightened the tension and the uncertainty. There had been little confidence before; now, there was none. The new powers given to the KGB (described, even by Tass, as 'very extensive') could be used against Soviet citizens and against Western joint ventures alike. All efforts were being made, it seemed, to push the economic changes into reverse.

By now, cynicism was total. There were, according to one joke, two possibilities for the recovery of the Soviet economy. One: the Soviet Union sorts out the problems by itself. Two: Martians land in a UFO and set everything to rights. Naturally, it was emphasized, the second possibility was much more realistic.

Pavlov's decrees in January 1991 appeared to indicate continuing attempts by the authorities to fend off the ultimate surrender – the scrapping of the old economy and a new start. For the moment, there was a new kind of stagnation. It looked increasingly as though it would take a fatal crash before a true change of direction would be introduced. Pavlov, as his later actions made clear, had no intention of introducing changes that might dismantle the existing system. Still, he was good at reciting the right lines, insisting that Moscow's problems in moving towards the market economy were not ideological but technical – all of which was just what the West wanted to hear. After the Baltic crackdown, the European Community suspended the billion-dollar aid package that it had agreed in Rome in December 1990. Gorbachev was not amused. When a trio of Community foreign ministers arrived in Moscow a month later, he exploded, insisting that the Europeans failed to understand the complexity of the situation in the Baltic republics. Hans-Dietrich Genscher, the German foreign minister, declared that it was important not to alienate Gorbachev, and others agreed. The upshot was that the Community reversed its freeze on aid, a month after the massacre, even as sporadic pro-Kremlin violence continued in Lithuania and the other Baltic republics.

Meanwhile, the union treaty, which Gorbachev had rejected and now embraced, topped the agenda. A referendum was announced, for 17 March, which asked the citizens of the Soviet Union if they supported the new union treaty. The Balts declined to take part, using the old argument that they had never been part of the Soviet Union in the first place. But, as a half-compromise, they organized their own referendums (which they described as opinion polls). Gorbachev declared the republican polls illegal and accused the Lithuanians (accurately enough) of trying to generate support for their separatist aims. The Balts ignored him. All three republics saw a turnout of more than 80 per cent for the polls on independence. In Lithuania, with an 80–20 ethnic split, 90 per cent voted yes. In Estonia, with a 60–40 ethnic split, 78 per cent voted yes. And even in Latvia, with a 50–50 ethnic split, 74 per cent voted in favour. With results like that, it was perhaps hardly surprising that Gorbachev wanted to ban the poll.

Elsewhere in the country, the union treaty got a yes-vote, of a kind. There were some absentees. In addition to the three Baltic republics, Georgia, Armenia and Moldavia boycotted the referendum, which asked: 'Do you consider it necessary to preserve the Union of Soviet Socialist Republics as a renewed federation of equal sovereign republics, in which human rights and the freedom of all nationalities will be fully guaranteed?' Two-thirds voted yes. Gorbachev triumphantly announced: 'Our Yes guarantees that never again will the flame of war scorch our land.' In fact, even after the vote was taken, there were as many arguments as before about what had, or had not, been agreed. Nothing was yet decided.

Meanwhile, the pressures on Gorbachev continued to build. Sometimes, the pressure came from surprising places. Only a year earlier, the opposition in the western republic of Belorussia was still harshly repressed. Zenon Pozniak, president of the republic's Popular Front, only gained his parliamentary seat in the face of considerable official harassment. Now, however, even once-calm Belorussia showed that it, too, could be radical. In April 1991, 100,000 went on strike. As so often, the trouble began with economic grievances, against the introduction of sharp price rises at the beginning of that month. Soon, however, there were demands for the abolition of Communist Party cells in factories and for the resignation of Gorbachev. By this time, opinion polls suggested that barely 10 per cent of the population supported the Soviet government.

Meanwhile, Boris Yeltsin was ever more powerful. Gorbachev banned a pro-Yeltsin rally (for reasons of public order and safety, he said), on 28 March. The rally was called to coincide with a new session of the Russian parliament, in protest at Communist moves to unseat Yeltsin as Russian leader. As had happened in so many contexts before, the ban served only to make the tone of the rally more radical and more defiant. Again, there were scarcely veiled official threats that the demonstration would be violently dispersed. None the less, among the thousands who defied the dangers, there was little sign of fear, as they confronted the troops in the swirling spring snow. Slogans included the demand: 'Save Russia from the Communist Party' and 'Say No to the Gorbachev Threat'. Yeltsin was, more than ever, the adored hero. One woman held a banner which read: 'Boris Nikolayevich, we are proud of you, not one step back.' She declared that she was not afraid: 'Let them shoot, let them shoot.'

The Russian stoicism, which had once worked in favour of the authorities, now seemed in danger of working against the system. Two years earlier, Russians were reluctant to become involved in public protests and preferred to stay at home. 'There's nothing you can do,' was a frequently heard phrase. Now, the balance had shifted: once people decided to go on to the streets, they were determined that nobody should scare them into going back home. This was a crucial change. In the end, the demonstration was yet another stand-off between the authorities and the people. The troops who poured into Moscow and lined the streets merely stood and watched as the demonstrators returned peacefully home. But the fact that so many people were ready to brave the expected violence – in other words, the Leipzig factor – should have been a lesson for the hardliners, who even now were trying to work out ways of putting the whole show into reverse.

Throughout this period, *Pravda* and the Communist press continued to snarl at Yeltsin, with his support for the Balts and his calls for a reduction in Communist power. But it was not only the Communists in Moscow who were reluctant to hear what Russia's elected leader had to say. Western politicians were almost equally impatient with Yeltsin's criticism of Gorbachev and the Soviet leader's hardline team. During a visit to the European parliament in Strasbourg, Yeltsin was told that he was excessive and irresponsible because of his clashes with Gorbachev. When Yeltsin tried to defend himself, Jean-Pierre Cot, the host of the meeting, told him sharply: 'We're in a democratically elected parliament here. If you don't want to hear what I have to say, the door is open.'

Others were almost equally abrupt. The president of the European Parliament, Enrique Baron Crespo, noted, with some understatement: 'The sympathies of the European parliament are rather on the side of the Gorbachev line.' For politicians in the West, the sympathies of the Russian people seemed, for the moment, an irrelevant element in the equation. It was the Communist Party leader who was – to use the familiar old phrase – the man they wanted to do business with. President Francois Mitterrand refused the Russian leader a proper meeting (though he grudgingly agreed to meet him for a handshake). As though to rub salt in the wound, Mitterrand received, on the same day and with full honours, Anatoly Lukyanov, the speaker of the Soviet parliament – an old party trusty and a friend of Gorbachev for four decades. Like most of the people who still surrounded Gorbachev, Lukyanov would soon show himself to be as unreformable as the Communist Party itself. Britain's new prime minister, John Major, on a get-acquainted visit to meet politicians in Moscow, 'did not have time' to fit in a meeting with Yeltsin, as requested by the office of the Russian leader.

In Moscow, all this seemed odd. By now, many of those who had been Gorbachev's key liberal advisers had defected. In the economic field, almost all the leading radicals were part of the Yeltsin team. Yeltsin himself remained, for many, an ambiguous figure whose long-term commitments to democracy were unclear. None the less, on any democratic checklist, he clearly scored better than Gorbachev, whose main advantage was the illusory stability that he provided. Yeltsin understood that the Baltic republics could not and would not stay in the Soviet Union; he worked hard to establish good relations with the Balts as they moved towards independence; and he tried to reassure other republics that Russia did not wish to dominate them, as it had done in the past. His commitment to radical economic reform was clear (his own grasp of economics sometimes seemed hazy, but he was prepared to give full backing to the radical team that he had gathered). And, above all, he constantly emphasized that the brain-dead but still-ruling Communist Party must give up its hold on power.

Gorbachev, on the other hand, publicly raged at the Balts and appeared to believe that the January massacre was their fault; his understanding of other republics' aspirations was patchy at best, chauvinist at worst. On the economy, he praised the hardline Pavlov and surrounded himself with old-time apparatchiks; when his best people deserted him, he blamed them for betrayal. And at the same time, he continued to proclaim constant loyalty to the genius of Lenin and to the Communist Party's vanguard role.

Thus, whatever queasiness some Russian liberals still had about Yeltsin, few were prepared to stake their money on Gorbachev. Some insisted that there should be a plague on both Yeltsin *and* Gorbachev. Others argued that Yeltsin, despite his unpredictability, was the man to stick with — for the moment, at least. The radicals' strength continued to grow — despite the fact that they were in permanent disarray. The hardliners in the Russian parliament were embarrassingly routed in their bid to dethrone Yeltsin at the end of March. They failed to get the no-confidence vote that they wanted and, after a split in the Communist vote, with reform Communists defecting to the Yeltsin camp, the Russian leader ended up in a much stronger position than he had been before. He was now on track for direct presidential elections — which would give his electoral credibility yet another boost.

Sure enough, on 12 June, Yeltsin was elected president with an overwhelming mandate. He gained a clear majority in the first round, with more than three times as many votes as his nearest rival, former prime minister Nikolai Ryzhkov. For Yeltsin, it was a triumph. Already, however, there was a hint of the worrying dangers that still lay ahead, as Russia emerged from the seven decades of totalitarian rule. In third place in the presidential race was a demagogic nationalist called Vladimir Zhirinovsky, who claimed to be an anti-Communist, but who consorted with Communist hardliners and anti-Semites. The vote for Zhirinovsky was a reminder of how simple were the answers that some people were looking for.

Meanwhile, though the style of the Russian leadership was becoming ever more radical, the style of the *vlasti* was not. On 3 June, Nikolai Trubin, the Soviet prosecutor-general, produced a remarkable report which claimed that the victims of the 'tragic events' in Vilnius had been 'shot and killed by Lithuanian militants who assembled around the radio and television centre, or were crushed by cars'. The report was startling in its blithe disregard for reality. Echoing Gorbachev's words in January, Trubin concluded that the violence had been triggered by the anti-constitutional activity of the Lithuanian leadership. As though in celebration of the Trubin report, there was another show of Soviet military force in Vilnius that very evening, with military checkpoints set up throughout the city. Thousands of Lithuanians again gathered outside the parliament in case it should be attacked.

The brief military takeover of central Vilnius was just one of many signs that conciliation was not yet the order of the day. Black Beret troops constantly attacked customs posts in the three Baltic republics — there were several dozen attacks in just a few months in which guards were beaten and customs posts burnt down. The worst attack came at the end of July, when seven Lithuanians were shot dead in an attack on a customs post near the village of Medininkai. The Soviet interior ministry denied responsibility; but few were convinced. *Moscow News* described the Medininkai killings as 'but a link in the chain of state-sponsored terror against Lithuania'.

There was, at this time, a twin-track policy. Gorbachev, wearing his conciliatory hat, met leaders of nine of the Soviet republics for talks about a new union treaty, at a government dacha at Novo-Ogaryovo on the outskirts of Moscow. On 23 April, they signed what came to be known as the nine-plus-one agreement, in which the signatories agreed in principle to a new union treaty, with power greatly devolved to the republics. In one sense, this was a dramatic breakthrough. Certainly, it marked much greater co-operation between Yeltsin and Gorbachev than had previously been seen. It angered the hardliners, too, as later events would make clear.

Even at this early stage, however, there were doubts over just how real this agreement would prove to be. One small indication of what was to come was that the Ukrainian president, Leonid Kravchuk, effectively disowned the nine-plus-one agreement in the parliament in Kiev on the same day that the agreement was announced to parliament in Moscow. And, as importantly, there was still no answer to the question of what would happen to the six republics who were determined not to sign. They were still being punished for wanting out. Lithuanian television, for example, was still occupied by Soviet troops.

Gorbachev still seemed as keen as ever to ride a middle way, balancing the hardliners against the radicals. Certainly, the hardliners were getting restive. In April, the Soyuz group suggested that Gorbachev should impose a state of emergency — or step aside and let them do it. There was sharp criticism of Gorbachev at a Communist Party plenum. Then, in June, Pavlov made an ill-concealed bid to thrust Gorbachev aside. He demanded increased powers for himself as prime minister, at the expense of the president. At a closed session of parliament, Pavlov was backed (and Gorbachev was criticized) by what would, within a couple of months, be the key members of the coup plotters' team: Pugo, the interior minister; Yazov, the defence minister; and Kryuchkov, head of the KGB. Kryuchkov, always the man with the most colourful allegations, told the parliament that he had reliable information of a CIA plot to subvert senior officials of the Soviet state. According to Kryuchkov, CIA agents now occupied key posts in the economy and government of the USSR. That was why Pavlov needed increased powers. It was good holiday-thriller stuff, even if it made no sense at all. But the hardliners' bid failed. They found, yet again, that they could make a lot of noise, but were unable to force their agenda through.

Gorbachev was angry at the rebellion, but, as he said later, he continued to trust his comrades. Meanwhile, in the field of economic reform, all remained as chaotic as ever. By now, a drift towards the market was taking place, by default. Even the diehard Communists proclaimed themselves in favour of the market, with the same unanimity that politicians had once proclaimed their loyalty to *perestroika*. But there was no sense of direction. Pavlov produced an 'anticrisis' programme in April, which claimed that all prices would be freed within eighteen months and talked of widespread privatization. Still, though, there was no commitment on the private ownership of land, and the plan was, in any case, based on fantasy. Pavlov insisted that it must be agreed by all fifteen republics in order to work, yet it was clearly unthinkable that the most rebellious republics (the Baltics, Moldavia, Georgia and Armenia) would sign any piece of paper that still tied them to the Communist unitary state.

After months of knocking at the door, Gorbachev eventually received an invitation to attend the meeting of the Group of Seven industrialized countries in London in July 1991. Even now, however, he emphasized his don't-try-and-interfere-with-us-Communists line. In his Nobel acceptance speech in June, he insisted that the Soviet Union was entitled to expect large-scale support, but, he said, it would be futile and dangerous for the West to set conditions for aid. So far, the structural changes that might finally help the situation to change had scarcely begun, despite all the noises of five years of economic reform. In the field of agriculture, for example, there had been no real attempt to reverse Stalin's collectivization of the 1930s. Less than 0.4 per cent of agricultural land was in the possession of peasant farms. Equally, the joint ventures that had been so much discussed and boasted of counted for less than 0.5 per cent of Soviet national income. Stanislav Shatalin, who worked closely with Gorbachev in 1990, had left his team, in despair, in January 1991. He argued, in an article written just ahead of Gorbachev's visit to London for the G7 summit in July, that it was necessary for Mikhail Gorbachev, Soviet president, to overcome the doubts of Mikhail Gorbachev, Communist Party leader:

> The economy, as a working entity, simply does not exist. Instead, we have an ideologically bankrupt system, where state property remains all-powerful. A system of 'serf law' is in force, where the absence of motivation means that there is no effective use of resources. Such motivation exists only in a market economy based on free enterprise. This, in turn, is impossible without private property – including private ownership of land...
>
> In the grip of invented ideologies, we attempted to cross the abyss in two jumps. There was a naive belief by government that we could 'invent a bicycle of our own': there was a proclaimed attempt to construct a market economy within the framework of 'socialist choice' and 'Communist perspective'. If we do not come to our senses, and end this pagan dance, then economic collapse will be inevitable ... Our nation knows all too well what life is like without a normal market economy based on free enterprise. It is beggary. Things simply could not be worse.

When Gorbachev arrived at the G7 meeting in July, he brought with him yet another economic plan: this time, a mongrel version of the pro-market plan which had been hawked around Washington by Grigory Yavlinsky (who had co-written the Shatalin 500-day plan the previous year). The Yavlinsky Plan, also known as the Grand Bargain, was written jointly with an American economist, Graham Allison, and assumed huge injections of Western capital. It was merged by Gorbachev with Pavlov's more cautious plan. A peeved Yavlinsky stayed in Moscow, in protest. Shatalin said, with reference to Gorbachev's planned merger, that shivers ran down his spine when he heard about it. Shatalin's radical plan had been abandoned after Gorbachev insisted that it should be merged with the conservative plan of the then prime minister, Nikolai Ryzhkov; now, the Yavlinsky plan seemed about to suffer the same fate. The West was enamoured of Gorbachev's politics, but was less impressed by his economics. Gorbachev left London with fond farewells, but with no cheques. He was promised associate membership of the IMF, which meant advice, but strictly no cash.

At home, it was not just Gorbachev's economics, but his politics that were under attack. The West wanted to ignore the continuing Baltic violence, the complaints about Gorbachev's hardline allies and the battles with the radicals. In Moscow, however, things were beginning to come to a head. Impatient with Gorbachev's refusal to heed their repeated pleas to move against the hardliners, Eduard Shevardnadze and Alexander Yakovlev – both once so close to the Soviet leader – announced the formation of the Democratic Reform Movement, an alliance that was dominated by Communist reformers, but included non-Communist democrats. Gorbachev claimed to welcome the new group, and some believed that he had personally approved the idea, as a way of creating an 'acceptable' party of ex-Communists. But his welcome was, in reality, barely lukewarm. As he himself later made clear, he still regarded any independent actions by the reformers as a personal betrayal.

Shevardnadze was rebuked by the Communist Party and summoned for what he described as an 'inquisition'. He refused to go and handed in his party card instead. Yet again, Shevardnadze felt betrayed by Gorbachev's lack of support. 'How did he reply to me and my friends? How did the leadership of the Communist Party respond? With threats of a party inquisition and punishment. New insults and insinuations. We were attacked – but Gorbachev was silent.' Certainly, nobody could mistake the strength of hardline feelings. On 23 July, just ahead of yet another central committee plenum, came the most notable anti-reform blast since the Andreyeva letter more than three years earlier. This time, *Sovietskaya Rossiya*'s clarion call was headlined 'A Word to the People'. It had twelve signatories, including well-known conservative writers and several senior military figures. The hardline Communists and the extreme nationalists had formed a coalition, bound together by lashings of purple prose:

Dear Russians! Citizens of the USSR! Fellow countrymen!

An enormous and unprecedented misfortune has occurred. Our homeland, our country and our great state, given to us for safekeeping by history, nature and our glorious forefathers, is perishing, breaking up and sinking into darkness and non-existence. This destruction is taking place with our silence, tolerance and accord. Have our hearts and souls really turned to stone? Is there not in any of us the might, the valour and the love for the fatherland that moved our grandfathers and fathers, who laid down their lives for the homeland on battlefields and in dark torture chambers? . . .

Why have crafty and pompous masters, clever and cunning apostates, and greedy and rich money-grubbers, sneering at us, mocking our beliefs and taking advantage of our naivety, seized power? Why are they stealing our wealth, taking from the people their homes, factories and lands, cutting the country into pieces, causing us to quarrel, making fools of us, excommunicating us from the past and alienating us from the future, thus dooming us to a miserable existence of vegetation in slavery and subordination to our all-powerful neighbours? How has it happened that we, at our deafening rallies, in our irritation and impatience, having longed for change and, wishing the country to prosper, allowed into power those who do not love this country, who fawn on foreign patrons and who seek advice and blessings across the seas? . . .

We direct our voice to the army, which has won the respect of mankind for the selfless deed of saving Europe from the Hitlerite plague; to the army, which has inherited the best qualities of Russian and Soviet arms, and which opposes aggressive forces. Our glorious defenders are living through difficult times. It is not the army's fault that it has been compelled hastily to leave its foreign garrisons, to be the subject of unpardonable political speculation, and to be subjected to the continuous attacks of lies and slander by irresponsible political intriguers . . .

Among the Russians, there are statesmen who are prepared to lead the country to a dignified and sovereign future. There are economics experts who are able to restore production. There are thinkers, creators of spirit, who see a national ideal. The Soviet Union is our home and stronghold, built by the great efforts of all the peoples and nations who saved us from disgrace and slavery in the times of the dark invasions! Russia, our only and beloved! She calls for help.

It was apocalyptic stuff. But, given its signatories, it could not be dismissed. Lunatic, yes; but not fringe. The twelve names included General Valentin Varennikov, chief of Soviet ground forces, and General Boris Gromov, Boris Pugo's deputy at the interior ministry, appointed by Gorbachev seven months earlier. It was, in other words, the heavy brigade. *Rossiiskaya Gazeta* retorted contemptuously the following day:

Of course, the appeal is timed to coincide with the next CPSU central committee plenum and is intended to rouse its participants to the highest extreme of political ecstasy. And, judging by the vocabulary and the total lack of argument, it was written in a state of impotent malice, when swearing and flashing one's eyes are the only things left to do … But in general, the soul gets very weary after reading such manifestos. First we had one Nina Andreyeva, now here are a dozen more. Where are they calling us, and why are they stirring up passions? It passes understanding. Clearly, Russia has really inexhaustible stocks – of public figures, of fools, and provocateurs.

The hardliners were especially indignant at a decree that had been issued by Yeltsin on the removal of Communist Party cells from the factories, on 20 July. It sounded like a merely symbolic declaration, but it wasn't. It was the most serious challenge that the party had yet faced. As Alexander Yakovlev pointed out, the leading role of the Communist Party had been eliminated in a legal, but not in any real sense. The party could talk unceasingly about its alleged new democratic aspirations, but, unless it gave up the right to its own presence in every factory or collective farm in the land, its all-pervasive, deadening influence remained. The eviction of the party from the workplace was thus the most serious sign so far that Yeltsin really meant business. From the party, there were howls of rage. The central committee said that this was an illegal act, violating international norms of civil and political rights. Gorbachev complained that 'nobody has the right to forbid the party to work with collectives'. The ever-loyal Soviet television news did not report the decree at all for two days. When *Vremya* finally did, it did so by broadcasting ten minutes of Communist Party protests.

Everything was now spinning in different directions. Internationally, there were yet more successes for Gorbachev. At a two-day summit with George Bush in Moscow at the end of July, the two leaders signed the Start treaty – which had been argued over, in one form or another, for almost two decades. For the first time, the two countries committed themselves to *reducing* their nuclear weaponry, rather than merely slowing down the speed with which the weaponry multiplied. The signing was only the logical conclusion of everything that had come before. None the less, it completed an important hat trick: first, agreement on medium-range nuclear weapons, with the signing of the INF treaty in Washington in 1987; then, agreement on conventional forces, with the signing of the CFE treaty in Paris in 1990; and now, in 1991, agreement on long-range nuclear weapons.

Already, however, there were signs of how far Gorbachev was beginning to be sidelined. Invited to an official meeting with Bush and Gorbachev, Yeltsin declined to play second fiddle. Instead, as president of Russia, he had a separate meeting with Bush in his own Kremlin office. Yeltsin continued to show the way forward, too. The day before the summit began, he signed a treaty with Landsbergis, the Lithuanian leader, which recognized Lithuania's independence.

On 2 August, Gorbachev delivered a fifteen-minute televised address to the nation, in which he announced that the union treaty would be ready for signing by some republics on 20 August. There were still many unanswered questions – not least in connection with Ukraine, which said it could not approve the treaty until after a parliamentary vote in September. It looked increasingly likely that the Ukrainian parliament would vote against. Meanwhile, there was a clear sense of an impending showdown. Shevardnadze declared, in an article published on 12 August:

> The situation here is like the renewed activity of a huge, long-dormant volcano. We feel the shocks, we see the eruption of lava, the dangerous emissions. But what vulcanologist can say how long this will continue, and how it will end? . . . I am worried that we are all losing crucial time. Destructive forces are gaining momentum.

Yakovlev gave even more explicit warnings. After being threatened with expulsion from the party, he made a pre-emptive strike, handing in his party card and declaring that he considered it 'no longer possible and, indeed, immoral to serve the cause of democratic reforms within the framework of the CPSU'. He also warned publicly – this was on Friday, 16 August – that 'an influential Stalinist group has formed within the party's leadership core' and that reactionaries were planning 'social revenge – a party and state coup'.

Obedient Communists were quick to respond. On the night of Sunday, 18 August – in other words, for the paper of Monday, 19 August – *Pravda* published a poisonous article about Yakovlev, in which it said that his allegations about a possible coup exceeded the bounds 'not only of party ethics, but of moral norms'. *Pravda* had always been good on moral norms.

Meanwhile, Gorbachev's annual August holiday in the Crimea – with his wife Raisa, daughter Irina, son-in-law Anatoly and granddaughter Anastasia – was coming to an end. He was due to fly back to Moscow on Monday afternoon and to sign the union treaty with some republics the following day. Everything was under control. Gorbachev had left the day-to-day running of the Kremlin in the hands of Gennady Yanayev, his loyal number two.

13 From Coup to Revolution

The music was the first and most ominous sign. Everybody who woke up to hear Tchaikovsky and Chopin on the radio knew that disaster had finally struck. As one Russian later remarked: 'Here, Chopin is not music. It's a diagnosis. They always play it to calm us down.' Then, interspersed with the music, there were the endlessly repeated decrees — expected, and feared, for so long. At last, after months of waiting, the heavy thunderclouds had burst. Beginning just after 6.15 am, on Monday, 19 August, announcers read out the decrees, on radio and television, in the robotic, funereal tone which is generally considered appropriate for the proclamation of a coup.

In view of the inability of Mikhail Sergeyevich Gorbachev, for health reasons, to perform the duties of the USSR president, powers have been transferred, in keeping with paragraph 7, article 127 of the constitution of the USSR, to USSR vice-president Gennady Ivanovich Yanayev, with the aim of overcoming the profound and comprehensive crisis, political, ethnic and civil strife, chaos and anarchy that threaten the lives and security of the citizens of the Soviet Union and the independence of our fatherland . . .

Then came an announcement signed by the group who said that they now ruled the country: the State Committee for the State of Emergency in the USSR. In order to prevent society from sliding into national catastrophe, the committee said, a state of emergency had been imposed, from 4 am that day. Then came a dose of coup rhetoric, in the style that was already familiar from 'Word to the People' four weeks earlier:

Fellow countrymen! Citizens of the Soviet Union!
In a dark and critical hour for the destiny of our country and of our peoples, we address you! A mortal danger hangs over our great motherland! The policy of reform initiated by Mikhail Sergeyevich

Gorbachev, conceived as a means to ensure the dynamic development of the country and the democratization of the life of its society, has, for a number of reasons, come to a dead end. The original enthusiasm and hopes have been replaced by lack of belief, apathy and despair. Authority at all levels has lost the confidence of the population. Politicking has left no room in public life for concern for the fate of our country and of the citizen. Malicious mockery of all the institutions of the state is being implanted. The country has in effect become ungovernable. Taking advantage of the freedoms that have been granted, trampling on the shoots of democracy, which have only just appeared, extremist forces emerged which adopted a course of destroying the Soviet Union, seeking the collapse of the state and aiming to seize power at all costs.

And so it went on, for twenty minutes. It covered all bases, from the flourishing of speculation and the black economy to the octopus of crime and scandalous immorality. The appeal declared: 'Only yesterday, the Soviet person who was abroad felt himself to be a worthy citizen of an influential and respected state. Now, he is often a second-class foreigner, who is treated with disdain or pity.' As in the 'Word to the People', the humiliation was an important theme. Yesterday, the Soviet Union had been a superpower, respected and feared by all. Now, no longer. But the emergency committee would set that right. With them, the path to Utopia was clear.

Without delay, we intend to restore legality, law and order, to put an end to bloodshed, to declare a merciless war on the criminal world, and to root out shameful manifestations, which discredit our society and humiliate Soviet citizens. We will cleanse the streets of our cities of criminal elements, and put an end to the tyranny of those who plunder the people's assets. We stand for truly democratic processes, for a consistent policy of reform, leading to a renewal of our motherland, to its economic and social prosperity, which will make it possible for it to occupy a worthy place in the world community of nations ... A steady increase in the well-being of all citizens will become the norm in a healthy society.

The new committee tried to pull a few populist strings. Its talk of combatting crime and speculation would be welcome. So, too – by those who believed them – would the promises that living standards would no longer fall. This populist, quasi-fascist guff was the familiar rhetoric of all would-be dictators. Crime, poverty, immorality, the humiliation of one's country – all these things would be solved when the new people took over. The signatories were several of Gorbachev's closest associates and the people that the liberals had protested about for so many months, only to be slapped down by Gorbachev himself. Altogether, five of the eight members of Gorbachev's powerful security council were signed-up members of the committee. There was Pugo, the interior minister, appointed by Gorbachev in December 1990, despite the liberal dismay; Kryuchkov, Gorbachev's appointee as head of the KGB, who was obsessed with CIA plots and who Gorbachev later said he thought to be a man of dialogue; Yazov, the defence minister, who Gorbachev had chosen in 1987 and on whose reappointment Gorbachev had insisted in 1989 (parliament had initially refused to approve him); Pavlov, the bureaucrat who Gorbachev had described as profoundly gifted; and, as the new figurehead president, Yanayev – whose appointment Gorbachev had forced through in December, with threats of his own resignation. All in all, there was little to cheer the Soviet leader as he sat in the Crimea, wearily contemplating his past, present and future.

On the streets, there was little immediate sign of reaction to what had happened. People hurried to work and tried not to think about the future. If everything was over, then the important thing was to survive. Partly, too, it was a kind of taking stock. You do not rebel until you know what you are rebelling against. On some routes into the city, Muscovites heading for work passed a long line of tanks along the road. In most parts of Moscow, however, there was nothing to indicate that this was different from any other Monday morning. One Russian journalist later commented on the extraordinary tranquillity of the city in the first hours of the coup. 'There was nothing unusual going on at all. Not a single soldier or tank. Just sunshine, flowers in the gardens, birds, people. Everything completely normal. Normal. There has been a coup, and nothing has changed. It's a sort of surrealism, as if one had arrived on another planet where everything is just the same.'

By mid-morning, many of the tanks that had been waiting on the edge of the city had moved into the centre of Moscow – though with a strange tentativeness; on their way into town, some tanks still observed the traffic lights. Within hours, the first clusters of people began to gather. But nobody knew what had happened, nor what they could yet expect. There was little immediate rejection of what had happened. There were even mutterings, in the long queues, of *'Pravilno'* – 'Quite right, too.' There was a growing fear of chaos in the Soviet Union and a resentment of the new poverty. There was anger that the 400-rouble average monthly wage no longer bought anything at all. For a pensioner, sometimes on barely 100 roubles a month, making ends meet was impossible. Many people felt a longing for some kind of new security, for somebody who would set things to rights. Queues formed outside the bread shops, following the old, Communist-bloc habit: when in doubt, buy more than what you need. There was fatalism, too. 'What's the use of getting upset?' one man asked. 'That will not change anything.'

Later, the chronology of events leading to the declaration of the coup became clear. On Sunday, 18 August, Gorbachev was at his dacha at Foros on the southern tip of the Crimea, overlooking the Black Sea, halfway between Sebastopol and Yalta. The three-storey villa on Cape Sarich, in one of the most beautiful areas of the Soviet Union, had already become controversial, after being specially built for Gorbachev, the slayer of privileges, on the same stretch of coastline where Brezhnev and other Communist Party leaders had had their luxury villas. Gorbachev's holiday home certainly lacked for nothing. Decked out with chandeliers, marble and ornately carved furniture, it included a fully equipped sports complex, with jacuzzi and huge swimming pool, a floodlit tennis court and a personal cinema, with a removable roof for summer viewing. Not surprisingly, Soviet television had never been allowed to peep inside.

After lunch on Sunday afternoon, Gorbachev began working on the text of the speech that he was due to give in two days' time, on the occasion of the partial agreement on the union treaty. He spoke to Yanayev in Moscow, who was courteous as ever, thanked Gorbachev for letting him know the time of his arrival and promised to meet him at the airport the following day. Then, at ten minutes to five, the head of the bodyguard announced that a group of people had arrived and was demanding to see Gorbachev. Gorbachev was not expecting visitors, and was suspicious. In an attempt to find out what was going on, he picked up one phone after another – only to discover that each of the phones was dead. As he later noted, with dry understatement: 'I realized that for me this mission would not be the kind I was accustomed to dealing with.'

Gorbachev's uninvited visitors were his chief of staff and long-time close aide, Valery Boldin; Oleg Shenin, a central committee secretary; Oleg Baklanov, Gorbachev's deputy on the defence council; and

Valentin Varennikov, chief of Soviet ground forces – and a signatory of the 'Word to the People' appeal the previous month. They told him that they had come from 'the Committee' ('What committee?' snapped Gorbachev) and that they needed a decree to be signed by him, Gorbachev. But if there was one thing that the arch-rivals Gorbachev and Yeltsin had in common, it was an absolute stubbornness. Gorbachev did not like ultimatums and his response was abrupt: 'To hell with you. You will kill our country as well as yourselves.' When his uninvited guests demanded that he resign, he retorted: 'You will not live long enough to see that ... Tell that to those who sent you.' It was, he said later, like talking to deaf mutes.

Gorbachev demanded that he be allowed to return to Moscow, though he later acknowledged that he feared for his life. It soon became clear that he was not going to dissuade them. Then Gorbachev changed tack. 'At the end of the conversation, using the strongest language that the Russians always use in such circumstances, I told them where to go. And that was the end of it.' So the four plotters returned to Moscow, with empty hands, on Sunday evening and reported back to Kryuchkov and the other coup plotters that the mission had failed. The plotters then set in motion all the plans for the coup itself, which was to take place overnight.

Well-orchestrated, the coup was not. The plotters said afterwards that they were convinced Gorbachev would go along with their plans for a state of emergency and claimed that it had been discussed in the past. Certainly, that provides one possible explanation for the confusion of their own plans. Yeltsin was alerted to the news on Monday morning, on a telephone that was still working. He had time to hold an early-morning council of war with other Russian leaders at his dacha at Usovo, just outside Moscow, and then left for the Russian parliament. After he had left, a group arrived to arrest the bird that had already flown. All domestic and international phone lines continued working, so that it was possible for information to be exchanged, across the city and across the country, and for that information to be beamed back, on Western radio stations, into the USSR.

It was a bungled tale compared with the declaration of martial law in Poland on the night of 12–13 December 1981. Then, hundreds of Solidarity leaders and activists across the country were rounded up in a single, pre-planned swoop in the early hours. All telephones, local and international, were cut so that it was impossible for Solidarity activists to warn each other. When Poles woke up on Sunday morning, the job was already over: their phones did not work and they found themselves listening to the country's Communist Party leader, General Wojciech Jaruzelski, telling them, over and over again, how he had put tanks on the streets in order to save the country. During those days in Poland, the information block was almost total. Only rumours ruled.

In Moscow, on the other hand, the authorities seemed determined to pretend that nothing had changed. One problem for the coup leaders was that the leaders of the opposition were all elected politicians. In Poland, Jaruzelski could arrest the Solidarity troublemakers, none of whom had constitutional positions, and be done with it. In the Soviet Union, on the other hand, where should the arrests begin and end? There was an obvious shortlist of a few dozen of the country's most prominent and popular radicals who needed to be put away. But where did that get the coup plotters? What price the committee's populism, if they had to lock up all the people who had constitutional legitimacy and popular support? A difficulty for the plotters was that democracy was no longer just an irritating excrescence, which could be lopped off, but had already infected the political structures, the system itself. Even more important was that people's minds had been infected, too.

During the morning, as the tanks began to arrive in the centre of Moscow, even the soldiers themselves were often confused as to why they were there. Young conscripts in the tanks and APCs in the city centre seemed anxious to emphasize that they, too, had no hostile intentions towards the crowds. On the streets, resistance was initially small. There were knots of demonstrators – on Manege Square, traditional scene of demonstrations, on Tverskaya Street, by Moscow city council, and, further away from the immediate city centre, near the Bely Dom, or White House – the Russian parliament. Initially, there was no mass resistance. People were too stunned for that. In any case, people were divided as to where they should go. But, already by lunchtime on Monday, the resistance had gained its first small victory. At noon, tanks arrived at the Russian parliament and stood in front of the building. It seemed that there would be an attack on the building itself and that Yeltsin and other leaders would be seized. The number of people present was tiny. But Yeltsin, who revelled in his own tales of derring-do, seized the opportunity that presented itself.

Unprotected except by the strength of his own personality – which not even his greatest enemies had ever doubted – Yeltsin came out of the parliament, shook hands with the men in the first tank and clambered on to the tank itself. The commander assured those standing there: 'We won't shoot Boris Nikolayevich.' As if in conscious imitation of Lenin's speech on an armoured car, subject of endless heroic paintings, Yeltsin spoke before the small crowd – and, much more importantly, before the microphones and the cameras.

> You can erect a throne using bayonets. But you cannot sit on bayonets for long. The days of the conspirators are numbered ... Clouds of terror and dictatorship are gathering over Russia. But they must not be allowed to bring eternal night. Our long-suffering people will find its freedom once again – for ever.

The committee, he said, had carried out a 'right-wing, reactionary, anti-constitutional coup'. It was a vintage Yeltsin performance. In his autobiography, he tells how, as a boy, he blew two fingers off one hand after stealing two hand grenades; how, as a young man, he moved a stalled lorry out of the path of an oncoming locomotive; how he climbed a crane in strong winds, to prevent it from toppling to the ground and causing huge damage; how a man who was about to kill him with an axe was scared off when Yeltsin shouted: 'Get out!'; and so on, a dozen such stories, whose punchline always involved a mixture of recklessness, decency and fair play. The big gesture was Yeltsin's traditional style. But, if some of the stories in his autobiography improved in the telling, it was clear that this story of courage, just before 1pm on Monday, 19 August, needed no embellishment. His action was crucial in turning the tide so early.

At that time, the crowd was small, but Yeltsin's appeal was broadcast – by a radio station operating illegally in Moscow and by foreign radio stations broadcasting back to millions, in Moscow and throughout the Soviet Union. Later on Monday afternoon, Yeltsin issued bullish decrees, declaring that the emergency committee was illegal, its members guilty of treason and its orders invalid on Russian soil. He ordered all army and KGB units involved in the coup to stand down and said that he was assuming control throughout the Russian republic. In essence, he was repeating the axe-trick that he had used to such effect while working at the Urals Heavy Pipe Construction Trust more than thirty years earlier: shouting loudly at a man who was about to slice his head in two, in the hope (or belief) that the thug and would-be killer would be cowed by the apparent show of strength. Yanayev rejected Yeltsin's decrees as 'unconstitutional' (which was rich, in the circumstances); but he was clearly unnerved.

In Moscow, the emergency committee held a press conference on Monday afternoon, where, only hours after seizing power, they showed a distinct lack of confidence. Pavlov was absent; it later turned out that he spent most of the coup in a drunken daze. Yanayev fielded most of the questions, with difficulty. He was clearly a nervous wreck. His hands shook as he accused the Russian leadership of playing a 'very dangerous political game'. Gorbachev — who watched the press conference on television in his luxury prison — later remarked on the obvious irony of Yanayev claiming that Gorbachev's health was poor when it was he who shook uncontrollably as he spoke. Gorbachev commented: 'What made the greatest impression on me ... was not what the plotters said at the press conference, but their pitiful appearance.'

Yanayev expressed his commitment to 'the reform programme' and insisted that everything would be fine with Gorbachev at the dacha. 'Mikhail Gorbachev is still enjoying rest and recuperation at the Crimean holiday location where he was on vacation when taken ill. He has become very tired after all his years in power and he will need a good length of time to recover his health.' He suggested that Gorbachev might, in due course, return to his duties, and added the sickening tribute: 'Mikhail Gorbachev did a great deal to initiate democratic processes in our country in 1985 and he deserves all our respect.'

'Very tired after all these years' was an interesting illness to contract so suddenly. It seemed that the plotters did not seriously expect anybody to believe them. The only alternative was to say publicly that they had ditched Gorbachev, and good riddance, but that, they were unable to do. However unpopular Gorbachev might have been, the hardliners were more unpopular still. Thus, on the one hand — with their promises of continued reform, improved living standards and a new Utopia — they were desperate to be accepted and approved of. On the other hand, they could be seen to be cheap liars. It was an unhappy balancing act, which would soon, for the plotters themselves, prove to be disastrous.

Out on the streets, resistance quickly began to build. Many in the Western establishment were queasy about the growing opposition to the crackdown. A former British ambassador complained about Yeltsin rallying resistance to the coup: 'He is clearly set on confrontation ... That is bad news for everybody, including us.' Another Western observer, noting the calls for demonstrations against the coup, said that resistance would be 'ill-advised', given the ban on all rallies and given the growing military presence in the centre of Moscow. The phrase reflected, with deadly accuracy, the Western view, so sharply at odds with the reality of living with an unwanted regime. In the literal sense, it was indeed 'ill-advised' for protesters to go out on the streets: by doing so, they risked being arrested or killed. But in a more important sense, it misunderstood the nature of all the cataclysmic changes in the Communist block in the previous two years — just as Western politicians had done when they assumed that the East European revolutions happened because Gorbachev willed them to do so. The mass protests in eastern Europe, in the Baltic republics and now in Russia, had *all* been ill-advised. They had been about the art of the impossible. If enough people grasped for the impossible at the same time (it did not need to be an absolute majority of the population: many could stand idly by), then the impossibility turned into reality. It was a matter of belief. When the balance of fear changed, the game was over.

The question was not: do enough Russians have the courage to risk their lives and, by doing so, to force the regime to surrender? Russian courage, in extreme circumstances, could not be in doubt, as the battle of Stalingrad and other dramatic encounters had clearly shown. Rather, the question was: do enough Russians care, as the crowds cared in eastern Europe and the Baltic states? Three years earlier, the answer would certainly have been no. Two years ago, maybe. Now, despite the still-widespread apathy and confusion, there were more positive signs. The darkened stage, where individuals each asked, in despair, 'What can I do alone, anyway?', had long since been flooded in light. The radicals knew that they were no longer isolated. On the contrary, it was they who — despite their incomparable chaos — had made the political running throughout the past year, even while the apparat used and threatened violence in order to hold on to power. That was why the hardliners found themselves in such angry despair.

The resistance was not only in Moscow. In Leningrad, extraordinary dramas began to take place. Orders were given for the arrest of the city's mayor, Anatoly Sobchak, but, like Yeltsin, he grasped the hardline nettle. He strode into the military district headquarters, where the local Communist Party leader and the local head of the KGB were with Viktor Samsonov, military commander in the district, who had announced on television that he was taking power into his own hands. Sobchak, a lawyer, started bellowing at them, arguing that they had no justification for obeying the coup plotters' orders. Not permitting any of them to interrupt, he told the startled trio: 'If you stir a finger, you will be put on trial, like the Nazis were tried in Nuremberg.'

It seemed to be pure, magnificent bluff, but it worked. Nor was it just bluff. Sobchak was telling the truth when he told Samsonov: 'Don't you see, General, what nonentities these people are? They will not retain power, even if they succeed in seizing it.' Samsonov had every reason later to feel grateful to Sobchak for forcing him to endure such a dressing-down. If Samsonov had continued to carry out the conspirators' orders, and if he had used troops against the crowds, then – like all the other coup plotters – he would soon have been arrested, or dead. As it was, the coup leaders shouted down the phone at him from Moscow, accusing him of selling out. But Samsonov seemed more frightened of Sobchak and of the people of Leningrad than he was of the blustering Yazov and the trembling Yanayev. That evening, Sobchak appeared on Leningrad television – which can be received in Moscow – and delivered blasts against the plotters, whom he referred to as 'former vice-president, former defence minister and former interior minister', as if they had already been sacked or jailed. Leningrad was, in effect, a free city from the afternoon of day one.

On Monday night, the Leningrad papers were published normally. The Leningrad daily, *Smena*, was typical, and remarkable. Down the right-hand side of the paper were published the decrees of the emergency committee, as ordered by Moscow. But across the left-hand side, the main headline read 'The putsch will not pass' – and full-scale broadsides were delivered against the plotters, together with reports of the resistance in Leningrad and elsewhere in the country. Next morning, Sobchak addressed a crowd of 200,000 that overfilled Leningrad's Palace Square – in front of the Winter Palace, whose storming marked the beginning of the Bolshevik Revolution. 'We are gathered here to express our firm resolve to prevent a *coup d'état* in the country,' he told the cheering crowds.

In Moscow, meanwhile, the small groups who had loitered at the Russian parliament during the day, waving the red, white and blue Russian tricolour and shouting 'Fascism shall not pass!', had swelled to several thousand by Monday evening. By now, it was clear that the parliament would be the main focus of resistance – just as it had been in Riga and in Vilnius. This began to give purpose to those who were there. They were still relatively small in number. But there were enough to ensure that any seizing of the parliament would already be bloody. By their own personal courage, they had already raised the stakes. Demonstrators began building barricades all around the building and hijacked buses to block the roads.

Many of those on the buses, on the Metro, on the busy streets, decided not to take part in any rebellion. They continued going about their business as though nothing had changed. They looked away as the demonstrators — cheerful and confident in the choice that they had made — headed for the White House through the cold drizzle. But, throughout Monday evening, the crowds grew. A curfew was imposed, together with an order to the army to suppress 'all instances of spreading of provocative rumours' or resistance to the new regime. But it was ignored. There was something of the atmosphere from Vilnius and Riga here — the solidarity, the knowledge that this was a turning-point. The protesters sang as they sat in the rain around their campfires. Well-wishers brought food and drink (non-alcoholic — all vodka was banned) to the defenders of the parliament. As in the Baltic republics, stalls were set up which served tea and sandwiches through the night and, as in the Baltic republics, improvised field hospitals began to appear. Some Lithuanians even travelled from Vilnius in order — in the words of a Russian woman at the parliament — 'to teach us how to build barricades and how to conduct ourselves'. For our freedom and yours; for your freedom and ours.

That night, too, came important psychological victories. Ten tanks defected to Yeltsin's side and took up positions in defence of the parliament. They could not achieve military victory against the over-whelming firepower of the pro-coup forces. But they were not intended to. It was the symbolism of the defection that counted. Nobody could be in any doubt: those soldiers who had defected to Yeltsin enjoyed high morale. Those who remained in the Yanayev camp — if there was such a thing, which soon came to seem dubious — were often unhappy and confused.

Although nobody knew it at the time, the crowds and the resistance, simply by being there, already won another important victory during that first night. It was not only the army that did not behave according to form. The KGB's special Alpha squad, which was involved in the seizure of the Vilnius television tower in January, received orders to storm the White House and arrest Yeltsin. A reconnaissance took place and arms and ammunition were handed out. The attack was due to take place at 3 am on Tuesday morning. But the KGB officers finally balked at the order: even they, not known for their soft-heartedness, thought the bloodshed would be too great. Physically, it could be done — it would have taken about half an hour, the KGB said later — but the cost would be too high. A plan to use helicopters in an assault against the parliament was also abandoned, apparently after threats by Yevgeny

Shaposhnikov, commander of the Soviet air force, that he would scramble fighters against such an assault.

At the same time, there were other important (if less life-threatening) forms of resistance. For the first time, the newly independent press could test its mettle. Already, with one of their early decrees on the first day of the coup, the plotters paid implicit tribute to how much Soviet society had changed by banning most of Moscow's best-known papers. The journalists could feel flattered by the change in attitude. Back in 1964, when Leonid Brezhnev and Alexei Kosygin led the palace coup against Khrushchev, there was no need for a press ban. All that was needed was an overnight change of party line, which would immediately be obeyed. (*Izvestia* dropped an evening edition while the new party line was straightened out.) Obedience was total. Journalists were not expected to think for themselves. They were expected to be mere ciphers of this week's Communist Party version of the truth.

Now, in 1991, papers could no longer be remodelled to the latest party line. As Alexander Kabakov wrote after the crackdown in January, fear was no longer all-pervasive. 'We've drunk the antidote,' he had suggested, and the optimism now seemed justified. When it became clear, for example, that *Niezavisimaya Gazeta* would not be allowed to print, journalists and printers secretly carried out the galleys of type and the proofs so that the paper could be illegally produced elsewhere. That they were able to do so, unhindered, was an indication of the plotters' chaos. But the fact that the editors and the printers were prepared to disregard the obvious risks involved in producing the paper illegally was also a reminder that Russians now lived in a quite different world.

News bulletins were clandestinely distributed, or pasted up on the walls of the underpasses and the Metro. Thus an almost free flow of information continued even during the coup. Journalists had been as craven as every other group in Soviet society – perhaps even more so – but now many of them had gained a dignity, which they did not wish to lose. Some remained untouched. *Pravda* had thundered, on Monday, that Yakovlev's predictions of a Stalinist coup exceeded the bounds of party ethics and of moral norms. Then, the following day, it contained the decrees of the self-same Stalinist coup – even as Yakovlev limped, with his war-wounded leg, to the barricades. For *Pravda* – literally 'Truth' – it was business as usual. But *Pravda* and its fellow-liars were in the minority. When the coup was declared, eleven leading Moscow papers banded together to from the *Obshchaya Gazeta*, or 'Joint Paper', with a front-page editorial signed by all the editors – including several who had been rebuked by Gorbachev in past months. In an article entitled 'What should we do?', the joint paper – flyposted across Moscow – declared: 'Different people at different times have come with tanks and promised food, tranquillity, order and peace. But those who listened to them only saw chaos and blood ... The putsch is weak. The putsch is only strong if we are afraid.'

Niezavisimaya's own illegal edition, produced on the first day of the coup, was categoric: 'The new regime cannot hold out for long.' On the airwaves, too, there was a breath of freedom. The Moscow Echo radio station, despite the authorities' efforts to silence it, broadcast from a tiny room inside the Russian parliament. The BBC World Service, Voice of America and Radio Liberty beamed their broadcasts to Moscow and were heard by millions across the Soviet Union – including, as it later turned out, the Soviet leader himself, listening on a little Sony radio with rundown batteries in the Crimea.

On Tuesday, apathy was still widespread. Millions of Muscovites went about their daily business. As one woman said: 'What can we do? We must just wait and see what happens.' But more and more people stood up to be counted. A demonstration was called for in Manege Square, which was completely blocked with tanks, so the protesters swarmed up the hill to the imposing eighteenth-century mansion on Tverskaya Street which had until 1917 been the official residence of the governor-general of Moscow and which now housed the city council of Moscow. From a balcony that looked across to the equestrian statue of Yuri Dolgoruky, founder of Moscow, Shevardnadze and Yakovlev spoke to the crowds. Yakovlev declared: 'They want to return us to the tunnel of death and Stalinism.' The coup would, he said, be defeated.

During the day on Tuesday, more than 100,000 gathered at the parliament, which was, by now, the focus for all protests. The numbers swelled when a procession of protesters arrived from the rally near Manege Square. Crowds stretched as far as the eye could see. Young soldiers aboard their tanks – covered with flowers and portraits of Yeltsin – seemed overwhelmed as the crowds tried to express their thanks. Many in the crowds came loaded down with bags of food. 'No, really,' pleaded one young soldier beside the parliament as an old woman forced yet another huge pie on him. 'I can't eat any more!'

Yeltsin appeared briefly on the parliament balcony, surrounded by men who protected him with bulletproof shields from possible sniper fire. The Russian leader told the crowds what they wanted to hear: 'Without your help, I can do nothing ... But together with you, and with the Russian people, we are capable of the greatest feats of heroism: we are capable of defeating these putschists and ensuring the triumph of democracy.' It seemed as though the cheering would never stop. Again and again, there was optimistic defiance. Elena Bonner told the crowds: 'We'll show them we're not mere cattle ... They cannot stand over us; we are above them, we are better than they, more honest – and we are many!' One man by the Russian parliament declared: 'We have won already. They should have got Yeltsin in the first few hours. Now, they are doomed to fail. They are just grey puppets and we are not afraid of them.'

Already, there was a sense of the absurdity of the plotters' behaviour. A military officer complained about the endless showings of *Swan Lake*, on all television channels, as the plotters floundered. 'Could it happen in any civilized country,' he asked, 'that the army takes over and all the people get is *Swan Lake* repeated four times on the television?' The non-stop diet of *Swan Lake* was much commented on in the days to come. A mocking badge soon went on sale which showed a picture of Yazov, the defence minister, labelled 'ballet soloist, *Swan Lake*'. Yazov's speech bubble declared: 'Dance, EVERYBODY!'

Yazov's problem was that nobody would dance to his tune. Mstislav Rostropovich, the cellist who had been banned from his homeland until the previous year, flew to Moscow when he heard of the coup, 'to be with my people and if necessary to die with my people'. Later, he described the special quality of the changes that took place during those days. 'People demonstrated *civic* courage. Russians were always thought of as being brave on the battlefield, defending their motherland. But often, we were not so brave at home. To die defending freedom here has in our past been to be dishonoured, to have your family dishonoured or worse, by those who won. That is what made many people pause, even now. But others broke that habit, and the psychological release is – and will be – tremendous.'

Initially, there had been much pessimism in Moscow about the possibility of defeating the coup. Russians explained why their compatriots would not rebel. That pessimism was understandable. Throughout eastern Europe in 1989, too, it had been possible to hear people explain – with sadness, but with conviction – why their country would not rebel. East Germans said that they, unlike the Poles, were too obedient; Czechs said they always avoided conflict ('Why are we such cattle?' asked one woman, after a too-small demonstration in October 1989); Romanians argued that the climate of fear was too strong and that, unlike Prague, there was no organized opposition which could lead a revolution. In each case, the arguments were partly valid. But, in each country, the part-truth was finally outweighed by a stronger reality. Each of those countries finally rebelled. Even in Albania, as late as autumn 1990, you could meet many people who told you that their country was different, that the Stalinist regime was too strong and that – to their regret – Albanians would not rebel in large enough numbers to force change. One did not need an especially well-polished crystal ball to reassure them that, if so many people, individually, were visibly yearning for change, they did not have long to wait before the explosion itself. It was, yet again, the 'What can I do alone . . .?' argument. It was just a matter of switching on the lights. Only two months after those conversations in Tirana, the lid blew, with student protests that forced a headlong retreat from Stalinism; free elections took place just four months after that, in spring 1991.

Thus, in Moscow, too, some people wondered on that first bleak, rainy Monday: can we really do it? Some argued later that the coup plotters' show of military force had itself been counter-productive, so little resistance had there been to the coup in its first hours. The military presence was presumably intended to instil fear. But it is difficult to persuade people that you have come to provide them with a better future if you also deploy tanks on their streets. Equally, if the plotters had *not* put tanks on the streets, still more people would have had no inhibitions about going out to demonstrate. For the coupsters, it was the old, unhappy dilemma that Communist leaders had faced throughout the past two years. As Shevardnadze later noted: 'The coup plotters took many things into account, except the most important: the years of *perestroika* had rid us of fear and we were different people now.'

When the coup began, the West was confused. With Gorbachev out of action in the Crimea and with his phone lines cut, it was assumed that the one man who was able to keep Russia moving towards reform was now out of action. In other words: this was the end. Helmut Kohl talked of the conditions for further Western aid to the new regime. President Mitterrand talked about the 'acting president' Yanayev. George Bush – who had also refused a meeting with Yeltsin – initially merely described the coup as a frustrating and unconstructive step, though he later covered himself, by acknowledging tentatively that 'coups do fail'.

By Tuesday evening, the fear of a possible attack on the parliament was greater than it had been at any time. Yeltsin spoke on the telephone to several Western leaders. John Major seemed shaken by his conversation with the Russian leader. 'We concluded our conversation, not at all certain what will happen in the next few hours.' Meanwhile, the Russian resistance continued to spread. Half of the mines in the Kuzbass were at a standstill. There were strikes, too, in Belorussia and the Ukraine. Already, there were the first hints that the plotters' nerves were cracking. On Tuesday night, it was announced that the drunken Pavlov had been taken ill with 'high blood pressure'. Reports of the resignation of Yazov had to be publicly denied. On Wednesday morning, the KGB was even forced to deny that Kryuchkov had resigned. The illnesses, rumoured resignations and denials of resignations all combined to heighten the sense of panic in high places.

The KGB – whose men had sat around drinking tea all day on Monday, waiting for orders – realized by Tuesday evening that the end was nigh. One KGB officer later described the mood: 'Many, especially those who had been so happy at the beginning, looked depressed and their eyes showed a presentiment of evil, as a dog does just before an earthquake. The dogs know something very bad is coming soon, but cannot understand quite what it will be.'

But though the KGB was beginning to realize that the game was almost over, there was violence to come before the final retreat. The tragedy began just a few minutes before midnight, near Uprising Square – which, like the nearby Barrikadnaya metro station, took its name from the 1905 rebellion against tsarist rule. A column of eight armoured personnel carriers, firing in the air, crashed through barricades and moved through an underpass at the junction of Tchaikovsky Street and Kalinin Avenue, a quarter of a mile from the parliament. They were, it seemed, aiming to take up positions further down the huge inner ring road. But though some of the APCs got through, several found themselves trapped in the underpass, with trolley-buses blocking the road ahead of them and street-cleaning machines cutting off their retreat. A tarpaulin was thrown over one of the APCs – which then drove backwards and forwards in blind panic and fury. One man was killed. His body was dragged along as the APCs fired in the air, wounding another man who was trying to pull away the body. 'Fascists!' chanted the crowds, as the APCs roared back and forth. One of the APCs was set on fire with a Molotov cocktail and the crew was forced to come out and surrender. The commander emerged, shouting: 'I am not a killer, I am an officer! I don't want any more victims, soldiers are abiding by orders!' In the meantime, though, the APCs continued shooting: a second man was killed. A woman fell under one of the

APCs. Moving to save her, a third man was run over and died.

As the crowds' anger and despair grew, some soldiers from the APCs now emerged with their hands up; one officer carried an improvised white flag. Others stayed inside the tunnel, apparently at a loss as to what to do next, until it was eventually agreed — by now it was almost six in the morning — that the remaining APCs should head towards the Russian parliament, under the Russian tricolour flag. The shooting was over, and there would be no more. It was the worst clash between rulers and ruled that the streets of Moscow had seen since 1917.

Brecht wrote: 'Unhappy the land that has need of heroes.' Perhaps. It is easier to live life in a country without such dramas. But unhappy, even more, the land that has need of heroes, and finds none. The death of those three men — Vladimir Usov, thirty-seven, an economist; Ilya Krichevsky, twenty-eight, an architect; and Dmitry Komar, twenty-three, an Afghan veteran — became a symbolic purging for the Russian nation. Russia owed them, and offered them gratitude. By Wednesday morning, near the intersection where the three young men had died, flowers were piled at makeshift shrines, amidst the tangled metal and shattered glass of the trolleybuses that had been used as barricades. Following the Russian tradition of placing food on memorials to the dead, there were sweets, apples, a meat sandwich and a glass of tea among the gladioli and roses.

If the fatal clash by Kalinin Avenue marked the worst point of the coup, it also represented the point at which the coup began to crack. The sense of popular confidence was growing, fast — just as the plotters' plans were descending into farce. Yeltsin suddenly announced to the Russian parliament that a 'group of tourists' had been seen on the way to Vnukovo airport. The plotters were seeking to flee. Plans were made to intercept them at the airport before they got away. What followed was an extraordinary made-for-the-movies race against time. Those who tried to chase the plotters to the airport arrived too late. The cavalcade of Zils had already swept through and the committee's plane, whose passengers included Yazov, Kryuchkov and Lukyanov, had taken off.

Ivan Silayev, the Russian prime minister, and Alexander Rutskoi, Boris Yeltsin's deputy, took a separate plane down to the Crimea, an hour behind Yazov, Kryuchkov and the others — and still not knowing what they might have up their sleeves. Silayev and Rutskoi travelled together with Yevgeny Primakov, one of Gorbachev's leading foreign affairs advisers, and Vadim Bakatin, the man who Gorbachev had sacked in favour of Pugo. They took with them thirty armed para-troopers, in case the plotters were still ready to resist. In fact, they arrived just in time for the dénouement. 'Welcome, everybody,' said a beaming Gorbachev in shirtsleeves, as the rescue party arrived.

The plotters, it turned out, had arrived, all bows and polite smiles, keen to explain to Mikhail Sergeyevich that it had all been a terrible misunderstanding and that they had never planned a coup in the first place. Gorbachev, not surprisingly, was unimpressed and refused to see Yazov and Kryuchkov. He did, however, receive Anatoly Lukyanov, his old comrade from law school, who insisted to Gorbachev that he was quite innocent of the whole affair. In reality, as soon became clear, Lukyanov's support for the plotters was crucial.

By now, the coup was beginning to unravel, minute by minute. By Wednesday afternoon, the tanks were on the move again − but this time, they were leaving town. Just before 5 pm, the ever-obedient Tass began talking of the 'former' emergency committee. Sixty hours after the committee's first solemn announcements, the coup was in tatters. Later that night, Gorbachev flew back to Moscow, with Kryuchkov sitting in the back to ensure that any attempt to shoot down the plane would also mean the death of one of the chief plotters. Kryuchkov was promised a conversation with Gorbachev on the plane, but, once on board, he was promptly arrested. Yazov flew back to Moscow on a separate plane, where he, too, was arrested. Yanayev, the trembling 'president', drank himself into a stupor in his Kremlin office before being arrested, and could not be roused. Pugo, the interior minister, killed himself, with a gun in the mouth, when he knew that he was about to be arrested; his wife also died of her gun-wounds. Sergei Akhromeyev, a former chief of staff and defence adviser to Gorbachev, committed suicide, as did a clutch of other senior apparatchiks − some because of direct involve-ment, and others because they were disillusioned and the prospects seemed so bleak.

The coup was over. The changes, however, had only just begun. Now, the revolution itself was on its way. The field that stretched in front of the radicals was wide open and the hardliners' defences were laid bare.

14 Return to Another Country

When Gorbachev, in an open-necked shirt, V-necked sweater and wind-cheater, walked down the steps of the plane that had brought him back from the Crimea to the Vnukovo-2 airport in Moscow, in the early hours of Thursday, 22 August, he was — as he later acknowledged — returning to another country. His tragedy was that he did not yet seem to realize it. Gorbachev could never pick up where he had left off.

He owed his freedom entirely to his old rival, Boris Yeltsin, and to the crowds on the streets of Moscow, who had in recent months been so ready to criticize the Soviet leader. Gorbachev had constantly played the radicals off against the hardliners. Now, though, there could be no more excuses. The era of fudging was over. Gorbachev's liberation, and the arrest of the plotters, removed the best and only weapon that Gorbachev had been able to use in fighting off the radicals' demands. How could he talk about the danger of a hardline backlash when the crowds, without Gorbachev's help, had already destroyed the hardliners' power? Gorbachev did not yet seem to realize that the arrest of his conservative comrades — who had treated him so shabbily — meant that he was now bereft of allies, on either side. A banner held high among the red, blue and white Russian flags at a victory rally in Moscow on Thursday warned of the mood in the city to which he had returned: 'Mikhail — don't forget under which flag you were saved.' But Gorbachev was still keen to pin his colours to the Communist Party mast, just as he had consistently done for the past five years.

At a news conference in the foreign ministry press centre — sitting on the same platform where Yanayev and his comrades had sat just seventy-two hours earlier — he was showing the strain of the traumatic three days at Foros. In the first few minutes, he hesitated, stumbled and appeared confused. But, as he moved on to questions of the future, he picked up momentum and soon it was almost the old Gorbachev. His loyalty to Communism was unchanged:

I often hear that Gorbachev allegedly still swears by his socialist choice. I do not swear by it. But I am nevertheless a person of principle and I am not someone who turns where the wind blows, like a weathervane ... The main thing is encapsulated in one sentence pronounced once by Lenin, perhaps in passing, that socialism is the living creativity of the masses.

Not only was Lenin still the touchstone. The party, too – the party that had hampered every single reform in the past five years – remained sacrosanct: 'On the basis of this new programme, which we have put forward, I consider that there is the possibility of uniting all that is progressive, all that is the best thinking. When you talk about the party as a whole being a reactionary force, I cannot agree.'

And so it went on. He was critical of Yakovlev for declaring the Communist Party to be unreformable and for handing in his party card:

I should say that Alexander Nikolayevich has been hasty ... He started saying: 'Gorbachev believes that the party could be reformed and I no longer believe this.' Well, I am sorry that those who should be contributing to the reform of the party are leaving. I do not intend to give up the position that I have taken ... I shall fight to the end for the renewal of the party.

It was a remarkable performance – and it was also entirely in keeping with what he had said so many times in the past months and years. Some Western admirers – who had always insisted, though Gorbachev himself had never sought to mislead anybody, that the fulsome tributes to Leninism were purely tactical – were stunned. There were even suggestions that Gorbachev must have become mentally unhinged during his three days as a hostage. How else to explain his continued loyalty to the party now that the hardline bogeymen were gone? Yet Gorbachev admitted openly that his alliances with the hardliners had not been purely tactical. Bizarre though it seemed, he had genuinely trusted these extraordinary characters.

At the press conference, Yuri Karyakin asked the question to which the entire nation wanted to know the answer: 'Once I would have been afraid of these questions which I am going to ask you now, even to think them to myself ... These eight men, at the moment they were chosen, and even before that, were obvious scoundrels. It was written all over their faces. Therefore, the question is this: why were you blinded to that?'

This was not a question asked with the wisdom of hindsight: the radicals had been asking it, angrily or in despair, for months. The self-confident Gorbachev seemed almost shamefaced in reply. 'I see that the Congress [of People's Deputies] was right when it did not elect Yanayev as the vice-president at the first go, but I insisted and got my way. I shall also tell you frankly – because there are no bounds to my frank talking – I trusted Yazov and Kryuchkov particularly.'

It was an extraordinary reply. Gorbachev went on to say that Kryuchkov, the man who was responsible for one hardline assault after another, had seemed to him to be a man of learning, culture and dialogue. Yazov, the defence minister, he had thought of as a very balanced person. These were the men, he said, whom he had 'trusted particularly'.

Gorbachev later described a conversation, just after the coup, with James Baker, the US secretary of state. According to Gorbachev's account, Baker analysed Gorbachev's pre-coup hardline alliances thus: 'In the last few days, George Bush and I have given a lot of thought, Mr President, to your policy and we have now understood your course of manoeuvre and compromise. You wanted to gain time so as not to allow conservative forces to wreck the policy of reform.'

There is no reason to disbelieve Gorbachev's version of Baker's words. The Gorbachev-wants-to-gain-time interpretation was precisely the one that Western politicians fell upon, again and again, both before and after the coup. Gorbachev himself was eager to oblige, and comments: 'Yes that is how it really was. The policy of compromise was essential to reduce tension at moments of serious danger. That was the situation in September 1990 and December 1990, and again in the spring of 1991, when the shout went up: "Down with the General Secretary! Down with the President!"'

The reality, however, may not have been so statesmanlike. Gorbachev's frank, almost apologetic comments at the press conference the day after he was freed were almost certainly closer to the mark. The alliances were partly tactical: as Shevardnadze's resignation and the coup itself made clear, the hardliners were eager to sabotage reform. But the reason that Shevardnadze and others had been so angry was that Gorbachev had done so little to resist that sabotage. His alliances were not only tactical. As Gorbachev himself acknowledged, he genuinely trusted Karyakin's 'scoundrels' and thought them to be men of 'culture and dialogue'. Shevardnadze remarked:

When he returned and spoke at the press conference, I saw that he was still a prisoner − of his own nature, his conceptions, and his way of thinking and acting. I am convinced than none other than Gorbachev himself had been spoonfeeding the junta with his indecisiveness, his inclination to back and fill, his fellow-travelling, his poor judgment of people, his indifference towards his true comrades, his distrust of the democratic forces and his disbelief in the bulwark whose name is the people, the very same people who had become different, thanks to the *perestroika* he had begun. That is the enormous tragedy of Mikhail Gorbachev, and no matter how much I empathize with him, I cannot help saying that his tragedy almost led to a national tragedy.

Even on his first day back in Moscow, Gorbachev found time to criticize those who dared question his Communist views. He complimented the liberal Moscow press for its refusal to knuckle under during the coup, but he added: 'There is so much oxygen available to the press that sometimes you can see it gasping for breath.' He complained that some newspapers write 'in an insulting way, when analysing my opinions'. He did not appear to understand that the two qualities − outspokenness against Gorbachev and outspokenness against the emergency committee's decrees − went hand in hand.

The yes-men for Gorbachev became yes-men for the coup. Newspapers like *Pravda* − which had been slavish in praise of Gorbachev − simply slipped off their *perestroika* clothes, squeezed into a tight-fitting, pro-coup number and explained to the world that the plotters were entirely justified. With Communist friends like that, who needs enemies?, Gorbachev might have asked himself in the first days of the coup. The answer was that he did, to save him from his Communist friends. Those who had spoken out against Gorbachev's dalliance with the hardliners were also those who risked their lives and liberty to condemn the coup − and thus helped Gorbachev to walk free. It was a contradiction which he himself seemed reluctant to come to terms with, but which Shevardnadze described bluntly: 'In the final analysis, the people who defended Gorbachev were those he had betrayed, mistrusted, or seen as enemies: Boris Yeltsin, the people of Russia and Moscow, the democratic movements and parties, and his former comrades.'

When the coup took place, there was much breast-beating in the West. The cry went up: 'If only we had given Gorbachev more money. If only, if only ... But now, it is all too late. The possibilities of liberal change are lost and gone for ever.' The assumption appeared to be that nothing could happen without the magic presence of Gorbachev. Even as the large crowds gathered at the Russian parliament on Tuesday, one commentary declared:

> There is every reason to think that the coup will succeed. It will do so because military coups usually do succeed, because insensitive men can sit very comfortably on a throne of bayonets, because the indignation of the people on the streets counts for nothing ... Yeltsin anyway is pure cabaret ... People faced with tanks have a way, witness Prague 1968, of going quietly anyway. What, anyway, is being defended? A parliament building!

This was the self-confident tone of the clubbable establishment. Huge numbers of Russians were consciously risking their lives, and all for a 'cabaret'. The complacency was breathtaking. So, too, was the arrogance towards all those Russians who knew that they might die tonight, but who also believed in the possibility of change, for the first time in their lives. The references to Prague in 1968 were revealing. Why 1968 – why not 1989, the year that proved that everything had changed? The answer, of course, was that the people were perceived to have done nothing in 1989. Gorbachev, according to this version, had simply unlocked the door. Nobody had taken risks. In Leipzig, Timisoara and Vilnius, they had merely stepped outside and said: 'Welcome, freedom.' And the threats, the guns, the tanks, the corpses, that preceded the final victory – that was all an illusion. Equally, everything that had happened in Russia in the past two years – the mass strikes in Siberia; the demonstrations in Moscow that had defied military force; the rebellious press; the defiance of Gorbachev's presidential decrees – that, too, was ignored.

'The indignation of the people on the streets counts for nothing' – no room for ambiguity there. Only Gorbachev counted; nothing else was real. Pressure from below, or the personal courage of small, unimportant people – that, in the commentator's perception, did not exist. It was politicians alone who created change. The commentary concluded: 'As for the West, we should merely consider that it was open to us to save Gorbachev and liberalism. The president's problem was belly-failure, the food he couldn't deliver. Asking for aid and credits, he was given derisory help and graceful approbation.'

In Moscow, the radicals continued to argue the opposite. If only, they said, Gorbachev had not surrounded himself with a team of hardline boors. If only he had not kept dismissing us as unnecessary whingers, while describing his hardline comrades as trusted allies. If only the West had realized that the Soviet Union had changed and that the world no longer began and ended with Gorbachev. If only the West had taken more interest in some of the other political developments in the Soviet Union – then, perhaps, the hardliners could have been neutralized and the coup plans would never have got so far.

Certainly, few in Moscow believed that the coup was about wanting more money. Nor had the coup plotters done anything to give the impression that they wanted Western cash. On the contrary, they found the idea that they needed Western cash deeply insulting and implied that Gorbachev was responsible for things having come to such a disgraceful state of affairs. In their message to the Soviet people, Yanayev and his comrades had been explicit: 'Only irresponsible people can put their hope in some sort of help from abroad. No handouts will solve our problems; our salvation is in our own hands ... The pride and honour of the Soviet person must be fully restored.' Kryuchkov, too, had suggested that foreign aid was equivalent to blandishments from the CIA. And the 'Word to the People' in July – the proto-manifesto for the coup – poured venom on the politicians who 'fawn on foreign patrons and who seek advice and blessings across the seas'. In other words: if Gorbachev had come back from London with multi-billion-dollar cheques in his suitcase, he would, if anything, have been regarded as a sell-out.

The failed coup had nothing to do with making the Soviet economy richer, or about making it work. It had everything to do with power. Georgy Matyukhin, the bluff chairman of Russia's central bank, had no doubts on that score. Immediately after the collapse of the coup, he said: 'I don't think that if Gorbachev had received money from the West, we would have been progressing more rapidly. The money would have been used for other purposes – as before. The coup was motivated by a desperate attempt to preserve the positions of the coup leaders. Not just theirs personally, but those of all the old guard.'

One way in which power was slipping away was through the union treaty and the prospect of the signing of such a treaty provided a powerful incentive for the plotters to act quickly. But it was difficult on that black Monday, when the coup was declared, not to feel that the hardliners' action was based on a misunderstanding of everything that had taken place in the Soviet Union in the previous two years. The hardliners convinced themselves that, if they scotched the union treaty, they could hold the Soviet Union together in its present form and thus keep their power-base undiminished.

The hardliners saw the treaty as the ultimate, humiliating surrender for the Communist Party, and for Moscow. They resented it for the same reason that they resented Gorbachev: the union treaty represented the new, more liberal face of the Soviet Union and acknowledged the republics' aspirations — even if only partially — for the first time. They did not see that — just as the 'loss' of eastern Europe could not have been avoided — Gorbachev simply had no choice. Gorbachev had come to realize that regional resentments, and the centrifugal forces, were now so great that a more liberal union treaty was the only hope of keeping republics in the Union at all. The hardliners thought that the union treaty was the ultimate betrayal, but, for many in the republics, the treaty was barely a halfway house. Several republics — especially, but not only the Balts — believed it did not go far enough.

The prospects for the plotters were poor. From the first day of the coup it was already clear, as I reported then:

> The hardliners' hope is that they can turn the clock back. What they may succeed in doing is only to unite the opposition fully, for the first time. With Gorbachev in power, Soviet radicals have split down the middle: should they be with him or against him? Now that he is gone, there will be — as Boris Yeltsin made plain — no further need for the radicals to hesitate in their resistance to the present regime.

At last, after five years of shadow-boxing, the gloves were off. It was now a matter of self-belief.

An acquaintance in Moscow, a Communist Party member for many years who took part in the resistance to the coup, said: 'I am not a brave man. I would not like to go to prison. But, in recent years, we have read so many terrible things about what some people did, and what people accepted, during the Stalin years. I began to think about how things are seen by future generations. I did not want to feel ashamed, in the years to come, before my children and grandchildren.'

At last, Russia had a sense of its own history. And every one of the smaller rebellions in the previous two years had made it clear that rebellion on a much larger scale was now inevitable. I, for one, did not think for a moment that the whole show would collapse within barely forty-eight hours. That would have been too good even to dream about. I assumed that it would take several bloody weeks and perhaps months – Yeltsin in jail, shootings in Novokuznetsk, rioting in Volgograd, party headquarters burnt down in Sverdlovsk, strikes in Minsk, rallies in Moscow and mutiny in Vladivostok – before the hardliners backed down.

But if the time-scale was improbably short, the basic scenario was all too predictable. Gorbachev was now almost incidental to the process of change. It was clear even before the feared coup took place that the process could not be reversed in anything except the very short term. I had written a few months before the coup: 'Perhaps one day journalists will wake up and find that their phones have been cut and that the radio is playing solemn music by Tchaikovsky, interspersed with an endless speech by General Somebody about saving the country from anarchy. But ... that will not be the end. It will only be the last gasp of the *ancien régime*.'

Certainly, there was no way that the brakes could be applied for an entire year, let alone five. The economy was too disastrous; Communism was internationally too isolated; and people's attitudes had changed too much. This was not China, where the lid could be slapped back on – for some years, at least – after the massacre of Tiananmen Square. In China, the economic aspect of reform – Deng's version of *perestroika* – had run far ahead of the *glasnost*, or greater honesty, which was the most important early aspect of Gorbachev's reforms. China's economy was open to the world. But, unlike the Soviet Union in 1991, it had no rebellious press, no elected radical politicians, no non-Communist regional governments and no mass strikes. There was nothing which could back up the actions of the students who risked and lost their lives on the Square of Heavenly Peace in June 1989.

In the Soviet Union, the economy in 1991 still seemed locked almost in the Communist Dark Ages. Rebelliousness, on the other hand, was everywhere. An entire country had begun to change, in just a few years, because of what they saw, read, discussed and heard. Unlike in eastern Europe, the Communist system that Russians lived with had not been imposed upon them by a foreign power. The psychological break with Communism would therefore be much more painful – and more ambiguous. The problems of adjustment to any new system would be enormous. None the less, the distrustful mood in Moscow before the coup in 1991 had more in common with eastern Europe in 1989 than with politically unreformed China.

After the collapse of the coup, it was widely argued that, if it had been better organized, it could have succeeded. Clearly, the coup could have lasted longer if the repression had been better orchestrated. Not to have arrested the democratic leaders and not to have cut off all phones were signs of remarkable incompetence. But the coup was based on a wrong premise: that change could still be controlled from the top.

It was later pointed out, as though to dismiss the idea of pressure from below, that the numbers who gathered at the Russian parliament were relatively small in proportion to the population of Moscow. That was true, but revolutions do not happen at the flick of a switch. Even in Prague, where everything seemed so pure and simple, the band-wagon had only slowly begun to roll. The revolution on Wenceslas Square was a ten-day affair, beginning with police violence on a Friday night. The demonstrations ran every afternoon, 4 pm to 7 pm, for one week. Each day, people went to work before the demonstrations and went home afterwards for their evening meal. As an example of Czech-oslovak efficiency, it was unsurpassable. The crowds almost doubled in size every day – until Milos Jakes, the hated Communist Party leader, was finally sacked on Friday night and the city erupted in ecstatic celebration: car horns blared, flags waved and crowds wept with joy. Then the Czechs finished the job off with a one-hour strike on Monday, insisting that the Communists give up their right to rule (which they promptly agreed to do). It seemed magically simple; in many respects, it was. But during those early days, it was easy to find people who believed that this was all a fuss about nothing and who went home instead of going to Wenceslas Square. Many of them, no doubt, were out on the Square by the end of the week. And many more stayed at home, till the very end, neither approving nor disapproving. No revolution needs an entire population in order to succeed.

The crowds in Moscow grew much faster than they had in Prague. On the first day, people were still in shock. There were a few protesters in the morning and a few thousand in the evening. By Tuesday, there were already 100,000 during the day – and the determination was growing. As it happened, the coupsters were so chaotic that by Wednesday the crowds were no longer needed – barely two days after the tanks had first appeared. But the victories had already begun before that. Leningrad was in the democrats' hands from Monday onwards. And, in Moscow, the momentum was already growing for further change.

If Yeltsin had been arrested — and the fact that he remained free was undoubtedly an astonishing failure on the plotters' part — the resistance would have been more confused. The victory of the opposition would have taken longer and would have been bloodier. But, despite the crucial role that Yeltsin played during those days, it seems implausible that Muscovites would have given up their adored Boris Nikolayevich so easily. The committee sought to make populist promises, but nothing could have made the inhabitants of Moscow more united in their loathing of the committee — and more determined to resist, come what may — than the arrest of Yeltsin. Thus, each of the what-if scenarios seemed to lead, eventually, to the same conclusion: the coup plotters' defeat. The only question was how many days, weeks, or months; and how many dead.

This time at least, Russia was blessed with good fortune. The coup was announced on Monday morning; and it was over by Wednesday afternoon. For the moment, in a country so woefully short of miracles, Russia could revel in the miracle that had been wrought. On Thursday, there was a huge celebratory rally at the White House. The crowd cheered as Yeltsin announced that from now on the square in front of the parliament would be called the Square of Free Russia. The crowds knew that the old world had died, for ever.

But Gorbachev's reaction to the pace of change served as another reminder of the difficulty he had in coming to terms with what had taken place. On Lubyanka Square, just a few hundred yards up from the Bolshoi Theatre, stood a huge statue of the hated Felix Dzerzhinsky, the Polish aristocrat who founded the Cheka, the earliest incarnation of the KGB. The statue — Dzerzhinsky in a long overcoat — towered over the square, in front of the huge KGB headquarters, symbol of everything that was most hated about the old regime.

Dzerzhinsky was now the target of the crowds, intoxicated by the possibilities that lay ahead. On their television screens, they had seen Communist statues being toppled across East Europe, from Poland to Albania. Now, at last, it was their turn. The crowds spent several fruitless hours trying to bring Dzerzhinsky down with steel hawsers. Then Moscow city council stepped in, as the KGB officials watched helplessly from inside their once all-powerful fortress. Worried that, if the statue came crashing down, it might smash through to the Moscow underground, the city council arranged for a crane to do the job safely. Finally, five cranes together helped to swing the 14-tonne, 40-foot statue up into the air and down on to a waiting truck below. 'Die, fascist!'

shouted some in the crowd. The humiliating end for Dzerzhinsky was the clearest signal of all that there was no going back on what had now taken place. But Gorbachev was dismayed. The attacks on the statue were, he said, 'a disgrace'.

The next day, at the Russian parliament, Gorbachev seemed bemused by the pace of change. He behaved as if he could jump straight back into the driving seat and showed almost the same self-confidence as the Emir of Kuwait, who returned from a palace in Saudi Arabia to his own country – where many had been tortured or killed during the seven-month occupation by Iraq – and declared, in effect: 'Congratulations on the good work, my people. I am so glad that you fought for my return. Now, I shall take over again and reintroduce the undemocratic status quo.' In the Russian parliament, that did not wash. The deputies seemed almost as impatient with Gorbachev as with the coup plotters, despite his ordeal. Gorbachev acknowledged the distrust in the hall and told deputies: 'I know what's in your eyes and in your hearts.'

With Yeltsin at its head, the Russian parliament was determined to humble the Soviet leader. Yeltsin's killer-blows were delivered with glee, as he savoured his cruel revenge. Despite Gorbachev's protests, Yeltsin insisted that the Soviet president read aloud the report on a cabinet meeting which took place on the first day of the coup, at which all but a handful of the twenty cabinet members approved the coup. After reading the incriminating document, Gorbachev had no alternative but to say: 'I think the correct approach would be for the entire government to resign.' Whereupon he received louder applause than for anything that he had said thus far.

Yeltsin then twisted the knife still further. 'On a lighter note,' he said, 'let us turn to the suspension of the Russian Communist Party.' Whereupon, he signed the decree, with his slow, careful signature. The parliament erupted in applause. Gorbachev protested, but in vain. The questions from the floor were brutal, rubbing salt into Gorbachev's wounds. 'It is not we who need you, but you who need us. Have you understood this?' If he had not understood, when he returned from Foros – he did by the end of that day.

Every few hours, another symbol of the old regime was crushed. Moscow city council ordered that the building of the Communist Party central committee on Old Square – the very heart of Communist power – be closed up. Investigatory commissions began to go through the incriminating evidence that was left behind. By order of Yeltsin, *Pravda* and five other pro-coup papers were suspended (strictly, Yeltsin had no authority to close the papers, but nobody was ready to argue).

And the unbelievable changes rolled on. On Saturday came the funeral of the three men who had died near the Russian parliament. Hundreds of thousands turned out to pay their last respects. In many ways, the funeral represented another kind of turning-point. There was mourning for those who died, but the bright sunshine, after several days of rain, also seemed to contain a symbolism of its own. One mourner said she had come because this was 'a symbol of the burial of the Communist regime'. Another put it more positively: this, he said, was 'the resurrection of Russia'. Perhaps, too, the funeral indicated a tiny seed of possible reconciliation, in that one of the three who died, for a free Russia, was Jewish: Ilya Krichevsky's parents gave special permission for their son to be buried on a Saturday, so that the funeral of all three men could take place on the same day. For a brief moment at least (and it was all too brief), it seemed that Russia's traditional anti-Semitism might find itself on less fertile ground.

Meanwhile, as Russia hurtled into a new era, Gorbachev showed himself, yet again, to be the master of the volte-face. By Saturday – after seeing the Dzerzhinsky statue torn down, the Russian Communist Party suspended and the central committee headquarters sealed, he was beginning to realize, yet again, that he was about to be punished by life itself. Following the Lenin dictum which he had quoted so approvingly, he suddenly began to abandon even those ideas which he had sworn, two days earlier, never to give up. On Thursday, he had talked of the need to renew the party and insisted that he was not a weathervane. On Saturday, however, in a statement read out on the television evening news, Gorbachev declared: 'I don't think it is possible to carry out my functions as General Secretary of the Communist Party of the Soviet Union – and I am relinquishing those powers.' He called for the dissolution of the party's central committee, which had effectively acquiesced in the coup – and through which the Communist Party had always ruled. He was, in effect, signing the death-warrant of the Soviet Communist Party itself – whose activities were suspended a few days later.

By now, Gorbachev himself was prepared to admit that he was reeling at the pace of events. On Monday, 26 August, just seven days after the tanks had appeared in the streets on behalf of the coup, he confessed to the Soviet parliament: 'People are saying that I came back to another country. I agree with this. I may add to this that I returned from the Crimea to this different country as a man who looks at everything – both the past, the present and the future – with different eyes.'

The radicals wished that a coup had not been necessary in order for Gorbachev to look differently at the past. Still, he promised that from now on there would be no more compromises with those 'with whom it is impossible and impermissible to seek agreement'. But, by now, Gorbachev was beginning to seem a marginal figure. A poll just after the coup suggested that only 2 per cent believed he held the keys to power (the same proportion had a good opinion of the Communist Party). Most startling of all, as an indicator of popular distrust, was that more than 60 per cent of those questioned believed that Gorbachev was somehow aware of or implicated in the failed coup. This was at odds with all the known facts – except inasmuch as he had permitted the coup by failing to act against the 'scoundrels'. It was, however, a reminder of just how cynical the population had become.

Moscow was not the only place where extraordinary changes were now beginning to take place in the wake of the coup. In the Baltic republics, too, history was locked on to the fast-forward button. In a region that had already seen so much pro-Kremlin violence in the past, nobody was surprised that there had been yet more deaths during the coup. A driver was shot dead by the Black Berets in Riga on the first day and another man died after his car was hit by an APC; the deputy head of Latvian TV and radio died when troops seized the radio building; and on Wednesday – even as the coup collapsed in Moscow – a Lithuanian was killed when Soviet soldiers attacked guards near the parliament building in Vilnius. The overall death toll of four in the Baltic republics was thus greater than in Moscow. None the less, once the show was over, the life went out of the Soviet occupation with remarkable speed. On Wednesday, Soviet troops evacuated the central TV tower in Tallinn – after occupying it earlier the same day. On Thursday, even the Lithuanian television tower was at last evacuated by Soviet troops, seven months after the lethal assault. It was a powerfully symbolic retreat.

The commander of the Omon unit in Vilnius, perhaps with a black sense of humour, asked for political asylum in the West for eighty of his men, because he feared for their safety in Lithuania. In the event, he need not have worried. The Black Berets, who had been the most active participants in the attacks in the Baltic republics, were quickly and humiliatingly forced to withdraw. They left scrawled messages behind, declaring: 'Till we meet again soon!' But the threats were little more than bravado. The special troops from Riga were put on a military plane to Tyumen, in western Siberia. Quite apart from being an uncomfortable place in itself (not nearly as pleasant as Riga or Vilnius), the workers in Tyumen seemed likely to give a chilly welcome to their Russian comrades. Tyumen, an important centre for oil and gas, had gained a reputation as one of Russia's most radical cities in the past two years.

There could be no more bars to the restoration of Baltic independence. Yeltsin had already recognized Lithuanian independence at the end of July and a treaty had been signed; but the West had not, at that time, been eager to follow Russia's lead. Now, it was clear that there were no more reasons to say no. Even the Soviet Union — inasmuch as such a country still existed — finally recognized Baltic independence, seven decades after it had first recognized the independence of the Baltic states and five decades after reoccupying them. Gorbachev's insistence on sticking to the drastic terms of his tightly framed law on secession was quietly forgotten. Once they were certain that Gorbachev no longer minded, the United States, Britain and others also followed suit with *their* recognitions of independence. The Balts suddenly found themselves rejoining the world community — the CSCE, the International Olympic Committee, the United Nations and dozens of other organizations besides — at a pace that they themselves could scarcely have dreamed of.

Elsewhere in Russia, too, impossible changes were taking place. When I had lived in Russia's second city, fifteen years earlier, it was clear that the city's name — Russianized from St Petersburg to Petrograd during the First World War and then renamed Leningrad in 1924 — would never change. One wistful set of questions and answers asked:

Where were you born?
St Petersburg.
Where did you go to school?
Petrograd.
Where do you live now?
Leningrad.
And where would you like to live?
St Petersburg.

At that time, everybody knew that this was pure fantasy. Now, however, the fantasy became real. Shortly after the collapse of the coup, the Soviet parliament gave its blessing to a referendum in Leningrad, which voted in June in favour of changing the city's name back to St

Petersburg. Gorbachev had angrily insisted, at the time of the vote, that there were neither political nor moral reasons for the change. 'This great city,' he said, 'bears the name of a great man, a great thinker of our century.' Now, in yet another change of mind, he accepted the new name with good grace.

The introduction of the change was startlingly sudden. Only one day after the parliamentary vote, the departure boards at Moscow's Sheremetievo airport showed the flight not for Leningrad, but for Sankt Petersburg. On arrival in the city, it turned out that *Leningradskaya Pravda* had vanished: it had been replaced by *St Petersburg News*. The new-old name for the city was a telling indication of how dramatic the changes had been, and would still continue to be.

Throughout the Soviet era, writers continued to refer to this hauntingly beautiful city – with its crumbling palaces, bridges and canals – as if Petersburg had never ceased to exist ('We will meet again in Petersburg,' wrote the poet Osip Mandelstam, who later died, for his poetry, in a Siberian camp). Now, the seventy-year experiment had, at last, come to an end. One young woman near Kazan Cathedral – when I lived in Leningrad, it had been the Museum of Atheism – declared simply: 'It's like being reborn.' Not all the inhabitants of Leningrad were in favour of the name-change. Some regarded it as an insult to those who had died in the Nazis' horrifying 900-day siege of Leningrad fifty years earlier. Some were loyal, too, to the old creed. One woman, fifty-one years in the party, declared: 'Lenin was a thinker, who is famous in all the world ... What the devil is "St Petersburg" for?' But the younger generation were overwhelmingly in favour.

In Moscow, too, extraordinary changes continued, even as the excitement descended into chaos. Several days of special parliamentary sessions ended with one, on 5 September, in which the Congress of People's Deputies, the full Soviet parliament, voted itself into oblivion (the deputies, canny as ever, voted to keep their electoral perks until 1994), as the Union itself collapsed. In effect, the Union of Soviet Socialist Republics was being put into receivership, after seven troubled decades, as a politically bankrupt enterprise. And yet, like so many moments of history, it did not feel quite like it that day. Rather, the proceedings resembled a local council meeting that had lost its way. The drafted and redrafted motions were so complicated and confusing that delegates sometimes had to take the vote a second time. 'A misunderstanding, was there?' asked a weary Gorbachev. 'Yes!' the deputies shouted back. 'OK, we'll vote again.' And they did.

When it came to voting themselves out of existence, the congress three times ducked the challenge and finally cleared the hurdle at the fourth attempt. They applauded themselves and got ready to go home. In the hall downstairs in the Palace of Congresses, notes told deputies where they should meet if they wanted to take part in a final group photograph. Outside, Sputnik tourist buses waited to take the out-of-town delegates back to their hotels. Finally, the curtain was ready to come down.

For the liberals, the death of the Communist system was a moment for rejoicing – if only briefly – before the real problems began. The weekly *Kommersant* introduced its front-page article, after the collapse of the coup, with a quotation from Nostradamus: 'The nightmare shall continue for seventy-three years and six months . . .' The headline was simple and unambiguous. '*Perestroika* is over – thank God.'

During the coup, change had come more suddenly than seemed possible. In the wake of the coup, one popular saying declared: 'Naturally, the plotters are criminals and bandits who should be severely punished. Before that, though, they should be given medals – for outstanding services to democracy.' The paradox was real. The men who had used force in order to stop change had accelerated the changes, immeasurably. The collapse of the coup provided a kind of catharsis. One Muscovite remarked: 'It was the happiest day of my life, happier even than when my child was born.' Another said that she no longer wanted to emigrate. 'Now, I feel a great joy and pride.'

That early optimism did not, however, last for long. Within days, the problems started crowding in. One early and alarming sign of the difficulties that lay ahead came shortly after the defeat of the coup, with an announcement by Yeltsin's office that Russia was prepared to question the borders between Russia and the two largest republics – Ukraine and Kazakhstan. Both Ukraine and Kazakhstan have large Russian minorities. Much of eastern Ukraine has a Russian-speaking majority; and in Kazakhstan the numbers were evenly balanced between Russians and Kazakhs as the single largest ethnic group. Russia's argument was that the borders had been drawn without regard for ethnic intricacies, at a time when nobody contemplated the possibility that the Soviet one-party state might one day fall apart. True enough. Yet it was Yugoslav-style fantasy to suppose that a re-drawn border could create a nominally 'correct' border. On both sides, tolerance was needed. Without it, Russia and its neighbours faced the prospect of what one Muscovite described — with apparent equanimity — as 'a thousand Yugoslavias', with reference to the bloody war between Serbs and Croats that was just getting under way.

The Russians insisted that by making threats against Ukraine and Kazakhstan they would make the two republics 'come to their senses'. In reality — as Yeltsin's officials could easily have discovered by talking to Kazakhs or Ukrainians — the threats had the opposite effect. Much of the goodwill towards Yeltsin quickly drained away. Once seen as a benefactor, he began to be seen as a potential threat. In Ukraine, they started talking of a 'new chauvinism' and a 'drive for a tsarist empire'. Yeltsin insisted that nothing had changed: 'The Russian state, having chosen democracy and freedom, will never be an empire, nor an older or younger brother. It will be an equal among equals.' But the scepticism remained. The president of Kazakhstan, Nursultan Nazarbayev, commented: 'The Russian leadership lost the chance to win the peace.'

Yeltsin dispatched a peacemaking mission — including Sobchak, the mayor of St Petersburg — to the two republics and the quarrel was partly patched up. But the mutual suspicions remained. It was made worse by the fact that even the most radical politicians, including, for example, Sobchak himself, seemed to come down on the side of Russian nationalism.

Throughout autumn 1991, various cobbled-together agreements were proclaimed which were supposed to keep the Soviet Union in one piece. On 2 October, the twelve remaining Soviet republics (following the departure of the Balts) initialled an agreement which theoretically paved the way for the creation of what was described as an 'economic space' in the territory of the USSR. Two weeks later, on 18 October, eight republics turned up for an official signing ceremony with Gorbachev in the Kremlin (Azerbaijan, Georgia, Moldavia and Ukraine had by now dropped out). The economic union went hand in hand with a new form of political union — in other words, a revamped version of Gorbachev's ill-fated union treaty. If you believed the official line, then a new 'Union of Sovereign States' was on its way, to replace the Union of Soviet Socialist Republics. The signing on 18 October, amid much smiling for the photographers, was described by Gorbachev as a 'tremendous event'.

In reality, however, all this was just empty words. All talk of economic co-operation was meaningless until some form of political agreement had been achieved. Many Soviet republics had officially declared independence in the wake of the coup (including republics like

Belorussia, where the declaration was – for the moment – more rhetorical than real). It was now unclear whether the Soviet Union was one huge country or a dozen smaller ones. Gorbachev continued to threaten the republics with dire consequences if they failed to sign up for the new union. The threats, in turn, made the republics much less eager to comply. In that sense, it was the same old story. The country was falling apart, even as Gorbachev insisted that it must come together.

The huge Ukraine, linked to Russia for centuries except for a brief period after 1918, began to move with ever greater determination towards independence. As the coup collapsed, the Ukrainian parliament had voted for secession, in name at least. At that time, many contradictions remained. The Soviet hammer-and-sickle flag continued to fly over the Ukrainian parliament building even after the independence vote. (In the western city of Lvov, by contrast, the blue and yellow Ukrainian national flag had flown over the town hall for more than a year.) The Soviet flag came down in Kiev only after popular protests demanding its removal.

But, if 'independence' was initially confused, the momentum was clear. By dint of nimble footwork (and despite co-operating with the coup committee in August), Ukraine's leader, Leonid Kravchuk, a former Communist head of ideology, was one of the most popular political figures in the republic. He was overwhelmingly elected president after proclaiming a new loyalty to the independence cause.

On the same day as the presidential vote, 1 December 1991, a referendum confirmed the parliamentary vote on independence that had taken place three months earlier. On this day, yet more nails were hammered into the Soviet coffin. Gorbachev insisted: 'There can be no Union without Ukraine, and no Ukraine without the Union. These Slavic states, Russia and Ukraine, were the axis along which, for centuries, events turned, and a huge multinational state developed. That is the way it will remain. I am convinced of it.' But, if Gorbachev was convinced, the Ukrainians were not. By December, the spirit of rebellion that had begun in western Ukraine, and then spread to Kiev, had infected the Russian-speaking eastern parts of the republic, too.

In the December referendum, more than 90 per cent of Ukrainians voted in favour of independence. If you believed Moscow's account – proclaimed again and again, in the weeks leading up to the Ukrainian vote – Russians living in Ukraine felt dangerously threatened by Ukrainian nationalism. But the vote indicated that things were not quite like that. In the eastern Ukraine, a clear 80 per cent voted in favour of

Ukrainian independence. Even the russified Crimea — which had only been given to Ukraine by Khrushchev in 1954, after two centuries of belonging to Russia — produced a narrow majority in favour of independence. Partly, this pro-secession sentiment reflected fears about the economic prospects for Russia. As one Russian admitted, in Donetsk in eastern Ukraine, 'If Russia had more sausage than us, then people would probably have voted against independence.' None the less, the direction was clear.

Until now, the West had repeatedly refused to accept the transformation of the European map until the changes were almost over. After the Berlin Wall came down in November 1989, Margaret Thatcher said that German unity would not come for 'ten to fifteen years' (in reality, it took less than one year for the process to be complete); her foreign secretary, Douglas Hurd, echoed that view, declaring that unity was 'not on the immediate agenda'. Those statements sounded as bizarre then as they do today. On the Baltic republics, too, the West insisted repeatedly, through 1989 and 1990, that the Balts should pipe down, and argued that the Balts' desire for restored independence was unrealistic. And, on Yugoslavia — in spring 1991, long after it was clear that the country was on the point of disintegration — President Bush declared that he 'would not permit' the country to fall apart. This had exactly the opposite of the desired effect. Belgrade took Bush's words as *carte blanche* for the use of military force to keep the federation together; Belgrade launched a war against the rebellious republics, which ensured that the already inevitable disintegration also became unimaginably bloody. Then, in Kiev, just weeks before the coup in 1991, Bush warned Ukrainians that independence was a 'suicidal' path.

Western leaders had seemed determined not to contemplate the immensity of transformation that was under way. A few lone parliamentarians, on left and right, persistently argued that it was necesary to formulate policies which could help to cope with tomorrow's realities, not just with yesterday's status quo. But those voices were ignored; they were regarded by those in power as 'unhelpful'. In relations with the Soviet Union, the West had staked everything on Gorbachev. Especially from 1989 onwards, political leaders seemed mesmerized by the dramatic pace of change.

Following the pro-independence referendum vote in December, it was clear that there could be no turning back. Western leaders at last began to accept that there was no point trying to put the brakes on history, and that it was only possible to help the momentous changes to take place with minimum instability – in itself, a giant task. Gradually, the West tried to get used to the idea of dealing with republics, not just with Moscow. Within days of the vote, diplomatic missions began opening up in Kiev. The central European countries – Poland, Czechoslovakia and Hungary – were the first to give full diplomatic recognition, and seemed eager to show solidarity with their immediate eastern neighbour. Canada, with a large Ukrainian minority, was also quick to move. Even the United States and Britain, which had been ardent supporters of the keep-the-status-quo school of diplomacy, dropped all talk of 'suicidal' behaviour and declared that they were ready to extend diplomatic recognition in due course. Gorbachev continued to insist that Ukrainian independence was impossible; but it was already becoming real.

Yet more talks were planned, in connection with Gorbachev's intended Union of Sovereign States – in which the Soviet president would continue to bear overall responsibility for the economy, defence and foreign policy. In other words, the union would again be a union on Moscow's terms. For republics like Ukraine, this was unthinkable. Moscow wanted to call the shots; but the vote on 1 December emphasized that Ukraine was determined to prevent that happening. Without a radical change of course, the prospects for any kind of settlement looked poor.

15 The Flag Comes Down

The Bialowieza forest, on the border with Poland, had until now been famous, above all, for its bison; this was one of the few places in Europe where they roamed wild. Even in pre-Revolutionary times, the bison in Bialowieza were considered so rare that hunting them was forbidden except by special permission of the tsar. Now, however, there would be a different reason for Bialowieza to be remembered. The meeting that began on 7 December 1991 at the Viskuli hunting lodge, deep in the pine forests, was billed as being about improved co-operation between the Slav republics. That made it sound almost routine – more talks about talks, which would again reach no real conclusions. As Yeltsin later admitted, he and the others at the meeting 'did not advertise' the true agenda of the meeting, which began just six days after the Ukrainians voted so overwhelmingly for independence. This was the occasion when the killer blow to the Union was officially administered.

Boris Yeltsin of Russia, Leonid Kravchuk of Ukraine and Stanislav Shushkevich of Belarus (as Belorussia was now officially called) stayed, together with a clutch of advisers, at Viskuli, a government guest-house near the Belorussian town of Brest, for two days of intensive negotiations. On 8 December 1991, they signed an agreement which drew an absolute line under everything that had come before. It proclaimed:

> We, the Republic of Belarus, the Russian Federation and Ukraine, being founding member states of the USSR, being signatories to the Treaty of Union of 1922, and hereinafter referred to as the high contracting parties, state that the USSR, as a subject of international law and a geopolitical reality, ceases to exist.

The three republics declared that they had formed a 'commonwealth of independent states'. Yet again, they were defying Gorbachev. Only two days earlier, he had insisted: 'We must move as fast as possible to sign the new union treaty ... They say there is an alternative to the

Union. I do not think so.' Gorbachev and Yeltsin were in agreement that the Union was unthinkable without Ukraine, which had voted for independence a week before the Bialowieza meeting. But the conclusions they drew were very different. Gorbachev said that Ukraine must stay in the Union, under all circumstances. On the very day that the commonwealth agreement was drawn up, Gorbachev said that he was 'absolutely convinced' that Ukraine would sign the union treaty. He insisted, too, that he was not ready to go. He declared: 'This is not a topical question . . . I shall not participate in the collapse of the country. I have not exhausted my role, and I believe that the people will not allow their present leaders to do that.' Yeltsin, on the other hand, argued that if Ukraine was not prepared to sign the union treaty, then some other accommodation must be found.

In many respects, the rhetoric of the new 'commonwealth of independent states' was reminiscent of Gorbachev's 'renewed union', with its talk of co-operation between republics. But there was a crucial difference. The official co-ordinating centre for the new commonwealth would not be Moscow, but Minsk – the capital of Belarus, the smallest of the three republics which signed the founding agreement. (As with Moldavia-turned-Moldova, Belorussia's 'change' of name was more apparent than real: Belarus had always gone by that name in Belorussian.) The choice of Minsk made it absolutely clear that the commonwealth should not be seen as the continuation of the tsarist empire and the Soviet Union, under a new name. In theory at least, nobody would be seeking to give orders any more. Yeltsin declared:

> During the past seventy years, we have all become well aware of what the *diktat* of the centre means, and that is why everyone fears like the devil the restoration of this *diktat*. So, when the republics saw that, verbally, the centre was in favour of the republics' autonomy, but in practice was retaining one, two, three, four, five union ministries – and in addition was forming new 'central' structures – well, then it became clear to everyone: the 'radical' Novo-Ogaryovo reforms [i.e. the union treaty] were merely an attempt by the centre to retain its influence in a different form. And when this was understood, the disintegration, the separation of the states began. The process has to be reversed. But how?

Answering his own question, Yeltsin drew a comparison with the European Community. A historic EC summit, which paved the way for

European economic and political union, began in the Belgian town of Maastricht just one day after the meeting in the Bialowieza forest ended. Yeltsin believed that the dissolution of the Soviet Union at the Bialowieza meeting and the federalism of Maastricht were two sides of the same coin – complementary, not contradictory. He declared: 'There was only one way: to unite, not within the framework of a single state but within a community of states. Just, for example, as the European countries are now doing. And thus was born the commonwealth of independent states.'

Even the semantic label given to the politicians' new creation was intended to emphasize the leaders' wish to distance themselves from the past. Gorbachev had talked only of *soyuz* – 'union'. *Soyuz* had long been one of the most Soviet words in the vocabulary and it was logical that hardliners had chosen it as the name for their powerful parliamentary faction, created in February 1990. The new word, *sodruzhestvo* – literally, concord, or friendship grouping – carried different historical baggage. It had traditionally been used, in the political context, for another loose group created from the ashes of empire – the British commonwealth, or *britanskoe sodruzhestvo*. For the leaders in Bialowieza, the parallels were clear.

Gorbachev promptly declared that the new commonwealth was illegal. He expressed indignation that he had not been invited to take part in the talks, nor even informed about the agreement, until after George Bush had been briefed:

This is a shame, a disgraceful shame. This is not a fair game. Shush-kevich informs me, while Boris Nikolayevich talks to Bush ... I shall not participate in this under any circumstances. Quite apart from anything else, I find such behaviour repugnant ... It is as though we are starting to cut this land up like a pie, to have it as a snack with a drink, as it were. No! I shall not descend to such a thing. Neither my convictions, nor my ethical code, nor my post allow it.

Georgy Shakhnazarov, one of Gorbachev's closest advisers, described the new agreement as 'a pure *coup d'état*'. But the position of the Soviet president was becoming untenable. Even Gorbachev gradually seemed to accept the inevitable and began to talk in valedictory terms. Just four days after the announcement of the new commonwealth, he concluded: 'I think it has been my fate to take on a great cause. That's all there is to it, I think ... It's all in the past now. The main goal of my life has already been accomplished. As for the rest – well, maybe other people will come along and do things better.'

The initial reaction of the Central Asian republics to the signing of the agreement – variously described as the Bialowieza, Brest or Minsk agreement – was almost as dismayed as that of Gorbachev. They were unhappy that they had been cut out of the decision-making process, as if their views on winding up the Soviet Union did not count. Within days, however – embracing the inevitable – the non-Slav republics, too, were queuing up to join. On 13 December, just five days after the commonwealth agreement was signed, all the Central Asian republics – Kyrgyzstan, Tajikistan, Turkmenistan, Uzbekistan and Kazakhstan – all met in Ashkhabad, capital of Turkmenistan, to discuss what had taken place in the Bialowieza forest.

There was more than a hint of bitterness when the Central Asians pointed out that the Minsk agreement 'came as a surprise to us'. They said it was 'unfortunate' that their point of view had not been considered, during the founding meeting of the commonwealth, and pointed out: 'The commonwealth of independent states cannot take shape on an ethnic, religious, or any other basis that infringes rights of the individual and of nations.' But the Central Asians also emphasized that they were not against the process itself, which was described as 'positive'; they declared their readiness to become 'equal co-founders of the commonwealth' and called for a meeting to be held with that aim. The eagerness to sign up was in itself an indication of how different things now were from the negotiations over Gorbachev's prized but elusive union treaty, which republics had kept trying to escape.

By now, it was clear that it was only a matter of days before the end came. On 21 December, eleven of the twelve remaining Soviet republics (the three Baltic states were gone for good) all met in Alma-Ata, capital of Kazakhstan to put their names to a new joint agreement. Only Georgia, racked by violent political clashes, stood aloof. Members of the new commonwealth of independent states guaranteed 'the fulfilment of international obligations, stemming from the treaties and agreements of the former USSR'. The eleven agreed that Russia should inherit the Soviet seat at the United Nations. Belarus and Ukraine already had UN seats – negotiated by Stalin, who insisted that the USSR needed one seat for each of the fifteen republics; three had been the compromise figure that was finally reached. The three UN member states of the commonwealth agreed that they would press for full UN membership for the other former Soviet republics.

Gorbachev was not even invited to the Alma-Ata meeting. Yeltsin effectively gave him an eviction notice, announcing publicly that he was expected to quit the Kremlin by the end of the month. Yeltsin seemed to delight in giving orders to the once all-powerful Soviet leader. But he claimed that nobody wished to trample on Gorbachev. 'We respect Mikhail Sergeyevich Gorbachev and we do not want to follow the tradition that has taken shape since 1917 of burying each head and leader of state and subsequently reburying him or regarding him as a criminal. In a civilized state, that tradition must end.' The members of the newly formed commonwealth pledged that Gorbachev would receive a pension of 4000 roubles a month. That was almost ten times the average wage – or, put another way, $40 a month at the then-prevailing exchange rate.

Gorbachev, said Yeltsin, would be moved out of the presidential apartment on Kosygin Street ('perhaps we will give it to a scientist'), into a smaller one. He would also move out of the presidential dacha and be given a more modest one instead. He would receive two cars – two plain Volgas, or a Zil and a Volga – and twenty bodyguards. He would receive special health care. He would, in other words, be comfortable, by Soviet standards – and powerless.

At the heart of the Kremlin, there was no mistaking the fact that the show was over. Artyom Borovik, a television correspondent who interviewed Gorbachev on the day of the Alma-Ata meeting, noted that there were no longer any attendants in the permanently staffed cloakrooms. 'They say they went out to lunch a week ago. The Kremlin resembles a burst balloon, whose string is being strongly grasped out of habit by the hand of its once mighty owner.' Yeltsin and Gorbachev held a nine-hour meeting to discuss the handover of power. Then, on 25 December at 7 pm, the last Soviet leader appeared on television for a partly defiant, partly reflective farewell address to the nation.

Because of the situation which has developed with the formation of the Commonwealth of Independent States, I am ceasing my activity in the post of USSR president. I have been firmly in favour of preserving the union state and the country's integrity. Events took a different course ... With all my soul, I wish to thank those who during these years stood alongside me for a right and good cause. Some mistakes could probably have been avoided, much could have been done better, but I am sure that sooner or later our shared efforts will achieve results. Our peoples will live in a flourishing and democratic society. I wish every one of you all the best.

It was an extraordinary end to an extraordinary era. It sometimes seemed hard to accept the reality of what was taking place. As Gorbachev said his goodbyes, he might have added – echoing the words of his old friend and supporter, Margaret Thatcher, who had been ousted by her former supporters a year earlier – 'It's a funny old world.' The man who had come to power, six years earlier, to set to rights the ailing but powerful Soviet Union was now presiding over the dismantling of the seventy-four-year-old state. Just twenty minutes after Gorbachev finished speaking, the red Soviet flag that had always flown over the Council of Ministers building in the Kremlin was lowered. It was 7.32 pm. Ten minutes later, the Russian tricolour – less than three years ago, people had been arrested for carrying it – was hoisted in its place. Only the illuminated red stars on the Kremlin towers served as a last reminder of the Soviet power that was already becoming a part of history. To mark the occasion, the chimes rang out for several minutes in the ornate seventeenth-century Saviour's Tower, overlooking Red Square.

A young militiaman on duty outside the mausoleum – where waxy Lenin still lay, in his dark suit and blue and white spotted tie – returned from his dinner break to find that the flags had already changed. He commented: 'It was a good surprise.' Out on the square, however, there were mixed feelings, even now. One woman declared: 'I am sorry for the Soviet Union. I am sorry a great country is falling apart before my eyes.'

Before his television appearance, Gorbachev signed a decree giving up his powers as commander-in-chief of the army and transferring control of nuclear weapons to Yeltsin. Then, after his official farewell, he handed the briefcase with the nuclear codes to Yevgeny Shaposhnikov, who had been defence minister of the now defunct country. Shaposhnikov, in turn, gave the nuclear briefcase to Yeltsin.

The following day came the cursory funeral rites. Only a couple of dozen deputies bothered to turn up for the final session of the Supreme Soviet, which took it upon itself to endorse the changes that were already almost complete. The plaque was being taken down even as the session began. The speaker of the parliament, Anuarbek Alimzhanov, complained of those who 'dance round the lion that has not yet been killed'. Then, speaking to the almost empty hall, he declared: 'We have fulfilled our civil and parliamentary duty.' Alimzhanov said that the 'good, kind and fine words about the future of this vast country' expressed at the first session of the Supreme Soviet, after the Revolution, had not come to pass. 'Today we have reached the stage where the old has been destroyed, the new is beginning. We know very well what we have lost; but we do not know what is yet to come.' Outside the Kremlin walls — in the queues on the icy streets and in the empty shops — the mood was grim. There were fireworks and celebrations on New Year's Eve. But the abolition of a country brought with it none of the light happiness associated with the defeat of the coup plotters in August. There was little joy, and much fear of the hardship and chaos that lay ahead.

16 Into the Void

Nowhere is New Year's Eve celebrated with greater enthusiasm than in Russia. Vodka and champagne flow freely. Every year, millions of Russians wake up with heavy hangovers and know that the New Year has truly arrived. Come New Year 1992, however, many Russians were bracing themselves for a different kind of pain. It was not just the difficulty of buying vodka and champagne – though there was that, too. On 2 January, prices were due to jump, often fivefold. The shops had completely emptied over the previous days and weeks in anticipation of the price leap that marked the goodbye to the old and the hello to the new. Bread production was increased, by almost a half in some areas. And yet there were bread shortages, as people bought increased quantities of the only item that they knew they could still afford. People looked with trepidation at the changes that lay ahead.

Already, many felt that things could hardly be worse. The rouble was, by now, almost worthless. By the time that serious economic reform began at the beginning of 1992, a month's salary could be exchanged, at the official tourist rate, for approximately five dollars. A single Big Mac at the still-crowded McDonald's on Pushkin Square cost a day's wages. The peasant markets were well stocked, but impossibly expensive for ordinary Russians. It was easy to spend a month's Soviet wages on a single, small shopping trip to the market. None except those with access to foreign currency could easily survive. Perhaps not surprisingly, hard-currency prostitution was considered to be one of the most desirable professions. According to one opinion poll, more than half of Moscow's teenage girls considered sex for dollars to be an attractive career option. The *valyutnaya*, as the hard-currency girls were known, could earn $150 – i.e. two annual salaries – with a single customer. By comparison, a teacher's monthly salary would not buy enough dollars for a snack at one of Moscow's hard-currency cafes, nor (if he or she somehow obtained the necessary entry visa into the UK) enough to pay for an underground ticket from Heathrow airport into central London. It was a humiliating situation and, in the short term at least, it would only get worse.

Russia's economic Big Bang, at the beginning of 1992, theoretically allowed the freeing of prices – described by Yeltsin as the 'painful and unpopular measure which for many years the country's leaders were unable to bring themselves to carry out'. In reality, prices were sky-high, but were not yet free; bureaucratic price-setting continued. In that sense, the early months of the reforms combined the worst of both worlds: the high prices were painful and, at the same time, the loathed 'speculators' could still find rich pickings. Yeltsin promised widespread privatization, including privatization of land. But, without the cash for small farmers to buy equipment, that process, too, was immensely complicated, especially while the old bureaucrats remained in place. The initial effect of the reforms was merely to hurt people's pockets, while improving little in their lives. Even within Yeltsin's government, harsh criticism of the new policies could be heard. Alexander Rutskoi, Yeltsin's vice-president (an Afghan war hero, chosen by Yeltsin as his running mate in 1991 in order to woo the military), and Ruslan Khasbulatov, the speaker of parliament, both complained that things were going too fast.

There was a deep, almost morbid pessimism. But Yeltsin insisted that he would not back down on the tough policies. He insisted, too, that there was room for hope. 'We have inherited a devastated land, but I think that we must not despair. Russia is gravely ill. Its economy is ill. But there are no incurable illnesses in the economy. However difficult things are today, we have a chance to struggle out of this ditch in which we find ourselves.' Gradually, the shops began to fill with products – at painfully high prices. In one respect, the widespread pessimism was no bad thing. It meant that people were already braced for the worst; any glimmer of light at the end of the long, dark economic tunnel would thus be a bonus. It would have been more dangerous if everybody believed that the advent of the market economy would bring the immediate answer to all their prayers. But support for the changes was grudging, at best.

Sometimes, Russia seemed to be seeing a replay of the charismatic-leader-meets-the-people show, which had enjoyed such success in the early Gorbachev years and which had started to go wrong in 1988. Like the former Soviet leader whose offices he now occupied, Yeltsin appeared on Russian television screens, seen in energetic conversation with the crowds in different parts of the country. Only weeks after Gorbachev's fall, he went on a tour of the provinces to drum up support for the cause. On a visit to the Volga region, he promised that things would get better 'within six months'. Such promises seemed a dangerous hostage to fortune. One man in the city of Saratov declared: 'He's a president like all the rest. It's all words.' Still, Yeltsin seemed braced for such disbelief. He insisted, even before the price rises were introduced, that he did not expect his economic policies to be a vote-winner. 'I have ventured to take unpopular measures. Therefore, I don't think I can expect ardent affection from the Russians. On the contrary, there is growing criticism of me. So, if portraits of me have sprung up in some places, then no doubt they will soon start tearing them down. I'm expecting that.'

The poverty, bitterness and chaos provided fertile ground for further revolt. There were plenty of politicians ready to capitalize on the resentments. Vladimir Zhirinovsky, the demagogic anti-Communist (whose views were flexible: he aligned himself with the hardline Communists during the coup and attacked opponents of the coup as 'rabble'), had been the third most popular candidate in the Russian presidential elections in 1991. It was a stark reminder of how easily one set of certainties could replace another. On the one hand, the army daily, *Red Star*, talked of the military as an additional republic, 'hungry and unsettled – but well armed and trained'. On the other hand, Zhirinovsky organized 'marches of the hungry queues', which criticized Yeltsin and drew support from both the Communists and the extreme right. Zhirinovsky shared a common agenda with men like Viktor Alksnis, a notable Communist hardliner and leader of the so-called 'black colonels' who had been at the forefront of the attacks against Shevardnadze in 1990. Zhirinovsky claimed that there were only three ways out for the country: another coup, a civil war – or electing him president. The rise of some kind of fascism, with or without generals, was a lurking danger. There were widespread calls for the *silnaya ruka*, the 'strong hand'.

It was a familiar story. Christopher Isherwood had written of such left-right political back-flips sixty years earlier. In his 'Berlin Diary', in *Goodbye to Berlin*, he describes how his landlady, Fraulein Schroeder, switched from voting Communist one year to being a Nazi sympathizer the next, with a dose of amnesia in between. Isherwood comments: 'If I were to remind her that, at the elections last November, she voted Communist, she would probably deny it hotly – and in perfect good faith.'

There were other problems, too. Many Russians found it difficult to come to terms with the joint responsibility for the survival of the system which had destroyed the country in the past seven decades. Stalin had not, after all, kept his nightmarish system together single-handed, any more than Hitler had been solely responsible for Nazi crimes. Just as in Nazi Germany, millions of Russians had been enthusiastic in their support for the Soviet system, however murderous it might have been. In sharp contrast to Germany after 1945, however, there was no attempt in Russia – as least in the initial period after the collapse of Communism – to come to terms with what had happened in previous years. There was little desire to take collective responsibility for Stalinism, so as to prevent a repetition of the horrors of the past – let alone to apologize to other nations which had been victims of the imperial politics of Moscow. Rather, many Russians simply believed that the Russian people had been 'punished' for the past decades and that the matter ended there.

In his New Year message in 1992, Yeltsin told his fellow-Russians: 'Our citizens are gripped by a feeling of bitterness for their country. We often bewail our backwardness, disorganization and many problems. But . . . it was not Russia which suffered defeat, but the Communist idea, the experiment which was conducted with Russia and which was imposed on our people.' 'Imposed on our people' was a dangerously comfortable phrase. After all, as Yeltsin himself acknowledged, 'Many of us believed in it and gave it our best years, energies and our lives.' Millions had for decades failed to protest against the Communist system, because of a mixture of fear and loyalty. If, as Yeltsin suggested, this was an experiment, imposed on the Russian people, then somebody must have been responsible for conducting the experiment.

For some, the answer was clear – they turned to the familiar scapegoat for a nation's ills. After the coup, anti-Semitic literature flourished. Typical was a new paper called *Russian Resurrection*, which published a cartoon showing a hook-nosed Jew, with horns and tail, sitting, with his flabby buttocks, on the head of Ivan, the honest Russian. The message was crude, but its potential effects were serious. In the past, some of the anti-Semitism had been orchestrated. After the August coup, bundles of anti-Semitic leaflets in numbered packets were discovered, ready for distribution, at the regional Communist Party headquarters in Leningrad – a reminder of the unholy alliance that the Communists and the KGB had formed with assorted persons of diseased mind, including the neo-fascist Pamyat. Now, the regime was no longer involved. But there was a real danger that such propaganda could easily take root.

Hardline Communism and Russian nationalism had always gone

hand in hand. Back in 1972, Alexander Yakovlev, then head of the central committee's powerful Department of Agitation and Propaganda, was, in effect, sent into diplomatic exile after publicly criticizing Russian nationalism. Now, as Russia stumbled into the new era, the old wounds were reopened. Yakovlev was again attacked as a 'russophobe', a standard phrase used against liberals by the anti-Semites.

Certainly, many people had lost all self-belief. With depressing frequency, Russians − living in a highly educated society − contrasted life in Russia with life in 'civilized countries'. The phrase was used almost without irony. 'In civilized countries, this would be done differently.' 'Does this sometimes happen in civilized countries, too?' 'Perhaps one day, our shops will be like shops in civilized countries.' Russia itself sometimes scarcely seemed to believe in the possibility of becoming 'civilized'.

It was true that the Soviet reputation for rudeness in public places was well deserved. Nowhere in the world, perhaps, were customers more routinely harassed and abused. London, Paris and New York − each of which likes to award itself the 'rudest city in the world' accolade − were all, by comparison with Soviet Moscow, models of charming courtesy. And yet, as any visitor to the Soviet Union could confirm, Russians' generosity and hospitality, inside their homes, went far beyond what the Westerner was used to. It was only when Russians stepped out of their apartments into the Soviet world that the law of the jungle prevailed. Rudeness was a form of revenge. Everybody was humiliated, in the shops and at work − and everybody, in turn, sought to humiliate others.

There was no intrinsic reason why such abusiveness should last for ever. One of the most startling changes in eastern Europe after the collapse of Communism in 1989 was the speed with which people began to show small courtesies, in shops and elsewhere, which would have been unthinkable during the old regime, when contempt bred contempt. Though it still seemed hard to imagine, there was no good reason why Russia should not see a similar change of public attitude.

Beyond Russia's borders, the fate of other former Soviet republics was almost as confused as that of Russia itself. There had been a long line of independence declarations in the immediate wake of the coup − not all of which were serious. In Central Asia, Communist leaders used nationalism as a way of protecting their own positions and even getting themselves elected president, in free elections. During the coup, hardline republics equivocated or worse. In Uzbekistan, the Communist Party leader and president, Islam Karimov, locked up the leader of Birlik, the main opposition group, on the first day and condemned the coup only when it was all over. Then, unabashed, he condemned the Soviet Politburo for its cowardly and unprincipled behaviour, and pressed for a declaration of independence for Uzbekistan. When the vote was passed, he demanded of his parliment: 'Why don't you applaud?' Whereupon, obediently, they did. There was a similarly unhappy combination of Communism and nationalism in Tajikistan and Turkmenistan. Only the tiny south-eastern republic of Kyrgyzstan showed itself more robust and denounced the coup from the start. In Kazakhstan, meanwhile, President Nursultan Nazarbayev, a Communist reformer, continued to press for radical economic change.

Once the commonwealth was formed, the Central Asian republics quickly signalled their desire to join. They gained 'independence', but without knowing quite what they wanted, or how they wanted to get there. Only a month after the dissolution of the Union, in January 1992, there were several deaths in protests against price rises in Uzbekistan, as the uncertainties continued to grow. Economically, Central Asia had gained more than other republics from being part of the Soviet Union. The average standard of living, though low, was higher in Soviet Central Asia than across the border in, say, Afghanistan. None the less, some kind of readjustment seemed inevitable. A clue to the possible nature of that readjustment could be seen as the restrictions on religious worship began to vanish. In 1989, there were just 160 working mosques in Central Asia and Kazakhstan. Two years later, there were more than 5000. New ones were opening up at the rate of ten a day. The long-banned Islamic Renaissance Party became the party with the fastest-growing support. There was little Islamic radicalism, but there was a much greater consciousness of Islamic traditions, which had been suppressed for so long.

Elsewhere, too, the instability remained, even after the commonwealth was formed. Moldova had supported Yeltsin and the 'incomparable heroism' of the Russian opposition, during the coup. The authorities in the republic arranged for banned Russian papers to be printed in Chisinau (as Kishinev was now known, losing the Russian name that it had been given for the past forty years), even while ethnic Russians in the self-proclaimed Dniester Soviet Socialist Republic supported the coup. There was thus the irony that non-Russians in Moldova supported the Russian parliament, while the Russian population in Moldova did not. In the wake of the collapse of the coup came an official declaration of independence and − in a reference to the annexation of Moldova in 1940 – a call for the 'illegally occupying' Soviet troops to be withdrawn. In a reminder of where Moldovans' hearts lay, the official anthem was changed to 'Romanians Awake' – the non-Communist Romanian anthem, dating back to the national revolutions of 1848.

After the creation of the commonwealth, talk of reunification with Romania – the ultimate goal for many in Romania and Moldova alike – was shelved for the immediate future, but soon came up again, with renewed force. Still, the breakaway would never be simple. As in Yugoslavia – and in contrast to the Baltic states – there was no simple border change that could satisfy all parties, since the borders of the former Soviet republic were not the same as the territory which Stalin had annexed from Romania fifty years earlier. Either Moldova would exclude some Romanians (who did not want to be left behind); or it would take with it some Russians and Turkic Christian Gagauz (who did not want to come). There were prospects of endless complications, further down the line. In late 1991, there were violent clashes and a number of deaths.

Elsewhere, too, the collapse of the Union was far from peaceful. The end of Soviet power meant still greater chaos in Nagorny Karabakh. The Kremlin's divide-and-rule policy was abandoned and Soviet troops were withdrawn. But there were constant skirmishes, so that the two republics were in more or less open war; as in Yugoslavia, whole areas became uninhabitable because of the fighting. Theoretically, the collapse of the Soviet regime meant that both sides could at last seek talks and understand the need for compromise. In the immediate wake of the coup, Yeltsin himself played the role of honest broker and achieved a peace agreement which was signed by the presidents of both Armenia and Azerbaijan. There was an agreement in principle on a ceasefire, exchange of hostages and return of deportees. Nevertheless, the killing continued.

Elsewhere, the bloodshed was even worse after the collapse of the Union than it had been under Communism. Some of the worst early clashes came in Georgia, where Zviad Gamsakhurdia, a veteran dissident who was freely elected as president with 87 per cent of the vote in May 1991, seemed to regard diversity of views and ethnic harmony as an optional extra. (His cavalier attitudes were not new. In 1989, Gamsakhurdia had argued that the solution to ethnic violence in Abkhazia, in western Georgia, was that all Abkhazians should be disarmed. I thought I must have misunderstood. 'You mean,' I asked, 'that *everybody* should be disarmed?' 'Why should Georgians be disarmed?' he replied irritably. 'They never use their weapons – except in self-defence.')

Soon, it was not only national minorities who President Gamsakhurdia wished to suppress. The Georgian opposition press was muzzled and Gamsakhurdia's rivals were arrested. Protests grew, and exploded violently, at the end of 1991. Gone were the peaceful demonstrations against Communism from 1989 and 1990. Now, even as the commonwealth was officially being declared in Alma-Ata, the streets of Tbilisi saw renewed bloodshed. This time, Moscow was uninvolved in the killing. Dozens died in clashes between Gamsakhurdia loyalists and armed rebels against the government. Much of the centre of Tbilisi was destroyed, after long gunbattles in the streets. Eventually, Gamsakhurdia himself, after spending two weeks holed up in the Georgian parliament, was forced to flee. But Georgia seemed condemned to suffer further violence, as Gamsakhurdia's supporters continued to battle it out with those who had ousted him. Gamsakhurdia had proved that 'anti-Communist dissident' did not have to be synonymous with 'peace-loving democrat'. None the less, the violence used against Gamsakhurdia's supporters (of whom there were still many) was an ominous sign.

Georgia was not the only former Soviet republic where getting rid of Moscow rule did not mean full democratic rights for all. In Lithuania, immediately after the coup, President Landsbergis imposed a form of direct rule on areas with a Polish majority (his reasoning being that the councils had failed to resist the coup). The idea that you could cudgel a national minority into being loyal citizens of a newly independent country was hardly convincing. But Landsbergis was unrepentant, talking of Polish 'Bolsheviks'. The hope was that intolerance in Lithuania would diminish as the country returned to non-Soviet normality. Nevertheless, the put-up-or-shut-up policies were not encouraging for the future stability of the region. Nor was any lasting settlement reached on the fate of what had once been known as Konigsberg in east Prussia, the birthplace of Immanuel Kant – and now the Kaliningrad region, a chunk of Russian territory surrounded on all sides by Lithuania. Talk of a Kaliningrad free trade zone that would be a 'new Hong Kong' was attractive, but seemed unreal. Equally, the widely touted idea that Soviet Germans should be imported into the territory seemed likely only to store up problems for the future.

As the Union collapsed, Western politicians were especially concerned by the question: whose finger is on the nuclear button? Ukraine insisted that it had no desire to be a nuclear power and that it wanted its nuclear weapons to be destroyed. But it insisted, too, that it did not wish to give the weapons up to the 'responsible' Big Brother in Moscow, nor did it wish to give Moscow sole control. There were other problems, too. The possibility that nuclear weapons might fall into the hands of any of the warring factions scattered across the Soviet Union was clearly nightmarish, and the West worried aloud about the possibility of Libya or Iraq buying up Soviet nuclear expertise. Still, the eventual destruction of Soviet nuclear weapons seemed a more likely outcome than their use by a lunatic group, at home or abroad. For many in the former Soviet Union, the greatest fear was of the lethal maelstrom that Russia itself could still become, with or without nuclear weapons.

Russia, which had always been the centre of the empire, was also, in many respects, the most unstable part. Officially, during the Soviet era, it had been the Russian Soviet Federated Socialist Republic (it was now simply the Russian Federation). Russia had always had a strong tradition of nationalism and a strong sense of what was 'a Russian'; but it had little geographical sense of identity. For centuries, it existed only as an imperial power. After the revolution of October 1917, Russia briefly renounced all its colonial possessions – but within a few years it moved to get most of them back.

France and Britain, as they lost their empires, suffered a loss of self-esteem. They could no longer strut so confidently on the world stage. But, even as their empires vanished for ever, the two imperial nations remained relatively prosperous – and at ease with their own identities. The contrast with Russia was clear. The 'core' Russia was unfamiliar, even for Russians. For them, Russia came as part of a package of nations, of which Russia was always seen as the most important. Many Russians were genuinely astonished to discover that Ukrainians and others did not necessarily see things in the same way. That sense of cross-purposes lay at the heart of some of the conflicts between Russia and Ukraine which emerged after the Union ended and which threatened to destroy the commonwealth itself.

It was not only with its neighbours that Russia's relationships remained difficult. Russia itself is several countries in one. Within the Russian-speaking territory, there is St Petersburg, the European city created by Peter the Great as a 'window on to Europe' and whose links with Europe are strong. There is western Siberia, with its coal mines, gas and oil, which is three time-zones east of Moscow (the same as from London to Baghdad, or from Los Angeles to New York). And there is the Russian Far East — Kamchatka, Yakutia and much more besides — eight, nine, and ten time-zones east of Moscow. The territory of Russia alone, ignoring all the other former Soviet republics, is almost twice as large as the United States.

Within Russia, there were many timebombs. The Russian federation contained sixteen autonomous republics — in effect, sub-republics — and several autonomous regions, many of which had no love for Moscow. Just one example of the trouble yet to come could be seen in the southern region of Chechen-Ingushetia, on Russia's border with Georgia, where trouble exploded in November 1991. Djokar Dudayev, the Chechen-Ingush leader (and an air force general) declared the independence of Chechen-Ingushetia from the Russian republic. Yeltsin responded by sending hundreds of troops and attempting to enforce a state of emergency. If the declaration of independence was one nightmare, Yeltsin's reaction was worse. As Gorbachev had found before him, there is nothing like the use of the big stick to unite your opponents against you. Eventually, Yeltsin was forced to back down when it became clear that his threats were merely making a bad situation worse. No permanent solution was found.

Other troublespots remained. Tatarstan, west of the Urals, refused even to take part in Russia's presidential election in June 1991. Instead, the Tatars elected their own president on the same day that Yeltsin was elected Russia's leader. After the collapse of the coup, the Tatar capital, Kazan (where Lenin had studied law), commemorated the anniversary of the capture of the city by Ivan the Terrible — 439 years earlier. There was growing pressure, based largely on the perceived intolerance of the Russians, for 'independence' from Russia itself.

To the east of Tatarstan, Bashkiria, the centre of the Soviet oil-refining industry, remained equally queasy about being further swallowed up in a powerful Russia. Many of these territories were islands in the middle of Russia, so that a complete breakaway was impossible. But the increased defiance of Moscow seemed likely to grow, especially if Yeltsin renewed his early attempts to bring rebellious regions to heel.

In much of the country, the nationalism and anti-Semitism was accompanied by a wariness of jettisoning old certainties. In eastern Europe, people had been pleased to be rid of the system with which they had been saddled for forty years by a foreign power. In Russia, though, nothing could be that easy. Near one of Moscow's main art galleries, an improvised outdoor sculpture collection was created immediately after the coup. The signposts pointed the way to 'Activists of totalitarianism'. Dzerzhinsky lay prostrate and paint-spattered in the grass after his ignominious removal from Lubyanka Square, alongside Khrushchev, Stalin and many more. Children clambered over the statues, laughing together.

Some visitors to the exhibition approved. As one man said: 'Everybody should be grateful that we went through this Communist experiment – so that nobody else should need to.' But there was a lingering loyalty, too. One woman gazing at the statues said: 'Stalin did lots of good, as well as some bad. He built up our industry – and there was discipline.' Others said that it was a disgrace that the statues had been pulled down, after so much good-quality stone had been used to make them. Even among the young, many still clung to the beliefs that they had grown up with. On October Square, near a huge Lenin statue, one girl said she was convinced that Lenin should remain. She declared: 'He was a genius, after all.' The dethroning of Lenin continued, especially after the official dissolution of the Union. But ambiguous support for the Lenin legacy remained.

Part of the problem was that there had not yet been a complete handover of power. In most of eastern Europe, it was all change at the top, after the revolutions were over. In the Soviet Union, real dramas had taken place: the locked-up central committee building on Old Square, and the non-Communist Russian flag that flew over the Kremlin, bore testimony to that. But, in many respects, this was unfinished business. A small example of the not-quite-revolution could be found inside the KGB headquarters, the Lubyanka, after the collapse of the August coup. The KGB's public relations man, the urbane and affable Colonel Oleg Tsaryov, gave a fluent description of how the KGB would, from now on, be a model of good behaviour. It all sounded impressive. But it was noteworthy, too, that Tsaryov – who had worked under journalistic cover in Britain for *Socialist Industry* newspaper in the 1970s, and who proudly described how he had found hidden MI5 microphones in his London flat – seemed unreconstructed when talking of the past. Unprompted, he dismissed the horror stories about the Lubyanka prison as nonsense; even Stalinism had not been so bad. 'Of course, you can always find people who overdo it. That's how it was in the Stalinist period, too.' It was a remarkable statement from somebody who was supposed to be convincing his Western visitor that we now lived in a brave new democratic world. Talk about the future and he was fluent. Talk about the past and it seemed that his views had not changed, in essence, since the days when he was a bright, up-and-coming agent in the Brezhnev era.

On the square outside the window, the red, white and blue Russian flag fluttered where the cast-iron Dzerzhinsky had stood until a few days earlier (the toppling of Dzerzhinsky had been been an act of vandalism and disrespectful to history, said Tsaryov). Anti-Communist slogans were painted around the base of where the statue had stood. Out there on the streets, a kind of revolution had already taken place – a confused revolution, but a revolution, none the less. Here, though, inside the corridors of power, the tidal wave of change had not yet swept through. Even after the Soviet Union had officially come to an end, men like Tsaryov remained at their desks. There was a continuing sense of instability. The greatest ructions were still to come.

After the dissolution of the Union, Russia officially took over the Soviet foreign ministry, one of the half-dozen huge Stalinist wedding-cake buildings that dominate the Moscow skyline. Eduard Shevardnadze, who had been reappointed as foreign minister in November, was once more out of a job (he even offered himself as a peacemaker in his native Georgia). But those who worked for him were still employed. Some were professional diplomats, whose skills were needed as the ministry entered uncharted waters. But others were born-and-bred Soviet apparatchiks, whose obstructive style of work remained unchanged, working for the new, 'non-Communist' foreign ministry of the Russian federation. It was the same in bureaucratic institutions across the country. Even more than in eastern Europe, the Communists showed themselves to be great survivors.

Meanwhile, the new structures seemed fragile. The commonwealth, which had been launched with reassuring statements about being a partnership of equals, soon seemed in danger of falling apart. Russia started issuing one ultimatum after another, just as Gorbachev, representing 'the Centre', had once done. Rumbling arguments between Russia and Ukraine over the ownership of the Black Sea fleet exploded less than a month after the commonwealth's formation. Ukraine, irritated at Russia's assumption that it was still in charge, argued that the fleet – based at Sebastopol in the Crimea – should belong to Ukraine. (Ukraine, whose defence minister was an ethnic Russian, admitted that it did not need the fleet – but argued that Russia did not need it either.) Yeltsin retorted that the fleet 'was, is and will be Russian'. The quarrel was patched up. But, like the question of borders, the dispute was shelved, not solved. There were frictions, too, when Ukraine wanted all troops remaining on Ukrainian territory to swear an oath of loyalty to Ukraine, instead of the previous oath to obey the Soviet authorities in Moscow; those who did not wish to do so were supposed to leave. As the diplomatic salvoes continued, the Russian parliament voted to reopen the question of the ownership of Crimea, which had officially been 'given' to Ukraine in 1954, in commemoration of the three-hundredth anniversary of the union between Russia and Ukraine.

With so many tensions — economic, political, military and ethnic — there were many reasons for pessimism about the future of what had once been the USSR. But there were reasons for almost-optimism, too. It had always been clear that the transformation of a seventy-year-old, insane regime (inheritor of another, less brutally repressive system) would not be a simple, upbeat affair. A democratic country or set of countries could hardly be expected to emerge instantaneously, like a butterfly fluttering out into the sunlight. The comforting stability of the old, totalitarian Soviet Union was always an illusion. As the bandages were removed from the festering wounds, it was scarcely surprising to discover an unpleasant mess underneath. Despite the chaos — which seemed certain to get worse — it was impossible to mourn what had been left behind.

Historically, Russia had never known democracy. The nearest it had come to it were eight months of political mayhem between February and October 1917.Thus, unlike in eastern Europe, there was not even a folk memory of a golden age to hark back to, unless you count — as some Russians did — the tsarist era. But the defeat of the August coup, and all the smaller rebellions that preceded that extraordinary, three-day victory, gave at least some hope that Russia's democracy might eventually prove to be the equivalent of the oak tree that Andrei sees in War and Peace, in a passage which Tolstoy presents as a metaphor for the possibilities of emotional and spiritual rebirth. The oak seems dead for ever when Andrei first notices it near the roadside, unyielding amid the fresh spring growth of the surrounding trees. 'It was an enormous tree, double a man's span, with ancient scars where branches had long ago been lopped off and bark stripped away. With huge ungainly limbs sprawling unsymmetrically, with gnarled hands and fingers, it stood, an aged monster, angry and scornful, among the smiling birch trees.'

Then, on a later visit, Andrei finds — to his astonishment and disbelief — that the tree has been transformed. 'Without realizing, without recognizing it, he admired the very oak he sought ... Through the rough, century-old bark, even where there were no twigs, leaves had sprouted, so juicy, so young that it was hard to believe that aged veteran had borne them.'

It often seemed that the Russian oak, even as it began to turn green, would bear hideous, mutant growth — like the trees that suffered the poisoning effects of Chernobyl. Never before, however — not in the tsarist era and certainly not in the Soviet era — had so many millions of Russians learned to question so much, so often. That could never be taken away, and it was the greatest legacy of Mikhail Gorbachev. Admittedly, Gorbachev had often been displeased when people used their new ability to question the old conventional wisdoms. But that scarcely mattered. What was important was that millions of people, from Minsk to Vladivostok, had changed.

As the old gave way to the new, a friend in St Petersburg expressed a mixture of foreboding and hope. 'Now, things are worse than ever before. I am frightened even to go on to the street — and I think things will get worse. But this is a period of disease, which will pass after a few years. One day, the disease will go.' As Russia reached the end of seven decades of the protesters' 'road to nowhere', the immediate prospects looked bleak. It seemed, however, possible — even now, it was unwise to put it more strongly than that — that the new-found ability to tell the difference between truth and lies might one day help Russia through to a time when some form of peaceful democracy might at last be born.

SOURCES

The daily BBC 'Summary of World Broadcasts' and the weekly Radio Liberty 'Reports on the USSR' have been valuable. Norma Percy's *Second Russian Revolution* series (Brian Lapping Associates, for BBC Television) included interviews with the key Kremlin players and some remarkable stories (it was no surprise to find that the series topped the ratings when it was shown on Russian television after the August coup). Angus Roxburgh's accompanying book, *The Second Russian Revolution* (BBC Publications, 1991), also contained useful material. Some of the other books and articles that I have used or quoted from are listed below.

1 Before the Deluge
Walter Duranty, 'Moscow to me', *Sovietland*, 6/1935; Natalia Gorbanievskaya, *Red Square at Noon* (Andre Deutsch, 1972); Vaclav Havel, *Living in Truth* (Faber, 1990).

2 Mikhail the Saviour
'Ten Days in May: A Soviet town in War and Peace', directed by John Blake, was shown on ITV, 11 September 1985; Boris Yeltsin, *Against the Grain* (Jonathan Cape, 1990); Andrei Sakharov, *Memoirs* (Hutchinson, 1990); *Izvestia TsK KPSS*, 2/1989.

3 Spanners in the Works
Hedrick Smith, *The Russians* (Sphere Books, 1976); *The Best of Ogonyok* (Heinemann, 1990); Irina Ratushinskaya, *No, I'm Not Afraid* (Bloodaxe, 1976).

SOURCES

4 Unlocking the Side Door
Conor O'Clery, *Irish Times*, 1 August 1988; 'Estonia looks ahead to secession', *Independent*, 17 March 1989; 'The crumbling of an empire', 11 April 1989; *Pravda*, 10 February and 22 May 1989.

5 Birth of Politics
Boris Yeltsin, *Against the Grain*; James Blitz, *Financial Times*, 28 March 1989; Marju Lauristin, 'End of the Baltic twilight', *Independent*, 31 July 1989; *The World This Week*, 'Estonia', directed by Ian Taylor (shown on Channel 4, 19 August 1989).

6 Fraternal Allies Wave Goodbye
Independent: 'A region where goalposts are on the move', 26 January 1989; 'The redundant symbol of the Berlin Wall', 8 November 1989; Vaclav Havel, 'A society at the end of its patience', 4 July 1989; 'Czechoslovakia "must be next"', 11 November 1989; Edward Lucas, 'The death of Comrade Fear', 29 December 1989.

7 What About the Workers?
Vladislav Starkov, 'No alternative to glasnost', *Independent*, 7 November 1989; Rupert Cornwell, 'Sakharov "was simply our conscience"', *Independent*, 19 December 1989.

8 The Unbreakable Breaks Up
Andrei Sakharov, at the Royal Institute of International Affairs in London, 20 June 1989; *The Nationalities Question in the Soviet Union*, edited by Graham Smith (Longman, 1990).

9 Going for Broke
Anatol Lieven, *The Times*, 12 March 1990; Edward Lucas, 'No Soviet visa, no problem for Lithuania', *Independent*, 29 March 1990; John Kohan, *Time*, 16 April 1990.

10 Russia Rises
Yuri Afanasiev, 'Fog remains over USSR's future', *Independent*, 15 September 1990; 'Gorbachev risks a retreat on Germany and Nato', *Independent*, 8 March 1990.

11 In Search of a Miracle
Tatyana Zaslavskaya, *The Second Socialist Revolution* (I. B. Tauris, 1990); Mikhail Gorbachev, *Perestroika* (Collins, 1987); *Economist*: 4 November 1989, 22 September 1990, 1 December 1990; Anatoly Sobchak, 'How Soviet Communists are subverting democracy', *Independent*, 16 February 1991; Eduard Shevardnadze, *The Future Belongs to Freedom* (The Free Press, New York, 1991).

12 Crackdown
Trevor Fishlock, *Daily Telegraph*, 14 January 1991; Helen Womack, *Independent*, 21 January 1991, 29 March 1991; Alexander Kabakov, Yuri Karyakin, Lyndmila Telen, *Moscow News*, 27 January 1991; Meg Bortin, 'On Yeltsin's European swing, some slights he won't forget', *International Herald Tribune*, 19 April 1991; Stanislav Shatalin, 'Take us to the market now', *Independent*, 7 June 1991; Eduard Shevardnadze, 'Democracy cannot wait', *Independent*, 12 August 1991.

13 From Coup to Revolution
Anna Husarska, 'The Apartment', *New Republic*, 16 September 1991; Igor Zakharov, 'There's been a coup. Try to get to the office a bit early', *Guardian*, 23 August 1991; Sian Thomas, *Independent*, 21 August 1991; John Lloyd and Leyla Boulton, 'The people find their voice', *Financial Times*, 24 August 1991; *Kommersant*, 26 August 1991.

14 Return to Another Country
Mikhail Gorbachev, *The August Coup* (HarperCollins, 1991); Eduard Shevardnadze, *The Future Belongs to Freedom* (The Free Press, 1991); Edward Pearce, 'A sacrifice on the altar of lethargy', *Guardian*, 21 August 1991; Susan Viets, 'Donbass votes for sausage and freedom', *Independent*, 7 December 1991.

15 The Flag Comes Down
James Clarity, 'What's next for new Russia? "History will show"', *International Herald Tribune*, 27 December 1991.

INDEX

Abalkin, Leonid 152, 154
Abkhazia 101, 236
Abuladze, Tengis 22
Afanasiev, Yuri 92, 138–9
Afghanistan 28, 60, 71
Aganbegyan, Prof. Abel 143
agriculture 147–7, 157, 179
aid 156–7, 173, 179, 199, 208
Airikian, Paruir 98
Akhromeyev, Sergei 38, 202
Aksyonov, Alexander 62
Albania 199
Alimzhanov, Anuarbek 228
Alksnis, Viktor 232
Allison, Graham 180
Alma Ata 97, 226
Amalrik, Andrei 9
Andreyeva, Nina 26–8, 132
Andropov, Yuri 10–11, 22, 143
anti-Semitism 127–8, 214, 233, 239
Arbat Poets 90
Argumenty i Fakty 65, 91–2
Armenia 51, 60, 97–100, 129, 174, 236
arms negotiations 19–20, 28, 155, 183
Article Six 94, 121–2, 124–5
Azerbaijan 97–8, 100, 107–10, 129, 219, 236

Babel, Isaac 4
Baedeker's Russia 6–7
Bakatin, Vadim 158, 201
Baker, James 205
Baklanov, Oleg 188
Baku 107–10
Baltic republics 50, 111–20, 139, 156, 221
  conscription 158, 161
  crackdown 160–7, 176–8
  during coup 215–16
  independence 119–20, 135
  pro-independence movements 42–53, 63–7, 69

  see also Estonia; Latvia; Lithuania
Bashkiria 239
Bat Cabaret 169
Belorussia (Belarus) 13, 174, 200, 220, 226
Beria, Lavrenty 32
Berlin, East 7, 76–7
Berlin Wall 76, 79–80
Bialowieza 223, 225–6
Birlik 103, 234
Boldin, Valery 188
Bonner, Elena 19–19, 166, 198
Borovik, Artyom 227
Brakov, Yevgeny 57
Brazauskas, Algirdas 112, 137
Brezhnev, Leonid 5–11, 32, 70, 73, 75, 103, 125
Brezhnev era 3, 19, 30, 42, 44, 84, 145
Brovikov, Vladimir 126
Bucharest 83, 113
Bukovsky, Vladimir 7
Bush, George 93, 110, 118, 140, 183–4, 199, 221, 225

Ceausescu, Nicolae 83, 105, 133
Cekuolis, Algimantas 111
Central Asia 103, 128–9, 148, 226, 234–5
Chagall, Marc 13
Chebrikov, Viktor 47
Chechen-Ingushetia 239
Chernenko, Konstantin 10–11
Chernigov 127
Chernobyl 16–17
Chernov, Sergei 164
Chikin, Valentin 26
Churbanov, Yuri 22
Commonwealth of Independent States 223–7, 235, 241
Communist Party (CPSU) 6, 54, 70
  central committee 13, 19, 24, 38, 66, 93, 112, 121, 124, 214

INDEX